Immigration and
European integration

MANCHESTER
1824
Manchester University Press

D1314363

European Policy Research Unit Series

Series Editors: *Simon Bulmer, Peter Humphreys* and *Mick Moran*

The European Policy Research Unit Series aims to provide advanced textbooks and thematic studies of key public policy issues in Europe. They concentrate, in particular, on comparing patterns of national policy content, but pay due attention to the European Union dimension. The thematic studies are guided by the character of the policy issue under examination.

The European Policy Research Unit (EPRU) was set up in 1989 within the University of Manchester's Department of Government to promote research on European politics and public policy. The series is part of EPRU's effort to facilitate intellectual exchange and substantive debate on the key policy issues confronting the European states and the European Union.

Immigration and European integration

Beyond fortress Europe?

Second edition

Andrew Geddes

Manchester University Press

Manchester and New York

distributed in the United States exclusively by Palgrave Macmillan

The right of Andrew Geddes to be identified as the author of this work has been asserted by him in accordance with the Copyright, Designs and Patents Act 1988.

First edition published 2000 by Manchester University Press

This edition published 2008 by Manchester University Press
Oxford Road, Manchester M13 9NR, UK
and Room 400, 175 Fifth Avenue, New York, NY 10010, USA

Distributed exclusively in the USA by
Palgrave Macmillan, 175 Fifth Avenue, New York,
NY 10010, USA

Distributed exclusively in Canada by
UBC Press, University of British Columbia, 2029 West Mall,
Vancouver, BC, Canada V6T 1Z2

British Library Cataloguing-in-Publication Data
A catalogue record for this book is available from the British Library

Library of Congress Cataloging-in-Publication Data applied for

ISBN   978 0 7190 7466 0   *paperback*

This edition first published 2008

17 16 15 14 13 12 11 10 09 08   10 9 8 7 6 5 4 3 2 1

Typeset by R. J. Footring Ltd, Derby
Printed in Great Britain
by Bell & Bain Ltd, Glasgow

Contents

Tables and figures

Tables

Figures

Preface

Writing the second edition of this book has been a challenging exercise for a number of reasons. Not the least is that, when the first edition was written in 1998 and 1999, the action of the European Union (EU) in these areas had begun to acquire some shape and form but was in its early and nascent phases, and moreover applied to only 15 member states, while now there are 27, with more in the queue, and there has been a huge increase in EU activity on migration and asylum, linked to EU enlargement. This required much more attention to be given to the period since 1999, when developments really began to speed up and to apply across a wider EU and beyond.

My thinking was that the book required a rather more fundamental rethink about the ways in which the analysis was structured; the second edition could not be an exercise in simply adding some new material or a new chapter to provide a simple chronological update. Much has changed empirically, which has necessitated major amendments to the structure of the book. It is now much more meaningful to talk about common EU policies on migration and asylum and to link these both to national policies and to broader questions about European integration and regional governance. These empirical developments also required a change in analytical focus. A lot of attention in the first edition was directed to analysis of a limited array of existing measures, to the framework within which they had developed, and to the potential for them to develop into something far more substantial. In this second edition, there is more analysis of substantive EU action and evaluation of its impact across the wider EU. A particular concern of this book has been to try to demonstrate links between migration and asylum and other important EU policy areas, such as enlargement, economic integration and social policy. This conforms with my own view – of course, heavily influenced by the work of others – that the best way to understand international migration is as nested within a much broader set of questions surrounding the development, consolidation and transformation of the European state system, of which European integration is, of course, an important component. By trying to think about migration and asylum in their broader context, the aim was to identify some of the social and political dynamics that underpin what can sometimes be a baffling and confusing array of EU measures and to place them in context. It is probably also the case that one of the most off-putting aspects of the EU is the arcane and obscure language in which it communicates its purposes. This should not disguise the fact that these measures are intensely political. They go to the heart of core questions for EU member states and impinge very squarely and directly on understandings of the EU as a group of states, as a supranational institutional structure, and as a regional organisation with powerful effects on surrounding states and regions.

It also became more and more apparent to me as the book was rewritten that the pace of change is likely to continue to be rapid over the next few years. My concern with this second edition was to put in place a framework for the analysis of these events that would not immediately become redundant in the face of the latest wave of developments. There can sometimes be too much of a temptation to focus on the 'new' and to imagine that all these developments mark some kind of radical departure from what has gone before or what happens elsewhere. While there are elements of novelty, I think there are longer-term continuities and points of comparison to similar, non-European states facing similar issues. What I have tried to do is locate elements of 'newness' in a broader context (both temporal and spatial) within which I hope they can be understood and which might possess some analytical utility for understanding developments that occur after this book has been published. And, if they do not, I could always try again and write a third edition.

The changes in the content of the book reflect far more than my own efforts. I am very grateful to my colleagues in the Department of Politics at the University of Sheffield for the supportive research environment to which they all contribute. I have also benefited immensely from discussions with a large number of friends and colleagues about migration, asylum and European integration over recent years. During the preparation of this second edition, I would particularly like to thank Alex Balch, Michael Bommes, Christina Boswell, Gary Freeman, Virginie Guiraudon, Randall Hansen, Jim Hollifield, Christian Kaunert, Gallya Lahav, Sandra Lavenex, Sarah Leonard, Tony Messina, Jan Niessen, Paul Statham and Eiko Thielemann. Their influence and those of many other authors are apparent in the bibliography, although all errors of fact, interpretation or omission are, of course, my own responsibility.

Another set of changes are more personal, but relate very straightforwardly to the writing of this book. Since the first edition, Federica, Jacopo and Beatrice within our European family have made all the difference in the world to my life.

Abbreviations

A8	Eight accession states – Czech Republic, Estonia, Latvia, Lithuania, Hungary, Poland, Slovakia and Slovenia – joining the EU in 2004
CEC	Commission of the European Communities
CFSP	common foreign and security policy
CIREA	Centre for Information, Discussion and Exchange on Asylum
CIREFI	Centre for Information, Discussion and Exchange on the Crossing of Frontiers and Immigration
DGFSJ	Directorate-General for Freedom, Security and Justice
EC	European Community
ECHR	European Convention on Human Rights
ECJ	European Court of Justice
ECRE	European Council on Refugees and Exiles
ECSC	European Coal and Steel Community
EEA	European Economic Area
EEC	European Economic Community
EFC	External Frontiers Convention
EMU	economic and monetary union
EP	European Parliament
EPC	European political co-operation
EU	European Union
EUMF	European Union Migrants' Forum
IGC	intergovernmental conference
ILO	International Labour Organisation
JHA	Justice and Home Affairs
MPG	Migration Policy Group
QMV	qualified majority voting
NGO	non-governmental organisation
RELEX	Directorate-General for External Relations
SAP	Social Action Programme
SCIFA	Strategic Committee on Immigration, Frontiers and Asylum
SEA	Single European Act

SIS   Schengen Information System
SIS II   Schengen Information System II
SLG   Starting Line Group
TCN   third-country national
UN   United Nations
UNHCR United Nations High Commissioner for Refugees
VIS   Visa Information System

1

Introduction

The book's focus

This book analyses the development of European Union (EU) migration and asylum policy since the origins of economic and political integration in the 1950s. The core question that it addresses can be simply stated: how have changed border relationships within and between EU member states affected understandings of and policy responses to international migration in its various forms? From this derive a series of questions about the timing, form and content of EU action on migration and asylum, and their relationship both to EU structures and to broader patterns of migration politics at national and international level.

The book derives its analytical approach from an important body of work that focuses on state borders as integral to the analysis of migration (for a seminal contribution see Zolberg, 1989; see also Donnan and Wilson, 1999; Anderson and Bort, 2001). It is the borders of states that make international migration visible, but it is also the case that European integration changes the location of borders, their meaning and associated notions of territoriality, territorial management and population control. International migration resides on what Rosenau (1997: 4) called the 'domestic/foreign Frontier', where:

> the international system is less commanding, but still powerful. States are changing, but they are not disappearing. State sovereignty has been eroded, but it is still vigorously asserted. Governments are weaker, but they can still throw their weight around. At certain times publics are more demanding, but at other times they are more pliable. Borders still keep out intruders, but at other times they are more porous.

Rosenau characterises the 'domestic/foreign Frontier' as an arena where domestic and foreign issues 'converge, intermesh or otherwise become indistinguishable within a seamless web.' This insight is particularly pertinent because of the ways in which responses to international migration necessarily involve both domestic and international politics, or, as Heisler

(1992) puts it, need to be understood as both societal and international issues, with linkages made across these levels. Yet, at the same time, international migration is an example of how borders as lines that demarcate one state from another have long performed the role of managing the contradictions and tensions of the international system, as they sift populations and decide who can enter a particular state's territory and on what basis. Walker (1998: 326) thus sees borders as the 'dangerous edges – the awful discriminations between us and them – that constitute our spheres of domestic comfort and external distress'.

The argument is that the shift to EU competencies may well have helped member states in the short to medium term to use the EU as a means of resolving domestic issues, by co-operating in an area where there are clear interdependencies and where EU action can be more effective than going it alone. At the same time, there are longer-term implications that are not captured by an 'escape to Europe' argument. One of these longer-term implications is the scope for policy convergence. Messina (2007) is sceptical of this and argues, with some justification, that there remain clear distinctions between EU member states. That said, the argument developed in this book is that there are some important elements of convergence that do arise as a consequence of European integration. Convergence can be understood as: 'Any increase in the similarity between one or more characteristics of a certain policy (e.g. policy objectives, policy instruments, policy settings) across a given set of political jurisdictions (supranational institutions, states, regions, local authorities) over a given period of time' (Knill, 2005: 765). There may be different forms of convergence, as marked by decreased variation, laggards catching up with leaders, the change of country rankings in specific policy areas and the measurement of domestic change in relation to some kind of exemplary model such as an EU standard. Convergence pressures may be more evident with regard to the migration and asylum policies of some states than others, while the policies around which convergence occurs may be limited. For example, this book shows that there are pressures on newer member states to converge around EU legislative norms and also that these focus particularly on border security. This convergence can be caused by 'trigger factors', such as security fears or demographic changes, or promoted by 'facilitating factors', such as basic institutional similarities between countries (Knill, 2005).

One reason for these pressures to converge is that there are important and intensive links between the national and EU arenas, with the effect that what happens in Brussels does feed back into domestic settings, through the legal, political and social effects of European integration. The nature of these linkages differs between member states, as some are more exposed to the effects of European integration, particularly newer member states in southern and eastern Europe. The shift to EU responsibilities in this area has also induced a depoliticisation of migration, in the sense that issues are now often dealt with in secretive European-level forums, often comprising officials with specialist expertise, and within agency-like structures that often possess a strong bias towards security concerns. While this form of EU politics may not correspond with more usual understandings of politics as open contests over policy alternatives, these EU-level developments do constitute a very particular form of social and political action centred on the mobilisation of expertise. This could be seen to accord with what Schmidt (2006) calls 'policy without politics'; that is, the EU now holds policy responsibilities without much, if any, political debate. The national-level counterpoint to this is 'politics without policy', as debate may occur but policy responsibilities have relocated to EU level. It is a contention of this book that 'policy' cannot be separated from 'politics', and that the decision to embrace and develop certain types of process and decision-making on migration and asylum are intensely political, link policy-making with particular kinds of politics (in this case a politics of expertise) and reveal to us integral and fundamental features of the EU that shape relations between the member states, influence the EU's identity as a regional organisation and, because of the economic and political power of it and its member states, shape relations with other states and regions.

To make this argument, the book develops a framework for the analysis of EU migration and asylum policy that explores the relationship between national and supranational responses to migration, but that also distinguishes between different types of border. The basic distinction that is made is between: *territorial borders* – the sites at which the sovereign right of states to exclude has traditionally been exercised; *organisational borders* of work and welfare that provide important points of access for migrants; and *conceptual borders* of identity, belonging and entitlement, which may be fuzzier than the other two in some ways but which also possess an important and powerful resonance in debates across Europe about migration (Geddes, 2005a).

The core contention of this book could also be seen as a claim about method. It is that international migration should not be viewed as some kind of external challenge to the European state system and to the EU. Rather, international migration in all its diversity is intimately connected to:

- the development, consolidation and transformation of European states;
- the underlying motives for European economic and political integration;
- the international system within which European integration is embedded;
- the ways in which organisational and institutional processes at national, European and international level 'make sense' of the complex human material that comprises international migration flows.

This does not mean that the book is concerned only with structures and that its claim is that institutional and organisational structures determine both migration and policy outputs. Rather, the core claim is that migrant agency (often embedded within complex networks) encounters the territorial, organisational and conceptual borders of European states and that processes at these borders are integral to the ways in which international migration is understood, to the categorisations of migration and migrants that develop, and to the policy responses that unfold at national and, increasingly, at EU level. As these borders change (including changes in their location, their meaning and their operation) then so too do the meanings ascribed to international migration as 'legal' or 'illegal', a 'threat' or 'opportunity', as 'wanted' or 'unwanted', as 'bogus' or 'genuine', as 'abusive' or an 'asset'. Borders are sites at which social and political meaning is ascribed to international migration. Consequently, analysis of European and EU responses to international migration requires investigation of the institutional and organisational processes that are constitutive of borders. This means more than looking at the location of borders; it also requires that attention be given to the meaning of borders and how these meanings change, and to how strategies of territorial management and population control can also change as the location and meaning of borders shift.

This understanding of migration is then related to institutional and organisational processes that have constituted European economic and political integration for more than 50 years. Until fairly recently, immigration and asylum from outside the EU were essentially irrelevant in this context. The only kind of migration with which the EU concerned itself was the movement by nationals of member states (now called EU citizens) to work, to provide a service, or to establish an enterprise, that is, for economic purposes. This has changed, particularly since the late 1990s. It is now much more meaningful to discuss a common EU migration and asylum policy, as evidenced by a series of legal outputs – directives and regulations in EU parlance – on visas, asylum, the rights of long-term residents and anti-discrimination, to name four areas.

There is much that is 'new' in these migration and asylum policy developments, not least that they are associated with a unique form of supranational governance; but it would be a mistake to focus solely on elements of newness. It is also necessary to show how migration is embedded within the European state system, how European integration has helped transform this state system, and then to explore the current dimensions of EU action on migration and asylum in this context. It is essential to do this because the setting in which EU action on migration and asylum has developed is all important. EU action has been constituted in particular ways, in relation to certain legal competencies, based on participation by certain kinds of actors and in relation to particular understandings of problems. It is necessary to identify and specify the constitutive elements of the EU policy field, the legal competencies that underpin it, the actors who participate within it, and the problems that have impacted upon it, if a better understanding of the timing, form and content of EU action is to be developed.

The politics of migration

Despite the often technical language of European integration, it is important to bear in mind that these are intensely political issues. Migration and asylum impact squarely and directly on the sovereign power, authority and capacity of states, on key social institutions, such as labour markets and welfare states, and on complex notions of belonging and identity, which could be labelled as the 'who are we?' questions that so consume public debate about migration and its effects.

It is precisely *not* this book's argument that migration drives these debates, because it is not on such a scale as to provoke such existential transformation. Rather, international migration can contribute to these changes but, equally importantly, provides an analytical lens through which we can view them in relation to a wide range of other factors. European and EU responses to international migration are thus nested within a much broader debate about the consolidation and transformation of the European state system. As such, they cannot be detached from the intensely political nature of international migration. Immigration has acquired a high political salience across the EU. In Austria, Denmark, France and the Netherlands, it has been a key election issue and given rise to major challenges to established political parties. There has also been a resurgence of right-wing populism in Europe, which can play on fears of immigration and also invoke nationalist opposition to European integration in the name of 'the people' and the nation to be 'saved' (Canovan, 1999; Meny and Surel, 2002). The growth and development of EU action also coincide with increased scepticism about the EU (Taggart, 1998; Szczerbiak and Taggart, 2000).

As noted above, focusing on the EU can leave us in a situation where we analyse policy as though it were detached from politics (Schmidt, 2006), in the form of highly technical, expertise-driven processes. There are very specific forms of political action at EU level which, as will be shown, are centred on what have been called networks of intensive transgovernmental co-operation; these draw in particular from national executives and from security professionals, who have been the most active in colonising this policy domain. 'Intensive transgovernmentalism' is then used to denote 'the greater intensity and denser structuring where EU member governments have been prepared cumulatively to commit themselves to rather extensive engagement and disciplines, but have judged the full EU institutional framework to be inappropriate or unacceptable, or not yet ripe for adoption' (Wallace, 2005: 87).

As the terms 'network' and 'transgovernmental' recur throughout this book, it may be useful to specify more clearly how they are used, how they are constituted and how they relate to 'action'. Networks are understood as modes of social action that link informal with more formal structures of political authority. This book does, in a sense, document the move from informal to more formal modes of action at EU level on migration. So, for example, throughout this book, reference will be made to active participation in the areas of migration and asylum by ministers and officials from interior ministries with an internal security brief. These officials can then be said to be operating within an internal security field constituted at EU level, within which modes of informal social action are connected to more formal modes of co-operation on policy. An example of this can be seen when reference is made to the 'wining and dining' culture (den Boer, 1988) that was evident in the internal security field during the 1980s and early 1990s; that culture represented a sound base for future collaboration in that it established regular and systematic channels of communication between ministers and officials in interior ministries (ministries which it could be assumed – albeit mistakenly – would be focused on national rather than European concerns). It can also be helpful to be more specific when discussing these officials. Many of the most active participants in the migration and asylum field are national interior ministry officials. They have tended to be the dominant actors at EU level. A key role has been played since the late 1990s by the Strategic Committee on Immigration, Frontiers and Asylum (SCIFA, a body comprising interior ministry officials); but interior ministries are not the only actors. For example, the development of an external dimension of EU action on migration and asylum (i.e. one that affects non-EU member states) has also drawn foreign affairs ministries and development ministries into EU-level structures, for example through the High Level Working Group on Asylum and Migration. These national officials interact with EU-based officials, particularly those within the European Commission's Directorate-General for Freedom, Security and Justice (DGFSJ). Interaction occurs at all stages of the development, elaboration, decision-making and implementation of EU measures on migration and asylum, which is where the more fluid notion of transgovernmentalism makes more sense than overly narrow intergovernmental or supranational foci. Member state representatives have tended to hold the upper hand in these areas because of the decision rules established in the 1980s and 1990s, but this has changed since the 2000s as the Commission and the European Parliament (EP) have attained more formal roles within decision-making on migration and asylum. Member state representatives thus not only need to work closely with the Commission but also more recently have had to take more seriously into account the views of the EP on some aspects of migration and asylum policy, particularly asylum. DGFSJ has a number of specialised units dealing with the various aspects of migration and asylum that have become EU concerns.

It is not only DGFSJ that has migration interests. For example, the Directorate-General for Employment, Social Affairs and Equal Opportunities has long held an interest in employment-related aspects of migration and anti-discrimination, while the Directorate-General for External Relations (RELEX) has increasingly played a role in migration and asylum, both in the context of EU enlargement and as a result of changing conceptualisations of security and the blurring of the distinction between internal and external security. The EP has tended to be a more marginal actor, although this has changed as key policy areas, such as asylum, have become subject to the co-decision procedure, which gives a bigger role to the EP. Beyond this institutional level are a range of non-governmental organisations (NGOs) and think-tanks that operate in Brussels and often have good links with EU institutions. It is not unusual for people to move from NGOs to jobs in the Commission or EP. NGOs and think-tanks may also receive funding for research projects, reports and evaluations from EU institutions. This adds a further level of intensity to relations within the migration and asylum policy field.

The kinds of routinised co-operation that have developed on migration and asylum can then provide a basis for the further development of policy integration, but they cannot necessarily be ascribed to some kind of supranationally led drive for closer European integration or to a neo-functional spillover, because the units within the Commission that deal with migration and asylum have thus far tended to be followers rather than leaders in migration and asylum policy. Many of those who are most active in this field may well work intensively at EU level, but their political background and career point of reference remain national. The constitution of networks of intensive transgovernmentalism can be seen to capture links between more and less formalised institutional resources and the resultant sectoral focus of action, with its strong emphasis on internal security. As has been argued above, this does not mean that the only actors present in this field are security professionals: there have also been an array of NGOs and think-tanks and other international organisations that have sought to intervene in the field through reports, proposals and other forms of mobilisation, for example around rights-based arguments.

There is another point to be made here, which relates to the form or type of politics being pursued at EU level; again, this can be seen as 'policy without politics' in executive-dominated arenas at EU level, which have provided routes for EU-level decisions that avoid domestic legal and legislative constraints (Freeman, 1998; Guiraudon, 2001, 2003). A point made in this book is that 'policy without politics' might work well in more technocratic areas of policy, but migration and asylum are not issues that can be passed off as largely technical concerns, because they relate fundamentally to core, constitutive elements of domestic and EU politics. To understand the 'politics' requires that attention be paid to the actors involved in these

processes and to the structures within which they operate. At all stages of
the policy process there are important questions to be addressed in relation
to the participants in that process, the prevailing understandings of policy
problems, the solutions that develop to these problems and the forms of
decision that result. So far, most EU action has been focused on 'talk' and
'decision' but, as Brunsson (1993, 2002) has shown, talk and decision may
suffice when issues are complex, the concerns of a compound and complex
polity need to be addressed, and 'action' in the form of policy implementation, especially in the pursuit of ambitious objectives, might actually be
very difficult anyway.

The international politics of migration

While immigration is a salient domestic political issue across the EU, it is
also the case that there is necessarily an important international dimension,
too. As well as assessing the reasons why states have sought co-operation
and integration in the areas of migration and asylum policy, it is also essential to consider the EU as a regional organisation within the international
or global system because, as Heisler (1992) has pointed out, immigration
is simultaneously a societal and an international issue, and links must be
made across these levels. The EU introduces a specific regional dimension
to the analysis. We explore the motives underpinning the development of
the EU, but also try to nest this analysis of EU action within the broader
international system. This is relevant both because international migration
is substantially motivated by global inequalities and because the EU now has
important effects on neighbouring states and regions as it seeks to 'export'
its migration and asylum policies to potential member states and even to
non-member states. This book is concerned to make connections between
the domestic, the regional and the international, and uses the analytical
framework provided by the distinction between territorial, organisational
and conceptual borders to explore these links and to show the origins of
this external action (Geddes, 2005a).

This interplay between the societal and the international explains the
subtitle of the book. The book analyses EU immigration and asylum policy
beyond fortress Europe. The reasons for this are twofold. The first is that
there has been an opening to new migration on the part of EU member
states, to offset perceived effects of labour market and demographic
change. The resultant large scale of movement across Europe's borders
makes it an unlikely fortress. This does not mean that immigration is 'out
of control' or that states have 'lost control' (Sassen, 1996). What it does
mean is that states seek to combine openness to some forms of migration
with closure to other, 'unwanted' forms, and the EU now plays a role in
attaining these objectives. The second reason is that the EU now seeks
to develop forms of external action that 'export' migration and asylum

policies to non-member states. Europe's reach now literally extends beyond any notion of 'fortress Europe'.

Terminology

Two key points about terminology need to be made from the outset. First, the term 'immigration' possesses little analytical utility when we are seeking to account for the sheer diversity of migration within and to the EU. The data that are available can be partial and also based on different national definitions. The Commission of the European Communities (CEC) is striving to establish some common points of reference for the gathering of data on international migration (CEC, 2005a). Table 1.1 presents some data on migration flows into EU states.

Data on migrant and foreign populations do need some explaining. The figures on foreign populations, for instance, may reflect nationality laws as much if not more than they indicate numbers of arrivals. For example, it has traditionally been easier for foreign nationals to become French citizens than it has for them to become German citizens. Nationality laws have changed, but the relatively large foreign population in Germany includes second- and third-generation populations born in Germany but who retain the nationality of another country, Turkish nationals being the largest such group. The very large foreign population in Estonia mainly comprises Russians, while in Luxembourg it is strongly linked to the presence of nationals of other member states working for the EU institutions based in that country. The numbers of asylum-seekers in EU states have fallen. In 1992, for example, there were over 600,000 of them in Europe, with around 480,000 in Germany alone. National and EU measures have intensified in a bid to reduce these numbers to their current levels. According to data from the United Nations High Commissioner for Refugees (UNHCR), by the end of 2004, Asia hosted 37 per cent of asylum-seekers, refugees and displaced persons, Africa 25 per cent, Europe 23 per cent, Latin America and the Caribbean 11 per cent, North America 4 per cent and Oceania 0.4 per cent (UNHCR, 2006: 10).

Migration to, from and within EU member states can also be related to broader international dynamics. Salient aspects of these have been captured by Castles and Miller (2003: 7–9), as follows:

- The *globalisation* of migration as more countries are affected by migratory movements and migration flows become more diverse.
- The *acceleration* of migration flows as numbers of migrants increase. While the vast majority of these migrants are not in EU states, the development of an 'external' dimension of EU action on migration and asylum (see Chapter 8) is closely related to this broader, global acceleration.

Table 1.1 Key EU migration data

Member state	Population figures (1,000s), 2003, by nationality					Immigration figures, 2004			Total number of asylum applications, 2004
	Total	Nationals	Other EU nationals	Non-EU nationals	% foreign nationals[a]	Total	Males	Females	
Austria	8,082.2	7,366.7	164.2	685.7	1.83	127,399	69,789	57,610	24,676
Belgium	10,355.8	9,530.9	578.0	2,740	8.22	77,585	39,147	38,438	15,358
Croatia	N/A	N/A	N/A	N/A	N/A	18,383	9,381	9,002	161
Cyprus	715.1	647.9	33.9	33.3	9.39	22,003	10,502	11,501	9,859
Czech Republic	10,203.3	10,076.4	48.1	78.8	1.24	53,453	34,385	19,068	9,859
Denmark	5,397.6	5,126.4	66.4	204.8	1.24	49,860	25,015	24,755	3,222
Estonia	1,356.0	1,084.5	4.0	267.5	20.01	1,198	544	654	15
Finland	5,219.7	5,112.7	34.6	72.5	2.05	20,333	10,130	10,203	3,651
France	59,635.0	56,314.0	1,260.2	2,060.8	5.56	140,033	N/A	N/A	58,577
Germany	82,536.7	75,565.5	2,085.9	4,794.3	8.32	780,175	455,605	324,574	35,613
Greece	11,006.4	10,239.2	79.5	687.7	6.97	12,630	5,452	7,178	4,466
Hungary	10,116.7	9,986.6	17.4	112.7	1.29	21,327	12,289	9,038	1,600
Ireland	3,963.6	3,682.7	145.8	135.2	7.08	70,000	39,100	30,900	4,766
Italy	57,321.1	55,978.6	174.0	1,168.5	2.34	440,301	216,015	224,286	N/A
Latvia	2,319.2	2,285.9	4.4	28.9	1.44	1,665	994	671	7
Lithuania	3,462.6	3,428.3	1.7	32.5	0.98	5,553	2,968	2,585	140

Luxembourg	448.3	282.2	143.6	21.9	36.91	12,495	6,910	5,585	1,577
Malta	397.3	389.7	4.9	2.7	1.90	472	251	221	997
Netherlands	16,258.0	15,555.85	224.3	477.9	4.32	94,019	46,200	47,819	9,782
Poland	38,218.5	37,518.4	14.4	685.7	1.83	9,495	4,800	4,965	8,077
Portugal	10,407.5	10,173.6	50.4	183.4	2.28	19,028	9,108	9,920	107
Romania	N/A	N/A	N/A	N/A	N/A	10,350	5,304	5,046	661
Slovakia	5,379.2	5,276.1	11.8	91.3	1.92	10,390	6,329	4,061	11,354
Slovenia	1,996.4	1,951.1	1.9	43.3	2.27	10,171	7,485	2,686	1,174
Spain	42,197.2	39,425.7	578.8	2,193.4	6.57	654,561	374,321	310,240	5,369
Sweden	8,975.7	8,499.6	207.0	269.1	5.30	62,028	30,786	31,242	23,161
UK	59,328.9	56,592.7	1,016.6	1,719.6	4.60	518,097	260,621	257,477	40,620

N/A, not available.
[a] Percentage of population comprising foreign nationals (EU + non-EU).

- The *differentiation* of migration into various migrant types – labour migrants, family migrants, asylum-seeking migrants, student migrants – each of which can then be broken down into sub-categories. These migration flows are fluid, can change in nature and purpose and, it must be remembered, are usually the outcome of classifications made by receiving states rather than some personal quality or characteristic of migrants themselves.
- The *feminisation* of migration, with a much greater presence of female migrants, which can then lead to distinct forms of labour market integration, as male and female migrants often have different occupational roles.
- The *growing politicisation* of migration, as evidenced by the high salience of migration and asylum across the EU.

The figures in Table 1.1 could also be interpreted as suggesting that there are many motives for immigration to the EU: to seek work, to study, to seek refuge, to join with family members. If migrants move to work, then it may be for the shorter or longer term, it may be in lower- or higher-skilled occupations and it may possess a strongly gendered dimension, as female migrants move into certain types of occupation and male migrants into others. The processes by which categorisations are made – still largely at the borders of EU states, although the EU plays an increasing role – are central to the politics of migration. Moreover, the definition of certain migration types as legal has the effect of denoting others as illegal (Bogusz et al., 2004). Forms of migration defined as illegal are thus epiphenomenal of types categorised as legal (Samers, 2004).

There can also be a demand for 'illegal immigrants' in certain types of economic activity that require a cheap and flexible labour force and where worker exploitation can be rife. It is, of course, almost impossible to know with any precision the numbers of such migrants. The more extreme form is found in sectors such as domestic work and the sex industry, which are associated with human trafficking, people smuggling and their facilitation, often by criminal gangs, in what amounts to a modern-day slave trade – 'the dark underside of globalisation', as the United Nations Population Fund (2006) put it (see also Anderson, 2000). As Kelly (2005: 236) notes, a new issue such as trafficking elicits considerable attention, but this may not always contribute to the development of a deeper knowledge base because 'publications may primarily reflect a claims-making process, vying for influence over how the issue is understood and where it is to be located intellectually, symbolically and materially'. This is an insight that applies more generally to migration, where there is basic uncertainty about the causes, effects and consequences of migration and a range of actors trying to carve out a role for themselves in the response to the issue (as they define it). Kelly argues that the strongest migration flows occur within Europe, particularly from and across the central and east European countries that joined the EU in 2004 and the states in south-west Europe that are moving – albeit at different rates – towards accession, including Croatia, Serbia and Montenegro.

These points about the knowledge base in the face of ostensibly new challenges point to two issues discussed at more length in the next chapter. First, the ways in which problems are understood are central to the politics of migration. The role of expert knowledge (and which kinds of expertise) and its inclusion within decision-making processes can be very important. Second, there has been a geo-political widening of migration in Europe such that the 27 EU member states (as of 2007) are sending, receiving and transit countries of migration, usually a combination of all three.

There can also be some confusion when analysing the EU. Over the course of the period of time analysed in this book, the organisation evolved from the European Coal and Steel Community (ECSC) established in 1951 to the European Union (EU) that we now know. Until the Maastricht Treaty on European Union came into force in 1993, the organisation was commonly known as the European Community (EC). It is still technically correct to refer to European *Community* law, not EU law. Throughout this book reference will be made to the EC and to the EU, but hopefully the reason for this will be clear in the context of pre- and post-Maastricht Europe. An additional element of complication is that the EU tends to assign the names of cities to its plans for action. So, for example, much of the recent development on migration and asylum arises from the Tampere declaration of October 1999, reinforced by the Hague Programme of November 2004. There are many examples of such city-linked declarations and reference to them is unavoidable. That said, this book aims to make clear the content of such measures and agreements that occurred at these places.

Plan of the book

The book adopts an essentially chronological approach to the analysis of EU migration and asylum. This allows us to explore the evolution and development of policy and also to see how the contemporary EU framework has been influenced by longer-established patterns of EU action on free movement, immigration, asylum and internal security. In order for this chronological approach to have some meaning beyond the merely descriptive, the following chapter identifies the book's analytical framework, which centres on the specification of different types of border as the means by which international migration is understood and policy responses develop. That chapter also makes clear the necessity of exploring EU migration and asylum in the context of the geo-political widening of the issues across an EU of 27 member states (and beyond), as well as the conceptual widening induced by the emergence of new migration challenges.

Chapter 3 then focuses on the EU's free movement framework and analyses the ways in which this has been central to the Union's development and creates clear linkages between migration and the EU's core economic purposes. These linkages are important because they created a legal base for future EU action and also a way of 'framing' subsequent claims for expanded EU action. For example, EU anti-discrimination legislation has been heavily influenced by core EU principles concerning gender discrimination and equal treatment, which had a strong market-making rationale.

Chapter 4 moves on to assess the linkages between free movement, migration, asylum and internal security, which became more clear following the Single European Act (SEA, 1986), which extended the level of economic integration to create a single market, defined as an area without internal frontiers. Even though the focus was on intra-EC migration, this did have major implications for migration and asylum from outside the EC, because the implications of a frontier-free Europe in terms of the relationship between security and freedom became the subject of intensified co-operation within the EC and in the parallel Schengen system.

Chapter 5 analyses the period after the (Maastricht) Treaty on European Union came into force in November 1993. Maastricht formalised EU action, but did so in the context of an intergovernmental 'pillar' that placed immigration and asylum in with other 'Justice and Home Affairs' issues, in a separate legal framework, where there was a limited role for the European Commission, the EP or the European Court of Justice (ECJ). As will be seen, this further reinforced forms of politics that were dominated by the executive.

Chapter 6 shows how and why the EU took co-operation and integration to a new level through the provisions of Title IV of the Amsterdam Treaty (1999) and subsequent developments, including the Reform Treaty (2007). Since Amsterdam, it is has been more realistic to talk about common migration and asylum policies, albeit these policies cover some but not all aspects of migration and asylum. A notable omission so far has been labour migration policies, which remain a national preserve. While Amsterdam did impart significant new momentum to EU migration and asylum policy, it drew from previous patterns of co-operation, particularly in terms of the executive-dominated mode of action. Amsterdam did, though, extend a greater role to the EP and more scope for involvement by the ECJ. This was further consolidated by the Reform Treaty.

Chapter 7 shifts the focus to analyse the ways in which social and political spaces for migrants have opened at EU level. The chapter identifies the key role of expertise in the EU policy process and analyses the role and activity of a pro-migrant lobby at EU level. It also explores in detail the laws that have been agreed on anti-discrimination, the rights of long-term residents and family reunion.

Chapter 8 reinforces the point made earlier about the need to make links between the societal and international levels by exploring the increasingly important external dimension of EU action. EU attempts to export migration and asylum policies to neighbouring states and regions have become an important part of the EU migration and asylum framework. This chapter analyses the export to accession states in central and eastern Europe and to what the EU calls its 'neighbourhood' (and beyond). It also shows that EU action on those forms of migration that it defines as unwanted are analogous to that taken in other parts of the world, such as the USA and Australia, that seek to combine openness to certain kinds of flows (of capital, goods and services) but retain highly selective immigration policies.

Chapter 9 summarises the book's key findings and addresses the questions raised in this introduction about the timing, form and content of EU action.

2

European integration and reconfigured immigration politics

Introduction

Since the 1990s, EU competencies in the areas of migration and asylum have developed rapidly. How can the timing, form and content of EU action be understood? There is much to understand, as a plethora of measures and new forms of co-operation and integration have produced 'harder' legal effects via the issuance of directives and regulations, and 'softer' measures, such as action plans and forms of co-operation both within the EU and with non-member states, as well as the emergence of new resources – such as funding opportunities – for political actors organising around migration and asylum issues. This chapter concerns itself with the issue of how we got to this point, where we need to seriously consider the implications of a common EU migration and asylum policy. To address this question, the chapter establishes a framework for the analysis of EU responsibilities for migration and asylum, and relates this to the key migration and asylum policy challenges that face EU member states when they seek to regulate international migration (in its various forms) and 'integrate', as it is often referred to, their migrant and migrant-origin populations. Strong links are made throughout the chapter between national-level responses to immigration and the EU framework, because it is necessary to understand when, why, how and with what effects member states' responses to migration have shaped and continue to shape EU action. Yet, a narrow, state-centred approach is insufficient if the intention is to capture the contemporary dynamics of EU policy co-operation and integration in the areas of migration and asylum, and their link to the consolidation of the EU as a regional form of governance. It will become clear as we look at the issues of migration and asylum that once member states have made decisions to co-operate and integrate, then the policy context and associated dynamics change, with the result that, while member states clearly remain key actors, they now routinely co-operate with each other and have created spaces for intervention in policy debates for EU institutions. Yet, as will also be seen, the impacts of co-operation and integration are uneven, as is made evident by the differential impact on states and on different migration types.

Migration and the nation state

The development of EU migration and asylum policy co-operation and integration is particularly challenging for national migration and asylum policy frameworks, which have often been viewed as paradigmatic and, as such, as rather difficult to shift because of their embedded nature. It would, however, be wrong to imagine that these national frameworks are cast in stone. They could, of course, change for a number of reasons. It would be difficult to pick up a newspaper or watch a television news bulletin in Europe without being aware of the way that some kind of 'multicultural challenge' has been identified for many European states. Similarly, emergent forms of political organisation 'above' the nation state posit a 'supranational challenge' to understandings of the organisation of political power in Europe. The extent of the supranational challenge, which is this book's primary focus, is, of course, closely linked to the distinct sources of legal, political, institutional and social power associated with European integration. The EU's core objectives, centred on the promotion of freer movement for people, services, goods and capital within the single market – what can be called the EU's market-making functions – raise questions about sovereignty, membership and identity, all of which have often been construed as delimited by state borders. But these questions are raised in relation to a particular kind of integrative project and hence to rather particular effects on migration and asylum policies that transcend state borders.

This chapter develops the argument that the best way to view these effects is through the analytical prism provided by borders of different types, understood as zones of interaction across which we see flows of people, services, goods and capital but at which we also see significant efforts to restrict those flows that are viewed as in some way harmful or threatening. The chapter distinguishes between *territorial, organisational* and *conceptual* borders as important zones of interaction that mediate the relationship between migrant newcomers and the societies they move to. Borders provide ways of seeing international migration and are integrally linked to European states and their development, consolidation and transformation (Bade, 2003). It is the categorisations made at state borders that make international migration visible (Zolberg, 1989), while what Bourdieu (1993) called 'state thinking' or what Wimmer and Glick Schiller (2002) call 'methodological nationalism' has been integral to the conceptualisation and analysis of international migration.

It will also become clear that the EU is a complex, multi-level system and cannot be analysed by relying entirely upon the familiar reference points of comparative political analysis or international relations. Multi-levelness challenges a vocabulary of political analysis that takes the state as its point of reference. Schmitter (1996b: 132) notes that:

> Our language for discussing politics – especially stable, iterative, 'normal' politics – is indelibly impregnated with assumptions about the state. Whenever we refer to the number, location, authority, status, membership, capacity, identity, type or significance of political units we employ concepts that implicitly refer to a universe featuring sovereign states.

State thinking and the power and resonance of the borders of states are necessarily challenged as the EU seeks what it calls free movement within its single market. This means that the ability of EU member states to determine who can and who cannot enter their territory is diminished, but, as will be argued in this chapter, a distinction between different types of border and their relationship to forms of international migration shows that there are significant processes of 'boundary build-up' at the EU's territorial, organisational and conceptual borders (Nevins, 2002). Such build-up can be seen in the reinforcement of territorial borders as well as in efforts to monitor immigrant populations construed as a threat. Consequently, while state power to regulate migration may well be inhibited by a wide range of factors – such as the effects of global inequality as a source of migration pressure, the operation of international labour markets or the operation of transnational migrant networks – it is also the case that European states do retain a formidable capacity to exclude, and that this capacity resides not only at territorial borders but also at key organisational borders of work, welfare, belonging, entitlement and identity. By making sense of migration, European states also make sense of themselves, by defining and redefining borders and boundaries that determine access, membership and notions of belonging (Weick, 1995).

The area in which EU competence in relation to migration is most marked relates to freer movement within the EU, which has been progressively and effectively supranationalised since the 1960s. This may be movement for employment or for other purposes, such as heliotropic migration as people retire from the cold north of Europe to warmer southern climes (Williams et al., 1997). This kind of movement was viewed as less problematic or, indeed, virtuous, if it fitted with economic integration objectives or if the migrants were relatively prosperous. The 'big bang' 2004 enlargement to include eight central and eastern European countries plus Cyprus and Malta led to movement within the EU being viewed as more problematic; indeed, such movement was represented not as 'virtuous' intra-EU mobility but as more problematic 'immigration', with a particular challenge posed to the organisational borders of work and welfare. The most obvious manifestation of this was the decision by 12 of the 15 existing member states (excepting Ireland, Sweden and the UK) to restrict movement for the purposes of work from the central and east European accession states (the

A8 as they were known – Cyprus and Malta were excepted if only on the grounds of size) for some part of a seven-year transition period.

Freer movement within the EU enabled by the framework of Community law can be separated from migration from outside the EU. The basis for this distinction is relatively clear, because movement within the EU was covered by a European legal framework while movement from outside the Community/Union was largely governed by national legal frameworks. Since the 1990s we have begun to see more development of the EU's capacity to act in relation to movement from outside the EU and to apply the EU's governance tools to manage this movement, such as issuing directives and regulations. When the period since the signing of the Maastricht Treaty in 1992 is examined, and particularly the accelerated rate of policy integration that followed the 1997 Amsterdam Treaty, it becomes apparent that it is now meaningful to discuss a common EU migration and asylum policy, with such a framework involving the authoritative allocation of capacity to act, albeit in relation to only some forms of migration and asylum, not all. There is certainly now a relatively highly developed capacity to 'talk' and 'decide' in relation to some elements of migration and asylum, but 'talk' and 'decision' are more difficult to turn into 'action' in terms of effective implementation of agreed objectives (Brunsson, 1993). The EU has acquired its most developed extra-EU migration competencies in relation to asylum and irregular migration flows, and has thus far been less able to develop regulatory competencies for labour migration from outside the EU.

This book concerns itself not only with policies designed to regulate international population movement, but also with those policies that are subsequent to such movement and are often labelled as concerning themselves with immigrant 'integration'. There are problems with many of the terms associated with migration. One of the more problematic is 'integration', because it is not clear who is to be 'integrated' into what and by whom. By this is meant that some, not all, migrant communities become the point of reference for integration policies, and that the idea of a community (often national and involving again 'state thinking') into which they are supposed to be integrated can be imprecise and contested, while it is also not entirely clear which actors or institutions will take responsibility for this process. Moreover, 'integration' is not an issue for migrants alone, as it must affect all members of European societies as they engage with a range of social processes and institutions that all in some way contribute to a notion of integration, such as schools, universities, the labour market, the political process and so on. That said, there is much emphasis within the public debate on the need for migrant newcomers to integrate or adapt to the societies that they move to, that this has social, economic, political and cultural dimensions and, as such, has also given rise to particular kinds of debate at EU level that reflect and refract often intense national debates

(Groenendijk, 2004). Since 2000 there has also been the introduction of EU anti-discrimination legislation and an EU directive that extends rights to legally resident third-country nationals (TCNs) after five years that are equivalent to those of EU citizenship. The EU has also drafted 'common principles' on integration and, as part of its softer, 'new governance' tools, applied techniques of sharing best practice and 'benchmarking' to immigrant integration (CEC, 2005b) .

These kinds of developments lead to what can be called a differentially empowered EU in relation to migration and asylum. This differential empowerment need not be entirely surprising, because this is also the picture across a wide range of other policy areas where European integration is marked by incompleteness (an endemic feature of integration) and is likely to persist given the complex dynamics of multi-level politics. The EU is not locked into some kind of straightforward teleological pursuit of a more complete form of economic and political integration, as though it was abundantly evident what this would mean. Far from it – the very essence of EU analysis, and perhaps its most compelling element too, is the implication of incompleteness within a multi-level system where power and competencies are shared across levels of government and dispersed through market and other types of non-governmental networks. In this context, the member states are not redundant or powerless, but their role has changed and, consequently, so too have understandings of their power, capacity and authority. Or, put another way, of their sovereignty.

By exploring the differential, incomplete, multi-level nature of EU competencies, we are also better placed to understand some of the underlying dynamics that have contributed to the emergence of an EU policy framework, because it is, of course, not by chance that EU responsibilities for extra-EU migration have grown precisely in those areas such as asylum and irregular migration that have been most troubling for domestic policy actors. Similarly, it has thus far proven more difficult to put in place arrangements for a common approach to labour migration, which tends to be linked to key national organisational variables, such as access to the labour market and to welfare state entitlements. Again, we are brought back to the issue of borders: their definition and effects, and changes in border relationships both within states and between states.

While a security frame or understanding of migration and asylum has tended to predominate, there is a body of scholarly work that has emphasised the importance of rights-based politics as a domestic political factor. This factor has created social and political spaces for migrants and their descendants at national level and thus militates against some of the harsher, more restrictive impulses of national governments (Hollifield, 1992; Joppke, 1997; Guiraudon, 1998). This insight involves distinguishing between the executive, legislative and judicial branches of government and arguing that, while the executive branch of national governments has tended to be the dominant player in the making of migration policy, the decisions of courts and sometimes bureaucrats – or decisions made behind 'gilded doors' as Guiraudon (2000) puts it in her analysis of France, Germany and the Netherlands – have often been rights-protecting or rights-expanding. The extension of this argument made by both Hollifield and Guiraudon is that the EU is then a supranational escape route for these national governments, as their executive branches use the EU as a way of avoiding domestic constraints.

The discussion of borders in this chapter does raise spatial issues associated with the location and effects of various types of borders and the location and effects of decision-making processes. It may also be the case that creating EU competencies can later have unanticipated consequences as, for instance, judicial decisions may confound the intention of current decision-makers. The impact of institutional rules put in place at time t_0 cannot be foreseen, with the effect that earlier decisions can have unanticipated consequences. The preferences of member states may also shift, leaving them with formal institutions and highly developed policies that do not fit their current needs (Pierson, 1996: 147; see also Hansen, 2002). Once gaps between initial decisions and their effects are opened, they can be difficult to close, because of supranational resistance, institutional barriers to change (political institutions are 'sticky') and high sunk costs and barriers to exit, which mean that even sub-optimal decisions become self-reinforcing over time.

Key policy dimensions

Two broad dimensions of migration policy and politics can be distinguished. The first of these concerns itself with the regulation of forms of population movement that involve the crossing of state borders. Hammar (1985) labelled these 'immigration policies'. This would seem to mean the authoritative allocation of capacity to regulate points of entry to the state territory, to determine residence conditions and rules governing access by family members and to determine the criteria governing access to key institutions, such as the labour market. There are then a set of concerns linked to post-migratory issues, which were characterised by Hammar as 'immigrant policies' but which are also often frequently referred to in public debate as 'integration policies'. These policies concern themselves with the debate subsequent to migration, and centre on a process of mutual accommodation, redrawing and re-imagination of organisational and conceptual borders. This means, in more practical language, conditions for participation and the complex interplay between rights and responsibilities for migrant newcomers. There are widely divergent European responses to immigrant integration, because of the national histories and institutional structures that provide a vital backdrop to them, as well as a temporal dimension linked to the point at which a country began to receive relatively large numbers of migrants, which then affects the maturity of the response. While Europe has 'older' and 'newer' immigration countries in terms of the timing of migration, the EU has had particularly strong effects on policy development in newer member states (Faist and Ette, 2007).

Regulatory immigration policies are focused on strategies of territorial management, while immigrant integration policies tend to address processes of inclusion and exclusion evident at the boundaries of welfare states, labour markets and rules governing access to national citizenship. However, when this broad distinction between immigration and immigrant policies is explored in more detail, it becomes apparent that it may well not capture the sheer diversity and complexity of contemporary European migration policy and politics. If we consider first the question of 'immigration' policies, then we immediately have to recognise that, as an analytical category, the term is so broad as to be effectively meaningless. There are many different forms of immigration. People may move to seek work, to join with family members, for the purpose of marriage, to study or to seek refuge. There are also irregular or illegal migration flows, which defy formal state policies but which may be strongly linked to the effects of restrictive policies or to economic informality in EU member states. Each of these can then be broken down into various sub-categories. For example, regular or irregular labour migration may be short term or longer term, it may be higher or lower skilled, it may involve movement into very different types of economic sector, and it may have a strong gender dimension, evident in the different types of employment undertaken by male and female migrants. In addition to this, one form of migration may turn into another, so that someone may arrive to study, may subsequently find employment and may then be joined by family members. Or people may arrive as irregular migrants but then be given the opportunity to regularise their status and become 'legal'.

A distinction could be made between labour and family migration, where there is an assumption of voluntary movement, and asylum-seeking migration, where there is a presumption of compulsion in the face of persecution. In public debate this distinction has been eroded because of the widespread use of the term 'bogus asylum-seeker' to denote asylum applicants for whom the motive for migration is deemed to be economic rather than a well founded fear of persecution. Faist (2000: 23) suggests that a stark distinction between voluntary and forced may not always adequately reflect the motives for migration, whereas a continuum with voluntary movement at one end and forced migration at the other may actually capture the situation better, with many migrants actually located somewhere between the two poles.

The legal context within which asylum-seeking migration is viewed also varies, because it is supported and legitimated by the United Nations

Geneva Convention on the rights of stateless people of 1951 and to which all EU member states are signatories. The Convention protects the rights of people fleeing persecution on the grounds of race, religion, nationality or membership of a particular social group or political opinion (Goodwin-Gill, 1996). After the Second World War, liberal asylum regimes were put in place in western Europe. The Federal Republic of Germany's was particularly liberal. Article 16 of the 1949 Basic Law stated that the 'politically persecuted enjoy the right of asylum'. What distinguished German provisions and made them particularly expansive was that Article 16 gave individuals the right to seek asylum, rather than recognising the right of the state to grant it (Joppke, 1997). Across western Europe, asylum was not considered too much of a problem in the 1950s, 1960s and 1970s, because the numbers involved were small. Many of those who did seek asylum were lauded as brave escapees fleeing from totalitarian regimes in central and eastern Europe. Attitudes began to change in the 1980s as 'jet-age asylum-seeking' (Joppke, 1997: 262) allowed easier access to European countries for those fleeing post-colonial trouble spots in Africa and Asia; at the close of that decade, the convulsions resulting from the end of the Cold War added an east–west source of displaced persons to more long-standing south–north patterns of movement. This was particularly evident at the height of the 1991–2 civil war in the former Yugoslavia. The number of asylum applications made to EC member states increased dramatically and reached its peak in July 1992, when 80,000 asylum applications were made in that month alone.

We will explore the relationship between EU action and international legal standards governing asylum more fully in Chapters 6 and 8. What can be noted at this stage is that the substantial elision in public debate that occurs between immigration and asylum demonstrates that distinctions between different migration types have been hard to maintain, with asylum-seeking often alleged to be a disguised form of labour migration and, as such, bogus or abusive.

It seems fairly clear that certain forms of migration are viewed as more problematic than others and it is these that tend to constitute the 'immigration problem'. Similarly, some migrant populations tend to be viewed as more problematic and it is these who then constitute the 'integration problem'. These populations do, however, constitute only a sub-set of the broader migration picture, which is highly complex – within that picture there are many and various migration flows and these have very different relationships to state and EU policies. For example, states may actively encourage sought-after migration, such as highly skilled labour migration, while restricting flows deemed as unwanted, such as asylum-seeking or lower-skilled migration. The other side of the coin of these efforts to restrict has been the growth of irregular forms of migration, which can involve the trafficking and smuggling of people and the facilitation of such movement, often by criminal gangs. The effect of these policies can also be to make a distinction between migrants from more and less economically developed countries. The borders of EU states that make migration visible also constitute significant borders of inequality. The effects of these inequalities become apparent when we look at the development of EU migration and asylum policy, particularly its external dimension, which is analysed in Chapter 8.

The borders of Europe

Europe's borders are necessarily central to the study of international migration. Early analytical approaches to population mobility did not distinguish between internal migration (i.e. within a state) and external migration (i.e. from outside the state) (Ravenstein, 1889). It was assumed that people would gravitate from poorer to richer areas and that the motives for movement within and between states were thus essentially similar. This approach was inadequate for a number of reasons. As Zolberg (1989: 405–6) points out:

> One important theoretical development of the past quarter of a century is recognition that it is precisely the control which states exercise over borders that defines international migration as a distinctive social process. This arises from their irreducible political element, in that the process entails not only physical relocation, but a change of jurisdiction and membership.

If we take global inequality as a key driver of international migration, then it is at the borders of states that we can identify those processes that give meaning to international migration as a social and political process distinct from internal migration.

As borders are central to the analysis of international migration, then it is necessary to specify what is meant by this term and to identify the different types of border that give meaning to international migration. A distinction can be made between three types of border: territorial, organisational and conceptual. Although there are clearly overlaps between the three, this classification is an heuristic device specifying processes that underlie the core features of the systems of categorisation and classification that are integral to the debate about international migration.

Territorial borders

These are the usual focus for analyses of immigration. Decisions made about who can or cannot enter the state's territory at air, land and sea ports of entry are indicative of that state's power, authority and capacity to exclude, and are the focus for much of the debate about immigration. Territorial borders have been challenged by the EU's single market as well as by new strategies of territorial management, which can see Europe's borders 'move' as controls are exerted in non-EU transit and/or sending countries (Guiraudon and Lahav, 2000; Guild, 2001). While Badie (1995) proclaimed the 'end of territories', it has been argued that this would be cataclysmic and improbable (Anderson and Bort, 2001) because there is still a highly developed sense of territoriality in Europe. This can be understood as 'a pattern of behaviour whereby living space is fragmented into more or less well-defined territories whose limits are viewed as inviolable for their occupants' (Glassner, 1993: 27).

One distinct and important aspect of the current European constellation is the intensification of data collection and data sharing, both between EU member states and with non-EU states, particularly the USA, as movement across borders is monitored and information pooled. Terror attacks since 11 September 2001 have accelerated and helped legitimise these developments, but tools such as the Schengen Information System (SIS), the Eurodac system of data sharing on asylum-seekers and illegal immigration, and the Visa Information System (VIS) predate these terror attacks and mark a concern by EU member states to develop new techniques to monitor and control people as they move into or across their territory. The VIS, for example, works in conjunction with the development of a visa sticker containing biometric identifiers; it stores information on TCNs who have requested, possess or have been denied a visa. Meloni (2005: 1358) notes that 'these measures have given rise to a number of concerns relating to personal information protection, the adequacy of individual remedies and, more generally, the development of a "control society"'. There have also been 'laboratories' outside the EC/EU Treaty framework for the development of such practices, such as the Schengen agreement in the 1980s, or more recently the Prüm Convention, agreed by seven member states (Austria, Belgium, Germany, Spain, France, Luxembourg and the Netherlands) in May 2005, which focuses on the gathering and sharing of data on border controls, illegal immigration, cross-border crime and terrorism.

Categorisations are integral to the sense-making processes that occur within organisations responsible for managing migration, such as border police forces. The legal framework will be determined a long way (both metaphorically and literally) from the locations at which decisions are made about who can and cannot enter the territory of a member state. Enforcement of immigration controls at territorial borders necessarily also involves a distinction between forms of migration defined by state and EU policies as regular/legal immigration and irregular/illegal. If substantial inequalities persist across state borders and border controls are restrictive, then the irregular/illegal route is the only option open to some would-be migrants. Moreover, there are differing capacities across the EU to actually enforce border controls. To match the rhetoric of control with the reality of restriction would be costly, so it is not entirely surprising that there may be some slippage in attainment of objectives (specified from national capitals or from Brussels) in those EU member states – particularly to the south and east – that border migrant-sending states and regions.

Organisational borders

These often exist within states and are those sites at which decisions are made about access by migrant newcomers to key social and political institutions, such as the labour market, the welfare state and national citizenship. There is some complexity here, too, which we explore later in the book. Not least, there are various types of welfare state and of labour market and, thus, interactions between migration, welfare and labour markets are complex and heavily dependent on context. A central theme within this book is the way in which changes in organisational borders of work and welfare in particular constitute an important pre-condition for – or way of seeing – international migration. As borders of work and welfare shift, then so too do perceptions of the 'usefulness' of different types of migration.

Organisational borders can also sharpen the distinction between regular/legal and irregular/illegal migrants because, for example, of the relatively large informal economic sector in some EU member states, which can provide a home for irregular migrants. Regularisation programmes thus usher irregular migrants into social locations where they are 'legal' and from which they can be more easily observed by the formal organisational structures of employment and the welfare state.

Conceptual borders

These constitute more nebulous, but no less important, notions, of identity, belonging and entitlement. They cannot be separated from, but cannot be entirely reduced to, the institutional settings that form the backdrop for debates about identity, belonging and entitlement, and thus are identified as a separate type of border. Debates about migration and asylum in Europe often boil down to the question of 'who are we' and then, by extension, the issue of how these self-understandings affect attitudes to migrant newcomers. There can be important relationships between organisational and conceptual borders because, for example, welfare state and labour market insecurity may well contribute to hostility towards new migrants when they are understood as a threat to a precarious status.

Thinking about borders is central to the analysis of international migration and has produced insights that are closely related to the analysis of EU migration and asylum policy. For example, Hollifield (2004) identified what he called the 'liberal paradox' as central to contemporary migration politics, whereby openness to movement of goods, capital and services has not been accompanied by similar openings to free movement of people. Ruhs and Chang (2004) point out that one reason for this is that people move as the bearers of rights, with more obviously profound implications for the societies that they move to. This tension between the various kinds of flow that make themselves visible at borders has been a central element of much recent work on migration and can also demonstrate how and why regional integration in Europe in this field is not necessarily distinct when analysed alongside other forms of regional integration. For example, processes of 'boundary build-up' on the US–Mexico border have imparted a spatial dimension (a 'thinning out' of place as a result of global migration flows) both to debates about borders and to the relationship between various types of flow across those borders. This is because:

> complex interchanges between state actors and groups of citizens produced a set of deep concerns about the ethno-cultural, socioeconomic, and bio-physical security of the nation, all of which are inherently geographical given their inextricable relationship to a particular territory. The boundary build-up was thus a territorial strategy to achieve that security and assuage those concerns. (Purcell and Nevins, 2005: 213; see also Nevins, 2002)

A rationale for European boundary build-up can be linked to a body of work on the securitisation of migration that broke out from a debate about the meaning of security in post-Cold War Europe. A shift in the terms of that debate led to a focus on a series of new security challenges, and particular forms of population movement being defined as unwanted or in some way threatening. Security can be understood as:

> a practice, a specific way of framing an issue. Security discourse is charac-terised by dramatizing an issue as having absolute priority.... 'Security' is thus a self-referential practice, not a question of measuring the seriousness of various threats and deciding when they 'really' are dangerous to some object.... It is self-referential because it is *in* this practice that the issue becomes a security issue. What we can study is the practice that makes this issue into a security issue. (Wæver, 1996: 106–7)

A strong security rationale underpins the development of EU immigration and asylum policy. This arose in part from established patterns of internal security co-operation, such as the Trevi Group of EC interior ministers and officials, set up in 1975. In post-Cold War Europe, the distinction between external and internal security was becoming blurred (Bigo and Leveau, 1992; Monar and Morgan, 1994). The 'securitisation' of migration emphasises the links between market relations embodied within the free movement framework and the control of population. Micro-level power relations are seen to determine the system of macro-level power relations that form the basis of capitalist class relations. Of particular importance are the modern technologies of surveillance, discipline and punishment. Attention is directed towards the practices of security agencies and the implementation and effects of new technologies of population control. From this perspective, it makes less sense to analyse the articulation

between liberalisation (free movement) and securitisation (involving techniques of population control) and to see security concerns as a knock-on
effect of single-market integration. Rather, processes of securitisation and
the control of the population are the foundation stones of liberalisation, with the effect that migration becomes a component of a security
field (Foucault, 1979; Huysmans, 1995; Bigo, 1996). Analyses of the
securitisation of migration then focus on the ways in which words such as
'foreigner' and 'asylum-seeker' are used to represent threats to cultural,
racial, labour market and welfare state identities (Huysmans, 2006). Shifting the discussion from the realm of conceptual analysis does still leave
open the question of the relationship between the number of properties
covered by the term 'security' (its intension) and the class of entities to
which the term applies (its extension) (Sartori, 1970). The analytical usefulness of a security story may be reduced if everything is a security story.

A particular argument about security in Europe is that the 'targeting'
of population has acquired an EU dimension through the development of
the Justice and Home Affairs 'pillar' after the Maastricht Treaty and the
designation of the EU as an 'area of freedom, security and justice' after the
Amsterdam Treaty. All these contributed to an intensification of co-operation
between security specialists and other officials, and a European-level representation of threats that reconfigures what Foucault identified as the
sovereignty–discipline–government triangle, 'which has as its primary target
the population and as its essential mechanism the apparatuses of security'
(Foucault, 1991: 102). The implication of this for sovereignty is that 'the
relationship between state and non-state sites is better viewed as heter-
archical rather than hierarchical' (Walker, 2004: 7). While the state remains
the key referent for many of the issues that are central to the EU politics of
migration, asylum and population control, it is also a central contention of
much of the work on this issue that networks of expertise now transcend
the borders of the member states, with the result that quintessentially
domestic issues have become a common European concern, with some form
of emergent multi-level governance of internal security.

Beyond fortress Europe

If responses to migration are nested within a much broader debate about
the meaning and effects of borders then, if we are to understand the relationship between various kinds of border and migration in contemporary
Europe, it is also necessary to explore some of the longer-term historical
patterns that have done so much to influence current EU responses. To do
this requires an examination of the contemporary history of migration to
Europe, which we now move on to consider.

The development, consolidation and transformation of Europe's territorial, organisational and conceptual borders play a key role in predetermining

and organising perceptions of this 'age of migration' (Castles and Miller, 2003; Geddes, 2005a). This section looks at attempts to characterise European migration politics since the end of the Second World War, with an initial focus on the idea of 'fortress Europe'. The next section provides an overview of the recent contemporary history of migration to Europe while attempting to identify the broader, shaping factors integral to the later analysis of the development of specific EU responsibilities. The aim is not to analyse in great detail responses across all EU member states, but to specify aspects of the development of contemporary European migration policy and politics that have become integral to the emergence of an EU response.

Although the origins of the term lie with protectionist elements of EU trade policy, the term 'fortress Europe' has become synonymous with debates about European immigration. Trade and migration are also linked because unfair trade in sectors such as agriculture, where the EU's Common Agricultural Policy has had a strong protectionist element, can exacerbate the economic inequalities that lead to migration. If we were to try to provide a definition of the supposed fortress, then it could be said to rest on a combination of tightly restrictive immigration policies and the social and political exclusion of settled migrants and their descendants. The term 'fortress' could appear paradoxical if it is borne in mind that millions of people cross the borders of EU member states every year. In such terms, this is a strange 'fortress'. Yet, if we shift the focus and look at the EU's southern frontiers, then we can see the sharp edges of fortress Europe made most evident by the dreadful death toll of would-be migrants lost at sea during perilous crossings as they try to enter countries such as Spain, Italy, Malta and Greece.

The EU and its member states clearly retain a strong commitment – at least at the rhetorical level – to the regulation of migration, but at the same time there are some openings to new migration. The EU in such terms pursues an approach to migration that rests on a balance between openness and closure, and is thus a reflection of the core dilemma for states, expressed most powerfully by Zolberg (1989: 406) when he noted that the analysis of contemporary international migration is about neither complete closure nor total openness; rather, it is about the walls that states build and the small doors that they open in these walls. European states have traditionally opened the door to certain types of workers, particularly the more highly skilled, and to small numbers of asylum-seekers. As Zolberg (1989: 406) presciently observed in an insight that still applies today: 'the future of international migration depends in large part on how these doors are manipulated'.

Even though arguments have been made for complete openness, they have not tended to prevail in the policies pursued by European states (or anywhere else in the world, for that matter). Rather, the debate about EU migration and asylum centres on the way in which member states have ceded some competence to collective forms of decision-making at EU level, particularly in relation to the development of pooled capacity to reinforce border controls. The broader geo-political and socio-economic dynamics that have characterised European societies and polities in the last few years have had the effect of pushing the debate about migration in a certain sense 'beyond fortress Europe', as European integration has led both to an intensified reinforcement of measures to counter 'unwanted' immigration and to some attempts to co-opt non-EU states into the EU framework, but also to a wider opening of the door to 'wanted' forms of migration, such as that by the highly skilled. EU liberalisation has also brought with it freer movement and the supranationalisation of certain rights and entitlements, supported by an autonomous supranational legal and political system at EU level with its own court, including relatively progressive anti-discrimination legislation and rights-extending measures for legally resident TCNs. Indeed, as we shall see when we analyse patterns of EU-level political mobilisation in Chapter 7, the claims of pro-migrant groups tend to centre on the need for 'more Europe', that is, more EU competencies in order to counter fortress-like tendencies that they see as emanating from national policies. The term 'fortress Europe' is not particularly well equipped to capture such dynamics.

This is not to deny that European states and the EU have pursued harsh and restrictive policies, but 'fortress Europe' has become associated more with a politics of symbols – of national and cultural identities and 'ways of life' that are supposedly threatened by immigration and are to be 'protected' – and less with the capacity of states to match the rhetoric of control with the reality of restriction (Cornelius et al., 1994). This is not the same as saying that immigration policies serve only symbolic purposes, because the effects of these policies can be only too real for those who seek to enter EU member states but who are deemed to constitute a 'threat'. It is no exaggeration to say that these policies have contributed to a shocking loss of life at Europe's frontiers, particularly those to its south. This is an important part of the picture and is closely related to broader strategies of territorial management and organisational change (such as in the welfare state and labour market) in EU member states that have forced some rethinking of the best and most appropriate way to 'manage migration', as it is now referred to. The debate about migration is thus inextricably linked to the ways in which borders, in their various forms, give meaning to migration and the ways in which changed border relationships within and between European states (and non-EU states) shape understandings of and responses to international migration, in its various forms.

The specificities of European migration also need to be connected with broader migration dynamics. When comparisons are made with responses to migration and asylum in the USA and Australia, it becomes clear that it is not necessarily the case that there is something distinctly and uniquely

'European' about the kinds of measures that are the focus of this book (Cornelius, 2001; Nevins, 2002; Maley, 2003; Rajaram, 2003). What is distinct is the governance structure within which these responses are located. The EU is a unique form of supranational governance in the sense that it possesses the capacity to turn treaties agreed between states into laws that bind those states (Sandholtz and Stone Sweet, 1998). It does this through its own institutional system, within which, as we will see, legislative roles are shared by the Council of Ministers and the EP, executive powers are shared by the Commission and the member states, and where the ECJ exercises judicial power in those areas where the EU has competence. It is this capacity to make laws – to issue regulations and directives – that is an important point of distinction between the EU and other forms of regional governance. There are, however, some important similarities between measures in relation to migration and asylum (from outside the EU) adopted at EU level and those evident in responses to migration and asylum in North America and Australia. EU responses can thus be connected with a more general salience of immigration issues in the late twentieth century. As detailed in Chapter 1 (see pp. 9–12), in their analysis of *The Age of Migration*, Castles and Miller (2003: 7–9) identify: the *globalisation* of migration; an *acceleration* of migration; a *differentiation* of migration; a *feminisation* of migration; and a *politicisation* of migration, at national and international level. The point here is that the EU has its own distinct processes, linked to its status as a unique form of supranational governance, but this does not necessarily mean that the forms taken by European and EU responses differ markedly from those seen in other parts of the world encountering similar dilemmas. So, if there are processes of boundary build-up at play on the US–Mexico border and there are some similarities to processes evident at Europe's external borders – particularly those to its south – then this suggests that this is not a distinctly 'European' issue or response (Geddes, 2007).

Migration and migrants in European history

As Bade (2003) demonstrates in his analysis of migration in European history, it is also necessary to locate migration within broader patterns of state development, consolidation and transformation. Adding historical depth to the analysis can show that migration is not some contemporary element of turbulence that 'challenges' European states. Rather, migration and migrants have been integral to the European state system during its formation, consolidation and more recent transformation as it has been affected by factors such as European economic and political integration. If we focus more closely on the post-war period, labour migrants made an important contribution to western European economic reconstruction and prosperity. Yet, even though both immigration and European integration were central to the post-war reconstruction of the west European nation state, it is European integration that tends to get the credit – the 'European rescue of the nation state', as Milward (1992) put it.

Large-scale movement of people in the immediate post-war period resulted from the devastation wrought upon the European state system by the Second World War. The ensuing vast displacement and resettlement of up to 50 million people, if the Soviet Union is included in the figures, was combined with the efforts of west European countries to restore their economies. One consequence was that the shake-up of the European state system was accompanied by labour market exigencies in the developed capitalist economies of north-western Europe – linked initially with economic reconstruction and then with economic boom – that prompted a demand for workers beyond the capacities of national labour markets (Kindleberger, 1967). Recruitment of migrant workers was an important part of the answer. Workers moved both within and from outside Europe (Castles and Kosack, 1973). Intra-European migrations saw migrant workers move from southern European countries, particularly Portugal, Italy, Spain, Turkey and Yugoslavia, to north-west European countries, especially Belgium, France, Germany, Luxembourg and Switzerland.

Intra-European migrations were supplemented by extra-European migrations, particularly from former colonies. Colonial connections played an important part in structuring migration. It was no coincidence that most migrants from the Maghreb moved to France; that people from India, Pakistan, Bangladesh and former British colonies in the Caribbean moved to the UK; and that people from Surinam and Indonesia migrated to the Netherlands (Entzinger, 1985). Moreover, many who moved from former colonies did so as citizens of the country to which they were moving. For instance, the 1948 British Nationality Act allowed citizens of the British Empire to move to the 'mother country', or at least it did until 1962, when the first of a series of restrictive immigration laws was introduced (Katznelson, 1973; Hansen, 2000). When they arrived as citizens, these migrants and their descendants had the same legal, political and social rights as other citizens, although extension of rights need not guarantee effective utilisation. This has had important effects on subsequent debates about migrants' rights. While all citizens are equal in terms of formal access to rights, experiences across Europe demonstrate that, when it comes to exercising rights, then, to paraphrase George Orwell, some citizens are more equal than others (see Layton-Henry, 1990). In contrast, migrants to Germany – or 'guest-workers' as they were called – arrived as foreigners and encountered exclusive nationality and citizenship laws, which led to a rather more basic debate about access to the formal status of citizenship (Brubaker, 1992; Green, 2004). Similarly, in newer immigration countries, in central, eastern and southern Europe, debates have tended to focus on access to status (e.g. of legal resident) rather than the use of rights.

Not all European countries had empires from which they could draw labour. Even for some of those that did, colonial links were supplemented by formal recruitment agreements. France's long-standing concerns about the demographic and economic implications of low levels of population growth led to an active recruitment policy in the post-war period (Noiriel, 1988; Weil, 1991; Hargreaves, 1995). France negotiated recruitment agreements with 16 European and non-European countries. Germany did not have recent colonial connections that could be exploited for labour market purposes so, when labour shortages became a problem in the late 1950s and early 1960s, recruitment agreements with Italy (1955), Spain and Greece (1960), Turkey (1961, 1964), Morocco (1963), Portugal (1964), Tunisia (1965) and Yugoslavia (1968) were concluded. In addition to France and Germany, three other EU member states had 11 recruitment agreements between them: Belgium had four, Luxembourg two and the Netherlands five.

Many migrant workers who moved to Europe were labelled as 'guests', which assumed return to their countries of origin when labour market conditions changed. Immigrant workers were wrongly perceived as a relatively malleable factor of production and the 'rotation' of workers was envisaged, whereby some would return to their country of origin after a period working abroad and be replaced by new immigrant workers. If rotation were to occur, then it would militate against permanent settlement and circumvent difficult questions about migrant integration into host societies, or so it was thought. The implication for migrant populations would be a form of displacement, characterised by Sayad (2004), writing about Algerian migration to France, as a 'double absence', with dislocation from the countries and communities of origin and a 'temporary', detached presence in receiving states. The clearest embodiment of this assumption of temporariness was evident in the West German *Gastarbeiter* (guest-worker) recruitment scheme. Article 2(1) of the 1965 West German Aliens Law stated that: 'A residence permit may be issued if the presence of the foreigner does not impair the interests of the Federal Republic of Germany'. This legislation thereby explicitly linked the presence of migrant workers in West Germany with the interests of the economy. It also introduced a principle of arbitrariness, whereby foreigners had a more precarious status and a vulnerability to techniques designed to encourage them to leave, such as the arbitrary denial of work permits.

The guests who stayed

What could countries of immigration do if the 'guests' decided to stay? Switzerland deported unwanted foreign workers (Hoffmann-Nowotny, 1985), but other European countries of immigration tended not to employ draconian measures that would evoke memories of wartime deportations and human rights abuses. Hollifield (1992) argued that it is on this point that economistic approaches to the analysis of immigration slip up, because they neglect the importance of politics, or what he characterises as the impact of 'rights-based politics' rooted in the 'embedded liberalism' of the post-war order (*pace* Ruggie, 1982; Gilpin, 1987). The forced return of migrant workers to their countries of origin would tend to infringe national laws and international standards protecting human rights. The same national and international legal framework meant that it was difficult to halt family reunification, although it could certainly be made more difficult.

An intergovernmental take on EU migration and asylum developments would argue that the shift or 'escape' to Europe was and is precisely about dodging these kinds of regulation-inhibiting and rights-expanding domestic constraints, by shifting decision-making to new supranational venues, where the executive branch of EU governments faces far fewer legislative or judicial constraints (Freeman, 1998; Guiraudon, 1998). An alternative account would contend that member states, even if they wanted to, have not been quite so easily able to slip these domestic political and legal constraints, and that European integration may have some rights-expanding and regulation-inhibiting effects, at least in the sense that competencies become pooled at EU level rather than national level. As will be argued later, the consequences – whether or intended or not – of EU-level action by member states has been to open new spaces for intervention by EU institutions that can constrain national-level decision-makers and create still more new spaces for particular forms of social and political mobilisation around EU competencies. This does not mean that member states have 'lost control' of immigration or that EU-level rights have replaced national-level rights, but it does mean that there are significant EU-level responsibilities that do need to be factored into the analysis if we are to understand the contemporary parameters of European debates about the regulation of migration and migrants' rights.

Restrictions on primary labour migration from the early 1970s onwards did not mean that immigration ended, because 'secondary' migration by families continued apace. Migrant workers and their families began to build new lives for themselves in Europe: they found employment, opened businesses, bought houses, their children attended schools, and so on. In short, migrants and their descendants became part of the social and cultural fabric of modern western Europe. Migrants and their descendants also, of course, paid taxes and became entitled to social benefits acquired as a result of legal residence. They were, however, usually denied the right to participate in the political process if they were not citizens of the country in which they resided, with some exceptions regarding local-level voting rights. Yet, despite facing social, economic and political disadvantages in their new countries, many migrants were still afforded a standard of living and economic and political stability that did not exist in their countries of origin. The result was that the 'guests had come to stay' and Europe's 'new ethnic minorities' were created (Castles et al., 1984; Rogers, 1985). The 'old' ethnic minorities are the indigenous or national minorities, such as the Scots, Catalans and Bretons. The 'new' ethnic minorities are post-war migrants and their descendants. Messina (1992) explores these 'two tiers of ethnic conflict' in Europe, although the complex relations between 'old' and 'new' ethnic minorities need not be understood solely in terms of 'conflict' or 'struggle'. Forms of political action that involve mobilisation in relation to ethnic or cultural identities can also be about attempts to seek incorporation into mainstream politics and acquire legitimate status; such attempts seek to draw 'identity politics' into the realm of 'normal' liberal politics, characterised by bargaining, accommodation and compromise (Koopmans and Statham, 2000).

There is also a distinct temporal dimension within the shift from an emphasis on the regulation of population movement to policies addressing 'immigrant integration'. Immigration policies became increasingly oriented towards restriction of labour migration after the oil price rises of 1973–4. They were supplemented by policies directed towards the social integration of settled migrants. These policies differed substantially across Europe, because they were usually refracted through different national traditions of nationhood and citizenship (Hammar, 1985; Brubaker, 1992; Geddes and Favell, 2004; Joppke and Morawska, 2003). Permanent settlement under-mined narrow, economistic approaches to migration analyses couched in terms of 'supply and demand' or 'push–pull', which saw migrants as rela-tively malleable factors of production. Such approaches failed to account for the various motivations for movement or the diverse social and political implications of settlement (King, 1993; Hammar et al., 1997). They also failed to account for the development of migrant networks and the links between these networks and formal organisational structures in sending and receiving states. A macro-level instance of the deficiency of economistic approaches was their neglect of the importance of prior contact between sending and receiving countries, such as colonial connections. These con-tacts helped shape the development and sustenance of migration networks. At the micro-level, recruitment and settlement patterns did not necessarily correspond with models of comparative economic advantage, models that predicted movement decisions by ego-centred individual economic actors founded upon reasoning about optimal cost–benefit ratios (Portes and Borocz, 1989). Kith and kinship could matter as much if not more than calculations of economic self-interest.

The acceleration of migration

Until the 1990s, most academic analyses of migration focused on the conse-quences of post-war migration motivated by colonial ties or by guest-worker recruitment for a relatively small group of receiving states in north-west Europe. The 1990s, however, saw a transformation of migration policy and politics in Europe that can justify the description of these politics as the *new* European politics of migration. Moreover, the backdrop against which such migration is set – the constitution of the different types of border referred to earlier – can be very different in southern, central and eastern Europe. Four particularly important elements of novelty can be identified.

Geo-political widening

All 27 EU member states are now sending, receiving or transit countries of migration, or more usually some combination of all three. No longer can analyses of European migration focus on a small group of north-west European countries and pretend that this provides adequate coverage of the debate. In the late 1980s and early 1990s, attention was directed towards the capacity of south European states to regulate migration. Greece, Italy, Portugal and Spain were relatively new countries of immigration, having previously been countries of emigration. They all have experienced – and continue to experience – migratory pressure at their external frontiers. These pressures have become European issues because of linkages within the single market. 'Older' countries of immigration sought the imposition of restrictive policies on newer countries of immigration. For instance, Spain's 1985 *ley de extranjería* (foreigner's law) was 'almost entirely the result of external pressure associated with entry into the EC' (Cornelius, 1994: 360). This suggests a process of international policy learning, although the learning curve appears steep, with marked implementation problems (Baldwin-Edwards and Schain, 1994). Consideration of migration to southern Europe also demonstrates how and why it would be a mistake to understand migration as some kind of external challenge without considering the ways in which migration is also linked to the labour market and employment patterns in these countries. A body of scholarship has highlighted the close relationship between both regular and irregular migration and the socio-economic structures of south European countries (although the insight applies across migration countries), with a relatively large informal economic sector accommodating considerable numbers of migrant workers. Analyses of economic informality in southern Europe demonstrated the necessity of accounting for background factors such as state–society relations and the organisational features of labour markets and welfare states (Calavita, 1994; Cornelius et al., 1994; Baganha, 1997; Baldwin-Edwards, 1997). In post-Cold War Europe there was also increased attention paid to the migration implications of the collapse of the Soviet bloc. There were some doom-laden predictions about large-scale east–west migration, with figures as high as 25 million migrants mooted (Brym, 1991; Heitman, 1991). In fact, although east–west migrations were substantial – around 2.5 million in the first half of the 1990s – they were not on the scale some had predicted. Predictions of floods of migration and invasions by migrants are a staple component of debates about immigration. Even though they may be exaggerated, they can have important effects and contribute to perceptions of a migration crisis. Codagnone (1999: 55) wrote that 'It can be argued that such scenarios have been at least partially instrumental in legitimating and reinforcing the concept of "Fortress Europe" and the restrictive immigration policies derived from this construction'. In their analysis of the institutionalisation of Europe, Turnbull and Sandholtz (2001) do seem to take at face value some of these apocalyptic forecasts and contend that predictions of large-scale migration from eastern Europe were a key factor at intergovernmental level impelling EU co-operation on migration at the time of the Maastricht Treaty. Other analysts have pointed to the way in which predictions of post-Cold War disruption of states, borders and security contributed to a 'securitisation' of migration as the security agenda expanded to include new 'societal' threats to order and stability (Wæver et al., 1993). Understandings of a so-called 'threat from the east' played an important part in structuring the debate about EU enlargement, with a great deal of emphasis placed on the reinforcement of migration control capacity in those countries seeking to join the EU at that time (Lavenex, 1999; Zielonka, 2001; Lavenex and Uçarer, 2002).

Conceptual widening
The ostensible emergence of new migration types and new forms of response to migration also challenges understandings of the politics of immigration predicated on 'older' flows seen after the Second World War. The word 'ostensible' is used because there is an 'old wine in new bottles' problem here, given that it may not be so much the motives for movement or countries of origin that have changed as the routes available for some migrants, the categories into which they are placed, and the types of policy response. In relation to migration flows, increased attention is now paid to asylum-seeking migration and to 'irregular' migrants. These have become the migration challenges that pre-occupy the EU and that motivate EU co-operation to strengthen and reinforce borders, particularly territorial borders. A range of non-state actors have been included as – sometimes unwilling – agents of the immigration control authorities. In practical terms, this means that truck drivers, airlines and ferry operators all face the threat of sanction if they transport migrants without the appropriate permits or documentation (Lahav, 1998; Guiraudon and Lahav, 2000). In relation to border control policies, it can be said that the borders of Europe have moved, in some senses, because the EU increasingly seeks to exert authority in transit and sending countries as a way of reducing the potential for migrants even to reach an EU member state (Guild, 2001). It is the reworking of migrant categories, the formulation of new types of response

and the development of new strategies for territorial management that are the most vivid representation of this conceptual widening.

Spatial reconstruction

The 1990s also saw another distinctly new element of European migration as EU competencies expanded. This marks a spatial relocation of the policy response to migration, with a growth in both policy debate and decision-making at EU level. The key actors have remained national governments, because the form that co-operation has taken has privileged them or, to be more precise, their executive branches. But the ways in which they discuss migration and asylum have changed, as has the context within which decisions are made. As will be extensively documented in the remainder of this book, there has been a significant increase in EU competencies. This leaves open the issue of whether there has been a more profound 'reconstruction', as marked by the redefinition of the interests and identities of actors involved in this policy area arising from the development of EU competencies and of the kinds of regularised interaction that accompany them. European integration could conceivably mean, for instance, that interior ministry officials, as a result of frequent interaction, set aside narrow national interest and 'become European'. If national actors operating at EU level do 'go native', this implies socialisation, understood 'as a process of inducting actors into the norms and rules of a given community. Its outcome is sustained compliance based on the internalization of these new rules' (Checkel, 2005: 804; see also Dawson and Prewitt, 1969). Beyers (2005) distinguishes between 'type I' socialisation, with a key role played by domestic political contexts, as well as other factors, such as career structures for senior officials, that remain nationally based, and 'type II', 'thicker' socialisation, which occurs when agents 'go beyond role playing and imply that agents accept community or organizational norms as the right thing to do'. Research suggests that the impact of EU socialisation is weak (Beyers, 2005; Hooghe, 2005; Lewis, 2005) and that EU dynamics are secondary to those operating at the national level (Zürn and Checkel, 2005), such as, again, career structures. The argument will be developed in this book that, while there is some evidence of refocused political activity, the main point of reference for key actors in the EU migration and asylum policy process remains national. The more important point may well be that the meaning of 'national' has changed, because of interaction within the EU and the development of networks of intensive transgovernmentalism (Wallace, 2005). Take the case of the British government, for example: formally, at least, it has opted out of key elements of the EU framework, such as those parts relating to asylum, but it cannot escape the entangling effects of the growth of EU action in this area and, indeed, may well not want to, because much of what happens at EU level maps quite closely to the policy preferences of the British government (Geddes, 2005b).

Temporal reconstruction

A particularly important component of the new European politics of migration has been the creation of new routes for migration, both regular and irregular, induced by labour market shortages and bottlenecks, as well as by the effects (actual and potential) of demographic change. Of particular importance has been a shift in the terms of debate away from 'immigration control' and towards 'managed migration', which signifies increased interest in new migration paths for the highly skilled and also some concern about the effects of an ageing population on European labour markets and welfare states. While it would be wrong to see immigration as a 'magic bullet' capable of resolving these problems, it is the case that some openness to new labour migration has been seen as a part of the answer and has acquired some supranational resonance through linkage to the EU's 'Lisbon Agenda' of economic reform that in 2000 declared the EU's ambition to be the world's leading knowledge-based economy by 2010 (an ambition that seems unlikely to be realised). This has also re-ignited the social and political debate about immigration and its consequences, and turned immigration into a hot issue in the first decade of the twenty-first century.

The EU policy context

The broad distinction that could be made between supranationalised free movement policy and a largely intergovernmental immigration and asylum policy never meant that the two were entirely disconnected and could be analysed separately. Indeed, the linkages have become even more obvious since the late 1990s. Linkages initially arose because freer movement for EU citizens brought with it tighter controls on movement by non-EU citizens, as a result of 'structural' and 'contextual' dynamics (den Boer, 1996). Structurally, the creation of the common market in the 1960s and single-market liberalisation since the 1980s focused attention on the implications for migration and asylum, particularly in the framework of internal security. Contextually, migratory pressures in the early 1990s raised the salience of immigration-related issues at both national and European level and also co-incided with an important shift in the terms of debate about security, with a broadening to include ostensibly new migration challenges such as migration and asylum. Although neither these structural nor contextual factors could dictate the form that policy co-operation and integration would take, the relationship between debates about member state immigration and asylum policy and politics and the development of EU responsibilities requires an approach that is sensitive to 'thick' horizontal national-level policy contexts and the emergence of a 'thinner' vertical dimension at EU level, contextualised by co-existent tensions between restrictive/expansive and inclusive/exclusive tendencies in national-level approaches to migration and asylum. This also suggests interdependence, interplay and entwinement

of the roles of national and supranational institutions, and allows circum-
vention of a narrow dichotomy arising from a misplaced focus on whether
it is member states or supranational institutions that control the scope and
direction of European integration. The issue of whether it is member states
or supranational institutions that are in charge may not be particularly
interesting in any case, because the answer is likely to be 'both sometimes'
(Putnam, 1988). State-centred intergovernmental accounts provide a way
of analysing intergovernmental preference formation and negotiation, but
can tell us less about subsequent institutional dynamics. Accounts that focus
on emergent forms of supranational governance tell us little about underlying national policy dynamics, but can capture important aspects of new
forms of social and political action linked to migration and asylum.

The EU's migration and asylum competencies and the development of
new locations for debate and decision-making about migration require
consideration of the shape and form of institutional interaction relating to
migration and asylum issues in a multi-level and multi-arena setting; here,
national debates about migration and asylum are nested within a wider
European debate. Institutions can be understood as 'the rules of the game
in a society or, more formally ... the humanly devised constraints that shape
human action' (North, 1990: 126) and as being '*constitutive* of actors', but
also arise from the preferences and power of the units that comprise those
institutions (Keohane, 1989: 161, emphasis in original).

The institutionalisation of an EU policy context can be conceptualised
as involving four stages: the *accommodation* at EU level of member
states' policy preferences; the formal *transfer of competencies* (laws, rules,
practices and decision-making capacity); the *expectations* of social and
political actors about the relevant location of decision-making power and
authority; and the *impacts* on domestic politics (Sandholtz and Stone
Sweet, 1998; Favell, 1998; Buller and Gamble, 2002; Radaelli, 2004). EU
action on migration and asylum has tended to focus on the first two of
these four stages, but there is some evidence of stages 3 and 4 becoming
more relevant (Faist and Ette, 2007). These stages could be seen to suggest
a neat heuristic, but are not discrete because, over time, previous transfers
of competencies and/or the impact of changed expectations will influence
the processes by which member states articulate their preferences and the
manner in which these are accommodated in negotiations.

The EU context may also affect the behaviour of these actors. It could
do so in a 'thinner', consequential manner, where domestic political contexts, as well as other factors, such as career structures for senior officials
who remain nationally based, still play a key role (Beyers, 2005). This
would accord with what March and Olsen (1989) identify as a logic of
consequentialism. Alternatively, agents may be influenced by new patterns
of intense interaction to 'go beyond role playing and imply that they
accept community or organizational norms as the right thing to do', with

the result that European integration induces far more profound changes, according to a 'thicker' institutional 'logic of appropriateness'. It is important to analyse the constitution of this new EU setting because, as March and Olsen (1998) put it: 'political actors ... calculate consequences and follow rules, and the relationship between the two is often subtle'. Moreover, they do so in a system within which constitutionalisation by treaty and institutionalisation as a result of EU-level interaction render 'the international system a bit less like anarchy, a bit more like a constitutionalized domestic polity' (Caporaso, 1996: 35).

Conclusion

This chapter has specified the key policy dimensions central to analysis of migration and asylum, as well as demonstrating the complexity of these categorisations and, by extension, the policy responses that then unfold. It did so by identifying two key components of the book's analytical framework. The first of these was the centrality of borders to developing an understanding of responses to migration. The distinction between territorial, organisational and conceptual borders is well placed to identify the ways in which European states make sense of migration, how and why the EU has acquired some competencies in these areas, and why the issues of migration and asylum have become more central to the European project. This analytical framework was then developed in relation to an EU with 27 member states. It is vital to factor in the impact of EU enlargement and to consider both boundary build-up and boundary shift as integral components of EU action on migration and asylum. The consideration of the meaning and implications of distinctions between different types of border and of the geo-political and conceptual widenings of migration will recur throughout this book. The next chapter begins to delineate the framework for EU action on migration by exploring the free movement framework that has developed since the 1950s and that made close links between migration and the core economic purposes of the EC/EU.

3

The supranationalisation of free movement

Introduction

Free movement for nationals of member states was central to the development of the EU, while immigration and asylum were not. Free movement chimes with the EU's fundamental market-making purposes and their contemporary restatement, such as through the 'Lisbon' economic reform process, but has also brought with it co-operation and some integration on migration from outside the EU, particularly in the 1990s and 2000s. Connections between free movement and immigration and asylum also demonstrate the blurred distinction between what Hoffmann (1966) called 'low' and 'high' politics, which arises because of the ways pressure can build for integration in policy areas that impinge directly on state sovereignty as a result of integration in areas where national sovereignty issues are less pronounced and where economic interdependence is more clearly evident. Analysis of events related to free movement since the signing of the Treaty of Rome in 1957 also indicates that these interdependencies need not dictate the institutional form taken by co-operation and integration on migration policy. We should not blithely assume that the EU is locked into some kind of trajectory of which the endpoint is a common immigration and asylum policy. European integration is more contingent and conjunctural than this teleological federalism allows. Despite the supranationalisation of intra-EU migration policy and significant development since the Amsterdam Treaty (1997), there remain obstacles to the initiation and implementation of common migration and asylum policies. Free movement for people has, though, created legal and political sources of power and authority that have implications for TCNs. By tracing the early stages of the debate about the rights of TCNs, we are better placed to locate more recent developments in their proper context. This chapter deals with three sets of issues: the ontological status of free movement in the European project as indicative of the EU's identity as a regional actor; the light that analysis of free movement casts on understandings of European integration; and the ways that free movement, migration and asylum are linked to the geo-political definition of the EU and of the practices of population control and territorial management associated with these understandings. The period from Rome (1957) to the SEA (1986) is covered; the latter is the subject of the next chapter.

Free movement in the common market

The essence of the 'European project' is its commitment to what are called the 'four freedoms', which means free movement for capital, goods, services and people. This has major implications for the territorial, organisational and conceptual borders of Europe, as becomes clear when we explore the development of the framework governing free movement for people and consider some early phases of EU action on extra-EU migration and asylum. The Treaty of Rome's provisions for free movement for capital, goods, services and people were central to the common market, which was, in turn, to be the keystone in the arch of European integration and ensuing political integration, or at least that was the plan. The establishment of a legal and political framework guaranteeing free movement also required the establishment of supranational legal and political competencies, to ensure that free movement arrangements were given full effect. The corollary of this was that member states' competencies and discretion were limited by the encroachment of supranational authority, which developed to ensure attainment of the EU's market-making goals. As a result of these developments, member states could no longer control migration by nationals of other member states moving primarily for purposes of work (who could enforce this right through the courts). The relationship of TCNs to this framework is a core issue. The inclusion of TCNs within EU free movement provisions requires an appropriate legal, political and institutional framework; in turn, establishing such a framework plays an important part in what could be called a European restructuring of immigrant inclusion.

Free movement was not originally intended to be a generalised right of free movement open to all people; rather, it was to be free movement *for workers* (CEC, 1977). Free movement was a functional right related to the economic purposes of building the common market. Neither was the freedom to move to be extended to TCNs, irrespective of how long they had lived in a member state. Free movement was to be for nationals of member states moving for purposes of work. Conditions of entry, residence and movement by TCNs were issues that resided squarely within the domain of competence of the member states. During the late 1950s and 1960s, it was also far from clear that the 'guests' (migrant workers) had actually come to stay (as described in Chapter 2). When it became apparent that permanent settlement had occurred, the member states displayed little intention to broaden the free movement framework to include within its scope legally resident TCNs. Immigration and asylum policies were squarely within the domain of national competencies, while the problems associated with melding diverse national policy paradigms highlighted the difficulties of what Pinder (1968) called 'positive' integration, and action in this area would require unanimity among member states. Immigration and asylum were sensitive national issues for which the Community had not been endowed with competence, and member states were prepared to resist Community encroachment into these areas. The result was that TCNs were largely excluded from the provisions of the Treaty. The question of the rights of TCNs still loomed large at the end of the 1990s and was an important part of the agenda of pro-migrant NGOs; in this area there have been major developments since the end of the 1990s, as will be seen in Chapter 7.

Free movement provisions were made in the Treaty of Rome, signed in March 1957, that established the European Economic Community (EEC) and put in place the legal, institutional and political structures of the EC.[1] The EC's market-making objectives and technocratic origins have led European integration to be perceived as an elite-driven process that emphasises efficiency in relation to capital rather than democracy in relation to participation and popular legitimation, despite the oft-quoted ambition to create a 'people's Europe'. A market-making rationale and fundamental economic purposes were central to the EC; the politics, it was thought, would follow once the complex web of interdependence had been woven.

When tracing the origins of free movement, it is actually possible to delve a little further back and observe its origins in the ECSC, created by the Treaty of Paris, signed in April 1951. The ECSC was the EC's forerunner and was itself indicative of far broader integrative intentions among the six founding states (Belgium, France, Germany, Italy, the Netherlands and Luxembourg) than its rather narrow focus on the coal and steel industries appeared to imply. Article 69 of the Treaty provided that member states were obliged to remove restrictions based on nationality upon employment in the coal and steel sectors for workers who were nationals of one of the six member states and held a recognised qualification. The Treaty of Rome built upon the Treaty of Paris' establishment of a common market for coal and steel with labour market provisions by seeking to create a broader customs union. It is important to be specific about actual provisions while keeping in mind the broader points that we are interested in, that is, those concerning the identity of the EU as a regional actor, the dynamics underpinning integration and the linkages between free movement, migration and asylum in the context of a wider Europe. This also leaves us better placed to explore the meaning of Europe's territorial, organisational and conceptual borders.

The Treaty of Rome's most relevant free movement provisions were contained in Title III, Part II (Articles 48–66). Article 48(1) stated that free movement for workers was to be attained by the end of a transitional period finishing on 1 January 1970. The functional character of the right of free movement is quite clear in the English-language version of the Treaty. The six signatories referred to 'workers' to indicate that the provisions applied to employees. As Plender (1988: 194) noted, this reference was even clearer in the German and Dutch versions, where the words *Arbeitnehmer* and *werknemer* are used. In separate chapters, three types of economic activity were defined by the Treaty as giving rise to a right of free movement (Handoll, 1995; Martin and Guild, 1996; O'Leary, 1996):

- work (Articles 48–51);
- self-employment (Articles 52–58);
- service provision (Articles 59–66).

The importance of these Treaty provisions should not be underestimated, because if the common market was to succeed, it was vital that free movement within it be facilitated, or at least not unnecessarily impeded. To reinforce this point, the ECJ has established a consistent body of case law enforcing these rights and has shown its ability to shape the parameters of supranational economic and political integration, or what international relations scholars call 'the domestification of international politics', which 'describes the process by which that system becomes less anarchic and more rule governed' (Caporaso, 1996: 38).

The legislation introduced in the 1960s to give practical effect to the Treaty of Rome focused on free movement for people who were nationals of member states, their dependants and those covered by agreements between the EC and third countries. This meant that the Treaty covered some TCNs, if they were a dependant of a Community national or covered by provisions of an agreement that the EC was to strike with countries such as Algeria, Morocco, Tunisia and Turkey. The Treaty's provisions did not cover TCNs *qua* TCNs. Possession of the nationality of a member state was the basis for access to Community rights. This raises the issue of post-national perspectives on citizenship and membership and ideas about entitlement derived from universal rights of personhood (Soysal, 1994). The specificities of supranational integration illustrate that rights beyond national borders were secured for nationals of member states moving for purposes of work but were difficult to secure for non-nationals, because of member state sensitivities about immigration and their own nationality laws. This was despite the fact that in Article 48(1) of the Treaty of Rome the words 'nationals of a member state' did not actually appear. Article 69 of the Treaty of Paris had been more specific, because it referred to 'workers who are nationals of Member States'. Plender (1988: 197) noted that it was possible that the drafters of the Treaty of Rome 'wished to leave open, in 1957, the possibility that the Community might develop a common market in labour corresponding with the common market in goods, accompanied by a common external policy towards labour from third countries and freedom of movement within the Community for established immigrants'.

This would require a common migration and asylum policy, which has begun to emerge – albeit in partial form – since the end of the 1990s.

Irrespective of whether there was serious intent to broaden the provisions to include settled non-EC nationals, the enactment of the free movement provisions made it clear that TCNs were not covered. Instead, attention was directed towards ensuring the effective operation of free movement for nationals of EC member states. Central to this was outlawing discrimination on the grounds of nationality for people moving for purposes of work. Article 48(2) of the Treaty of Rome stated that freedom of movement entailed the abolition of discrimination based on nationality between workers of member states as regards their employment, remuneration and other conditions of work and employment. Non-discrimination on the basis of nationality has long been the oil in the cog of free movement. Article 6 of the Treaty of Rome stated that any discrimination on the grounds of nationality was prohibited, and that the Council of Ministers could adopt rules designed to prohibit such discrimination. No provisions were made for the prevention of discrimination on grounds of race or ethnic origin until the Amsterdam Treaty in 1997.

Member state competencies with respect to intra-EC migration were severely diminished and even where there was scope for prevention of the exercise of the right of free movement there were limitations on the exercise of this discretion. Article 48(3) of the Treaty of Rome outlined some limitations on the right of free movement for workers that were related to public policy, public security or public health. Directive 64/221 dealt with the grounds for expulsion of EC nationals from another EC member state.[2] Member state discretion was constrained because the ECJ defined very narrowly the circumstances in which these powers could apply. In the *Bouchereau* case, the Court ruled that there must exist 'a genuine and sufficiently serious threat to the requirements of public policy affecting one of the fundamental interests of society'.[3] This meant that a member state's discretion to expel non-nationals was limited. The free movement framework empowers individuals who are nationals of an EU member state and gives them recourse to national courts and the ECJ to protect their rights of free movement.

Article 48(3) detailed other key practicalities. It specified that workers must be free: to accept offers of employment; to move within the territory of a member state for the purpose of taking up an offer of employment; to stay in a member state for the duration of that employment; and to remain in the territory of a member state after having been employed there. Aside from the limited public policy, public health and public security concerns that could be used by member states to prevent free movement, the only other significant limitation on free movement for workers was that it did not apply to employment in the public service. Most member states still reserve the right to appoint their own nationals to key public service jobs.

The Treaty did not actually define 'public service' – this was left to the ECJ (Plender, 1988: 209–13).

A key effect of the free movement framework was that it empowered supranational institutions and created scope for constitutionalisation, by which is meant the scope for EU institutions to turn treaties agreed in public international law between states into laws that bind those states (Sandholtz and Stone Sweet, 1998). Member states' discretion was limited because, for certain categories of people (EC nationals moving for purposes of work, the self-employed to exercise the right of establishment, or others to provide a service), they could no longer determine who could and could not enter their territory. State capacity to control immigration by EC nationals moving for purposes of work was effectively ended. Article 49 gave the Council competence to issue directives or make regulations which set out the measures required to bring about, progressively, free movement for workers. Directives and regulations are the principal instruments of EC law; they possess 'direct effect' and are supreme, which means they over-ride national law.[4] EC laws create rights and obligations; they exist 'above' member states and member states are obliged to uphold them. Most of the powers established by the Treaty of Rome for free movement were exercised in the form of directives. Directives were used because the powers contained in the Treaty were fairly substantial and the use of directives gave member states a degree of latitude when implementing them (Hartley, 1978: 7). Directives leave the actual method of implementation to the discretion of national governments and their bureaucracies. Regulations are supposed to be implemented in a uniform manner across member states. This does, of course, raise the issue of implementation in a Union of 27 (at time of writing), but the main focus of this analysis are what Brunsson (2002) calls 'talk' and 'decision'. As Brunsson also shows, there are good reasons to suppose that *talk, decision* and *action* may not be closely connected, particularly in complex issue areas such as free movement, migration and asylum. Decision-makers may seek to appease complex environments through talk and decision, but the very complexity of the environment means that action may be difficult to attain. For example, immigration is an area often characterised by strong rhetorical commitments to control that may not always relate very well to the realities of continued migration. In 2002, for instance, the Italian government introduced new immigration legislation (the Bossi–Fini Law) with the specific intention of severely curtailing migration to Italy. This could even, it seemed, include use of force against immigrants because, as one of the law's sponsors, the leader of Lega Nord (the Northern League), Umberto Bossi, put it: 'I want to hear the sound of cannons otherwise this story will never end'. Yet, during the five years of centre-right government in Italy between 2001 and 2006 there was the largest growth in the immigrant population in Italian history, from 1.3 million in October 2001 to 2.7 million in January 2006, while 646,000 people had their status regularised (Geddes, 2008).

The nuts and bolts

Free movement for nationals of member states has become a defining feature of the EU and integral to ideas and practices relating to such things as 'EU citizenship'. Free movement reconstitutes territorial and organisational borders while also drawing into view the 'who are we' questions that are central to the conceptual borders of the EU and its member states. As Maas (2005) demonstrates in his study of the 'genesis' of free movement rights, the underlying drive for this reconstitution was intergovernmental, with a key role played by the Italian delegation at the time of the negotiation of the Treaty of Paris creating the ECSC. These intergovernmental origins do not, however, require that all motives for future action also be intergovernmental. As will be seen, the development of a supranational legal framework covering free movement has created legal, political and social spaces for intervention by EU institutions such as the ECJ, the European Commission and the EP (Guild, 2001).

The Council adopted the most important implementing regulation for free movement of workers in 1968. Regulation 1612/68, of 15 October 1968, provided for 'the right to take up activity as an employed person'.[5] Until 1968, member states were still able to control entry, residence and access to employment. After this, they were no longer able to do so because their competence in this area was ceded to supranational level. TCNs were not covered by Regulation 1612/68, because Article 1 made it clear that the provisions applied to nationals of a member state. The possibility was expunged that a more general right of free movement open to all people legally resident in an EC member state could develop. Nationality laws were – and still are – none of the EU's business, as a declaration attached to the Maastricht Treaty (1993) attested. This does present some difficulties. For instance, definitions of entitlement to nationality can differ between member states. Germany, for instance, emphasised 'blood' descent, which led to an expansive notion of German nationality for ethnic Germans that exceeded the borders of what was, when the EC was founded, West Germany (Green, 2004). The 1949 *Grundgesetz* (Basic Law) defined a German as 'a person who possesses German citizenship or who has been admitted to the territory of the German Reich as it existed on 31 December 1937 as a refugee or expellee of German stock'. German nationals could be taken to mean those holding German citizenship (the narrow definition) or those falling within the broader definition provided for by the Basic Law, which included people deemed German by nationality law but who did not actually live in the Federal Republic of Germany (a broader definition). In a declaration attached to the Treaty of Rome, the Federal Republic of Germany stated that it preferred the second definition. This meant that free movement for workers within the common market also applied to people in what was East Germany, in parts of Silesia and Upper Prussia, which were part of Poland and the former Soviet Union, respectively, and to expellees and refugees of German descent. Similarly, the provisions made in the 1948 British Nationality Act prompted an expansive notion of nationality, encompassing British passport holders living in countries of the Empire/ Commonwealth. This position was changed by the 1981 British Nationality Act, which emphasised acquisition of citizenship by descent (*jus sanguinis*).

After it had been made clear that free movement for workers applied to nationals of a member state, the 48 articles of Regulation 1612/68 outlined in detail the rules for nationals of a member state. These covered their right, irrespective of their place of residence, to take up employment within the territory of any other member state. The right to take up employment was to be on the same terms as those afforded to nationals of that member state, that is, the application of the principle of non-discrimination on grounds of nationality. This applied to conditions of employment and work, remuneration, reinstatement and re-employment. Migrant workers who were EC nationals were also given the same social and tax advantages, the same access to training in vocational schools and retraining centres, and the right to equal housing treatment with national workers. If workers were to exercise their right of free movement, then it was also essential that their families could join them, otherwise incentives to move would be diminished. Article 10 of Regulation 1612/68 therefore provided for family reunification. Migrant workers had the right to be joined by their spouse as well as by descendants under the age of 21 years who were dependants, as well as by dependent relatives in the ascending line of the worker (parents, grandparents). Member states were also required to 'facilitate the admission' of other members of a worker's family if they were dependent on the worker or living under the same roof.

These details are important because they illustrate the connections between market-making and free movement and the distinct sources of legal, political and social power created at the EU level. If we want to identify a piece of EU legislation that goes right to the heart of questions about border control and national sovereignty, then we need look no further than Directive 360/68, of 15 October 1968.[6] This required that member states abolish restrictions on the movement and residence of their nationals and their families, and give workers the right to enter, reside in and leave member states. Upon production of a valid passport or identity card, migrant workers would be issued with a 'residence permit for a national of a Member State of the EEC', which would have five years' duration and be automatically renewable. Article 2 of Directive 360/68 stated that the family of a migrant worker who was not a national of a member state had the same residence, work and welfare rights as the migrant worker on whom they were dependent. This meant that some TCNs could move within the Community, but this was because they were dependants of an EC national. Council Directive 148/73 made similar provisions for self-employed persons.[7]

Social security entitlements were also important within the free movement arrangements, because workers would be reluctant to move between member states if their entitlement to social benefits were jeopardised. Territorial principles rooted in national systems of welfare provision underpin European welfare states. Bommes and Geddes (2000) discuss the centrality of organisational borders of work and welfare to our understanding of contemporary migration and, in particular, the relationships between migrant newcomers and the definition of a community of the legitimate receivers of welfare state benefits. TCNs acquired social entitlements as a result of legal residence. It is important to distinguish between territoriality (residence) and nationality as the bases for entitlement. Although they have been nationally based, welfare states in member states have also tended to operate on the basis of territoriality, which means that legal residence and contribution prompt entitlements. However, access to EU-level social entitlements derived from the right of free movement depended on possession of the nationality of a member state. European integration brought with it an element of deterritorialisation for member state nationals moving for purposes of work, while affirming nationality as the basis for access to these entitlements. The effects were that most TCNs could not move freely and, thus, were not entitled to what were otherwise transferable social entitlements.

The broader point here, and one to which we will return, is that the Treaty framework provides us with a rather specific set of migration-related issues that became EU concerns in the sense that an institutional and legal context at EU level was developed, with the capacity to shape policy. The longer-term patterning of EU free movement, migration and asylum policy is closely related to the market-making fundamentals of European integration, from which TCNs were largely excluded. Moreover, free movement, even at its origins, provided an area of contestation for member states as they discussed the desired form of economic integration. Despite the development of a common EU framework for the 'four freedoms', there remain important differences in the organisation of welfare states and labour markets across the EU and, equally importantly, differing ideas about the relationship between economic integration and social models (Ferrera, 2005).

The social rights of migrants and the relationship between migration and European welfare states demonstrate the ways in which European integration can challenge the organisational borders of work and welfare, which, particularly in the case of welfare, have been strongly linked to the national state. Article 51 of the Treaty of Rome provided that the Council, acting by unanimity on a proposal from the Commission, could adopt measures for social security provision for migrant workers who were nationals of an EC member state. These powers to adopt measures apply to: first, aggregation of entitlements when acquiring and retaining the right to benefit and calculating the amount of benefit under the laws of the member states; and second, payment of benefit to persons resident in the member states (Handoll, 1995: 21–2). The main implementing regulation was 1408/71, on the application of social security schemes to employed persons, to the self-employed and to members of their families moving within the EC, which also covered stateless persons and refugees. Regulation 574/72 laid down procedures on the application of 1408/71. Both were, as Eichenhofer (1997: 12–13) notes, the subject of hundreds of ECJ decisions. Certain welfare rights were placed on a 'personal' rather than 'territorial' basis and became portable within the common market. Social entitlements became portable for nationals of EC member states moving to other member states for purposes of work, but again TCNs were largely excluded from these provisions.

Other parts of the Treaty of Rome also had free movement implications. Article 100 gave the EC powers to approximate (i.e. render more compatible) national measures impinging on the functioning of the common market. Article 127 established the principle of non-discrimination on the basis of nationality in the provision of vocational training. Article 235 allowed the EC to attain one of its objectives where the Treaty had not provided the necessary powers. The Council must act unanimously on a proposal from the Commission and consult the EP before taking the appropriate measures.

Over time, rights of free movement have been extended to other categories of persons, such as students, pensioners and other economically non-active persons, so long as they are not dependent on the receiving state and have adequate health insurance. This helps illustrate the point that free movement was not a generalised right; rather, it was a right extended to those who fell within one of the categories of people entitled to move freely. The need for further refinement of the free movement framework was made clear by the report of the High Level Panel on free movement of persons, chaired by the French politician Simone Veil. The Commission responded to the report of the High Level Panel with its 1997 action plan for free movement of workers, which sought to improve and adapt the free movement rules. It did this by proposing: that the labour market be made more transparent by, for instance, encouraging cross-border dissemination of information on employment opportunities; that structures for assisting migrant workers to adapt to their new countries be strengthened; that education schemes to improve knowledge among EU citizens of the right to free movement be developed; and that projects to support free movement within the provisions of Article 6 of the European Social Fund be supported (CEC, 1997a). These objectives were reinforced by the 'Lisbon process' of putative economic reform and by efforts at better information on job opportunities across the EU. The 2004 and 2007 enlargements did, however, lead to the majority of member states imposing restrictions on movement by citizens of accession states (see Chapter 8).

The directives put in place to regulate free movement and the relationship to social security in the common market were complex because, for example, there was a separate base for workers, the self-employed, students and the economically inactive. A 2004 directive created a single legal basis for EU citizens and their family members to move and reside freely within the EU; it amended Regulation 1612/68 and repealed nine other directives.[8]

Agreements with third countries

The 'external' dimension of EU action has long been highly relevant to the discussion of free movement, migration and asylum. This section shows how, since the 1960s, the EU has located migration within the agreements it concluded with third countries. It also demonstrates that some TCNs acquired rights of free movement as a result of agreements between the EU and third countries (Guild, 1992; Peers, 1996). For instance, the European Economic Area (EEA), created by the Treaty of Oporto in May 1992, extended rights of free movement to nationals of Austria, Finland, Iceland, Norway, Liechtenstein and Sweden. The EEA was seen as a halfway house to EU membership, as indeed it was for Austria, Finland and Sweden, which joined in January 1995.

Association Agreements developed with third countries such as Turkey, Morocco, Algeria and Tunisia have involved reciprocal rights and obligations applying to EU nationals and the nationals of the third country. Guild (1998) argued that a key feature of EC law is its creation of a triangular relationship between individuals, member states and the EU. Although the principle of direct effect was a judicial invention (see above) and the empowerment of individuals was not necessarily its main intention, individuals have been empowered within this triangular relationship, while the discretion of member states has been limited.

A key issue is the place of TCNs within this triangular relationship. At the origins of the EC free movement framework, it was clear that TCNs *qua* TCNs were excluded from EU provisions, as they did not possess the nationality of a member state. However, the provisions of Association Agreements between the EU and third countries did mean that, for some TCNs, a more limited triangular relationship with implications for competence and discretion could develop. The basis for this argument is that Agreements with third countries have direct effect and their provisions must be interpreted in accordance with the equivalent principles of the Treaty of Rome. A series of ECJ decisions since 1986 has affected the rights of TCNs covered by these Agreements, although not all the judgements have pointed in the same expansive direction (Alexander, 1992). For example, provisions of the 1964 Agreement with Turkey were used as the basis for the case for the creation of a 'Resident's Charter' that would allow permanently settled TCNs to enjoy the same free movement rights as EU citizens.

Agreements with Turkey, Algeria, Morocco and Tunisia established Association Councils, with representation from the Commission, the European Council and the relevant governments. The decisions of these Councils were legally binding on all parties. The Agreement with Turkey (supplemented by an additional protocol signed in 1970) includes provisions for workers under the heading 'Movement of Persons and Services'. In 1980, the EC–Turkey Association Council provided that Turkish workers could benefit from the gradual elimination of employment restrictions, the same social security benefits, free access to the labour market for family members after five years' residence, equal educational, vocational and apprenticeship opportunities and a prohibition on future restrictions on Turks' access to employment. In the *Demirel* case, the ECJ ruled that Article 12 of the 1964 Agreement and Article 36 of the 1970 protocol covering progressive extension of rights of free movement for Turkish nationals did not have direct effect because they were general programmes, insufficiently precise and unconditional, and not specific plans for action.[9] However, in the *Sevince* case the ECJ decided that provisions made in the Association Council covering entitlement to free access to the employment of choice once residence requirements had been met *were* sufficiently precise to have direct effect (Guild, 1992: 3–11; Handoll, 1995: 323–9).[10]

The *Demirel* case was also interesting because the ECJ ruled that it had no jurisdiction to determine whether national rules on family reunification were compatible with the principles of the European Convention on Human Rights (ECHR). This meant that Demirel, a Turk resident in Germany, was unable to challenge a national ruling forbidding him from being joined by the rest of his family for a lengthy period. Handoll (1995: 329) argues that 'leaps of judicial imagination' could have prompted more ambitious interpretations of Demirel's rights under the terms of the Association Agreement, but that the ECJ was not prepared to take such bold steps, which 'would be seen as trespassing on sensitive national preserves'. In other areas it did display some boldness. In the *Kus* case, a Turkish worker without a residence permit following his divorce from a German woman was entitled to renew both his residence and work permits because he had legally entered Germany and, upon entry, lawfully obtained residence and work permits. The right to continue employment was, therefore, held to have direct effect.[11] This was described as 'a stunning example' of ECJ policy-making (Ireland, 1995: 252).

Co-operation Agreements were signed with Algeria, Morocco and Tunisia in 1978.[12] All three made provisions for co-operation in the 'Field of Labour'. Workers from any of these three Maghreb states were to be free from discrimination on grounds of nationality regarding their working conditions or remuneration. Workers of Algerian, Moroccan or

Tunisian nationality were able to receive social security treatment free from discrimination based on nationality in relation to the nationals of the member state in which they were employed. In the *Kziber* case, the ECJ ruled that the provisions of the Morocco Agreement in respect of social security entitlements had direct effect.[13] A similar decision was made with regard to non-discrimination. It was further argued that as the provisions of each of the Agreements with the three Maghreb countries were virtually identical, then decisions made in relation to Moroccan nationals also applied to nationals from the two other countries (Guild, 1992).[14]

The ECJ also dealt with what was known as the 'posted worker' problem, where workers from one member state were sent for employment to another member state. Court judgements on this issue and the 1996 Posted Workers Directive had implications for TCNs, although the right of establishment was the key issue. In the 1990 *Rush Portugesa* case, the right to post workers was affirmed by the ECJ. A Portuguese contractor had sent Portuguese workers to France while the transitional arrangements governing Portuguese accession to the EC (which occurred in 1986) were still in place.[15] The French Labour Inspectorate fined the Portuguese employer for not having secured work permits for the Portuguese workers in France. The ECJ used Article 59 of the Treaty of Rome (the right of establishment) to argue that Portuguese enterprises were entitled to equal treatment and the requirement that its workers had work permits was contrary to that right. There were also posted worker implications for TCNs. The *Vander Elst* case concerned a workforce of mixed Belgians and Moroccans sent from Belgium to France.[16] The French Labour Inspectorate fined the employer because the Moroccan workers were TCNs and did not have French work permits. The ECJ again upheld the right of establishment. A 1996 Commission directive on the posting of workers in the framework of the provision of services included TCNs within its remit.[17] The original proposal had been presented in 1991, but was held up because of a dispute between those countries with contractors sending posted workers, which wanted to maintain what they saw as competitive advantages associated with low labour costs, and those receiving them, which feared 'social dumping'. This was particularly evident in the German construction industry, where cheap labour from other EU member states, such as the UK and Portugal, undercut the domestic workforce and drew into stark relief the relation between free movement, migration and welfare in an integrating Europe (Hunger, 2000). Germany, Austria and France already had national legislation on posted workers, which was brought into line with EU standards. The posted workers directive made mandatory certain protections of the rights of posted workers, such as maximum work time and rest periods, but did not preclude that member states might legislate to improve these minimum standards (CEC, 2003a).

Immigration and asylum

Between 1957 and 1986, extra-EC migration and asylum resided squarely within the competence domain of national governments. The constitutional-isation and institutionalisation of free movement were not accompanied by similar developments for immigration and asylum. There was some intergovernmental co-operation outside of the Treaty of Rome between member states on internal security issues, but little inclination to seek a common policy in response to immigration and asylum, which were matters for national governments. A key factor was, of course, the absence of a substantive legal basis in the Treaty of Rome for immigration and asylum policy and the absence of political will among member states to establish such competencies.

An example of member state opposition to the development of migration policy responsibilities at supranational level occurred when the Council blocked the Commission's 1976 proposal for a directive against clandest-ine immigration.[18] The EP sniped from the sidelines and argued that the absence of EC competence made it more difficult to ameliorate growing social tensions in member states. As is its wont, the EP made an ambitious call for immigration and asylum responsibilities to be exercised at EC level, combined with policies for immigrant integration and action against racism and xenophobia. What actually did occur was of far less significance. The 1977 Joint Declaration by the EP, Council and the Commission on funda-mental rights affirmed respect for the 1950 ECHR, but it was a costless declaration, with no legislative teeth to deal with substantive issues related to TCNs, or to tackle racism and xenophobia.[19] As with many EU denunci-ations of racism and xenophobia until the Amsterdam Treaty (1997), the declaration was essentially symbolic and not backed by competence to act.

There was the possibility that more substantial and wide-ranging migra-tion policy development affecting national immigrant integration policies could arise from a Council resolution of 1974 establishing the Social Action Programme (SAP).[20] The Council resolution called for the achievement of equality for EC nationals and TCNs in relation to living and working con-ditions, wages and economic rights; it also promoted consultation between the EC and the member states on immigration policies vis-à-vis third countries. The SAP was an attempt to counterbalance the market-based purposes of the EC with activity in the areas of social policies and citizens' rights. In December 1974 the Commission published its action programme, which envisaged a migrants' charter, covering equality of treatment in living and working conditions, the granting of civil and political rights, the control of illegal immigration, and co-ordination of immigration policies (Handoll, 1995: 352). The Council preferred a less expansive understand-ing of the term 'migrant workers', one which encouraged (i.e. rather than legislated for) the achievement of equality, consultation on migration policies and co-operation on illegal immigration. When the Commission sought to put the first SAP into effect, it had to back down in the face of Council opposition to proposed legislation to extend social provisions to include TCNs.

European citizenship

The EU has been motivated primarily by a market-making imperative, but as Meehan (1993) has argued it is incoherent to suppose that European integration is just about economics. The creation of EU citizenship in the early 1990s introduced a more explicitly political dimension to European integration but, according to Maas (2005), the origins of free movement rights – which in turn are core EU citizenship rights – can be traced to legal and political developments in the 1950s. Could EU citizenship create pressure for the extension of rights at domestic and supranational level to migrants? The argument advanced in this book is that the limited package of rights on offer under the heading of EU citizenship from the EU has thus far made little impact on the rights and status of TCNs, but that what has been far more significant is the rights-based framework associated with economic integration that has accompanied the fifth and sixth enlargements (those in 2004 and 2007), and which has enabled fairly significant migration within the EU by nationals of EU member states. Thus, the expansion of the rights-based framework within the EU – albeit with some time limitations – has been a highly significant development, with important implications for organisational borders of work and welfare (see Chapter 8 for more details).

The legal, political and social components of the widely used Marshallian framework for analysing national citizenship have acquired an EU resonance as a result of European integration (Marshall, 1964). Debates about citizenship have acquired an EU dimension in the sense that questions about membership, democracy, social inclusion and participation have become questions addressed by EU-level political processes. That said, one risk of utilising a Marshallian perspective is that it could lead us to suppose that we are witnessing a rerun of processes of nation state formation; but the EU does not possess the once powerful agents of nation state socialisation. It has instead its single market, its economic and monetary union (EMU) and regulatory competencies.

The EU's institutions have played a prominent role in developing an EU citizenship agenda, prompted by overlapping of instrumental and idealistic motivations: more democracy and accountability would be good for Europe and at the same time be good for supranational institutions, in that they would acquire a greater role. The debate about European citizenship fits nicely within this kind of context, where the core purposes and social and political effects of European integration are considered, as well as the motivations of EU institutions. The EU's social and political role has strong roots in its core economic purposes. To neglect this is to risk misconstruing the nature of the EU and adopting a perspective within which the EU can solve the problems of Europe by acquiring responsibility for activities and purposes for which it has not been designed and for which it is not necessarily suited.

At the Paris summit meeting of the heads of government held in October 1972, the Belgian and Italian governments proposed that local voting rights be extended to EC nationals residing in another member state, but this was rejected. The December 1974 Paris summit meeting of heads of government asked the Commission to prepare reports on the establishment of a passport union and the granting of special rights to citizens of EC member states.[21] The heads of government also asked the Belgian Prime Minister, Leo Tindemans, to prepare a report that would examine the meaning of 'European Union'. The Tindemans report stressed the importance of countering the image of a technocratic Community detached from the concerns of the nationals of member states. Citizenship was seen as one way of bringing the Union closer to its people.[22] These rights were not seen as replacing national citizenship; rather, they were seen as complementary and creating added value. Tindemans proposed, for instance, that the protection of consumer and environmental rights be a priority. He also called for an attempt to create some form of European solidarity, through the use of symbols such as a European flag. The citizenship agenda had not exactly moved to centre stage, but substantive and symbolic aspects of the agenda, as discussed in the Tindemans report, began to be taken more seriously. However, it was not until 1993 that the Maastricht Treaty created EU citizenship, and even then it was a limited package.

A further risk in utilising a Marshallian perspective on citizenship is that the sequential progression he postulated that linked legal, political and social rights has broken down in EU member states for migrants. Guiraudon (2000) shows that many migrants received legal and social rights before they acquired political rights. There was discussion of the extension of local voting rights to foreigners and greater involvement of foreigners in local communities. In its 1976 proposal for an Action Programme in Favour of Migrant Workers and Their Families, the Commission had called for extension of local suffrage to TCNs. As a first step, greater involvement for non-EC nationals in the life of local communities was proposed, through local consultative councils based on Belgium's well developed system of Consultative Commissions for Immigrants. An EP resolution supported the Commission's proposal for the granting of special rights[23] but, once again, 'member state sensitivities precluded progress' (Ireland, 1995: 240).

In June 1984 the Fontainebleau European Council set up an *ad hoc* committee to examine the creation of a people's Europe.[24] Its proposals with regard to the free movement of people and wider opportunities for employment and residence fed into the Commission's 1985 White Paper on the single market (see Chapter 4). These concerns with building some kind of people's Europe were clearly directed at the nationals of the member states, as confirmed by the Commission's 1988 *Communication on a People's Europe* (CEC, 1988a) and a 1988 proposal for a directive on local voting rights for EC nationals in their member state of residence.[25]

The structure of EU citizenship as a complement to rather than a replacement for national citizenship was outlined in a memorandum circulated by the Spanish government, which sought a move in status for nationals of member states from 'privileged foreigner' to 'European citizens'.[26] The Maastricht Treaty built on the Spanish government's proposals and included provisions for EU citizenship derived from prior possession of the nationality of a member state. Citizens of the EU were to have the right to move freely (Article 8a(1)), although this freedom would remain associated with people belonging to one of the categories (workers, the self-employed, students, pensioners, etc.) already entitled to such rights. Article 8a(2) allows extension of these categories, but only upon the basis of Council unanimity.

The scope of EU citizenship created by the Maastricht Treaty was circumscribed by practical considerations (Meehan, 1993; O'Keeffe, 1994; Wiener, 1997). EU citizenship sprang from the market-making purposes of the common and single markets and was intended to oil the wheels of free movement. If the EU were to become a democratic federation, it would need its citizens, but as it stands the EU is not a democracy and its citizenship provisions are not particularly extensive. Promoting EU citizenship could be a way of closing the EU's so-called 'democratic deficit' and emphasis has been placed upon the constructive potential of EU citizenship in building some kind of community of Europeans (Wiener and Della Sala, 1997). The realisation of a *Gemeinschaft* imparting common European values, beliefs, a shared destiny and ties of solidarity raised concerns about new forms of exclusion (Kostakopoulou, 1997, 1998).

Maastricht also made it clear that EU citizenship was to be a right derived from prior possession of the nationality of a member state. This has reinforced the importance of member state nationality laws. This could be construed as paradoxical, because key citizenship rights, such as social entitlements, are often acquired as a result of legal residence in a member state rather than acquisition of the nationality of that member state (Bommes and Geddes, 2000). In Germany, for instance, restrictive nationality laws have made it difficult for migrants and their descendants to acquire German citizenship, while the labour market and welfare state have served as vehicles for inclusion and renegotiation of the terms of inclusion. Yet, despite inclusion within provisions for social rights at national level, access to entitlement at EU level largely depends on first acquiring the nationality of a member state. The form of 'post-national membership' created by

European integration has been circumscribed by the emphasis on acquisition of nationality for those who are not citizens of a member state.

Discussions of EU citizenship prompt invocation of 'inclusion'. It is rather ironic that the creation of EU citizenship appeared to reinforce the exclusion of TCNs, by affirming the importance of prior acquisition of nationality for access to free movement rights and access to social entitlements that at national level did not depend upon acquisition of nationality. Ironic it may be, but irrational or inexplicable it is not – nationality of a member state was central to acquisition of rights associated with European integration. A highly significant innovation of the first decade of the twenty-first century was the creation in 2003 of rights for long-term residents derived from residence status rather than nationality (see Chapter 7). The breaking of the link is, however, accompanied by the imputation of particular meaning to supranational rights, grounded in a series of inter-state compromises that focused on the core economic purposes of European integration and prompted a subsequent supranational-level institutionalisation of a free movement framework. As will become clearer in this book, this occurred in a setting that in some ways mimics national responses to migration, as member states seek closure against those forms of migration they define as unwanted while extending some rights to those legally resident migrants already on their territories, with a concomitant concern about their 'capacity' to integrate (Groenendijk, 2004).

International obligations and European regionalisation

Those who stress a post-national dimension that reconfigures the European politics of immigration and claims-making by migrants emphasise the importance of international agreements for migrants and the ways these agreements contribute to post-national forms of membership; these in turn create a universalised discourse of entitlement that renders national citizenship 'inventively irrelevant' (Soysal, 1998: 210–11). As a result, it has been argued, rights traverse borders and claims for membership no longer take nation states as their sole point of reference. Yet free movement in the EU has privileged nationals of member states and offered little substantive entitlement to TCNs. Moreover, claims for inclusion are made in respect of an organisation that constitutes 'a form of regional governance with polity-like features to extend the state and harden the boundary between themselves and the rest of the world' (Wallace, 1996: 16).

Have international legal standards offered scope for the protection or advancement of the rights of non-national migrants within the EU? This issue becomes particularly pertinent when we examine responses to asylum since the 1990s, because a rights-based dimension linked to international law has been a central component of the asylum debate in Europe. This question prompts examination of the relationship between EU member states, the free movement framework and international human rights standards that EU member states are pledged to uphold. Arguments for 'postnational membership' (Soysal, 1994) or 'rights across borders' (Jacobsen, 1996) are countered by those who contend that international legal standards were at best 'soft law' and, at worst, irrelevant and that the developments that did occur arose as a result of national legal standards (Joppke, 1997, 1998; Guiraudon, 1997, 1998). Joppke (1997: 261) writes that:

> the protection of human rights is a constitutive principle of, not an external imposition on, liberal nation states. The international human rights regime set up after World War Two is, after all, the externalization of principles that liberal states have internally long adhered to.

After the Second World War, the newly created United Nations (UN) was central to the construction of international human rights standards. Several UN legal instruments have relevance for migrants and TCNs, but there are two important differences between UN legal standards and EC law. First, UN agreements are more expansive in their scope, because they do not tend to distinguish between nationals and non-nationals when rights are granted. Second, the highly significant downside is that, even though they can claim the moral force of the 'international community', they carry little legal weight as a practical source of redress, because they are neither supreme nor possessed of direct effect in the way that EC law is. Even though the potentially expansive principle of non-differentiation between nationals and non-nationals is a key aspect of instruments such as the Universal Declaration of Human Rights (1948), the International Covenant on Civil and Political Rights (1966) and the International Convention on the Elimination of All Forms of Racial Discrimination (1966), the practical effects on EU member states are minimal. A good example of the lack of impact is the 1990 International Convention on the Protection of the Rights of All Migrant Workers and Members of Their Families, which covers civil, political, economic, social and cultural rights. The aim of the 1990 Convention was to provide a core of human rights for migrant workers that it was hoped would encourage legal immigration and discourage illegal immigration. Hune (1994: 79) argues that 'although there are inherent weaknesses in human rights legislation with regard to the universality of application for both men and women', the 1990 Convention 'advances human rights theory' because it 'obligates States Parties who ratify to extend the application of human rights to a vulnerable group of non-nationals within their own national boundaries and jurisdiction'. It addresses the rights of legal and illegal/undocumented migrants and also deals with rights of family reunification and 'equality of treatment'. Part II of the Convention consists of one article, which outlines the principle of non-discrimination and provides that no distinctions of any kind, such as those based on sex, race or colour, can be adopted by signatories. Bold intentions have little effect when EU member states show little inclination to ratify ambitious international declarations. By April 2008, the Convention had only just mustered the 20 signatures from states parties among UN members needed for it to enter into force. In its 1994 *Communication on Immigration and Asylum Policies*, the Commission invited EU member states to sign the 1990 Convention, but by April 2008 none had done so (CEC, 1994a: 43). Hune (1994: 89) points to ignorance of the Convention's existence as a factor, and also notes that states may fear that the Convention would prompt increased migration. EU member states are also likely to oppose the proposed extension of rights to undocumented and irregular migrant workers.

In 2005 the Council of Europe's Convention on Action Against Trafficking in Human Beings was opened for signatures. The Convention focuses on the protection of victims of trafficking and the safeguard of their rights, and applies to all forms of trafficking, whether national or transnational, whether or not related to organised crime and whoever the victim (women, men or children) and whatever the form of exploitation, such as sexual exploitation or forced labour. By April 2008, 16 member states of the Council of Europe, 10 of which were EU member states (Austria, Bulgaria, Cyprus, Denmark, France, Latvia, Malta, Portugal, Romania and Slovakia), had ratified the agreement.

Another organisation with clear migration policy responsibilities is the International Labour Organisation (ILO), which was set up by the UN to monitor workplace standards and seek improvements, but it similarly lacks real teeth. Convention 97, of July 1949, on the Position of Migrant Workers, establishes the principle of non-discrimination between migrant workers and workers who are nationals. Convention 143, of June 1975, Migrations in Abusive Conditions and the Promotion of Equality of Opportunity and Treatment of Migrant Workers, extends the principle of non-discrimination and provides for action against illegal migration. Conventions apply to all workers, irrespective of nationality and whether or not their countries of origin have ratified them. Both the above conventions, however, apply only to workers who are legally resident in the territory of the contracting states. Provisions for implementation and supervision of ILO conventions are weak and based on government reports and on complaints made to the ILO, which are then investigated by expert committees.

A key legal standard in the European context is the European Convention for the Protection of Human Rights and Fundamental Freedoms, which was adopted by the Council of Europe in 1950. By 2008 the Council of Europe was the largest pan-European organisation, with 46 members, covering all major policy areas except defence. All EU member states are signatories and pledged to abide by the standards of the European human rights framework. Within the Council of Europe, conventions and agreements are prepared and negotiated before culminating in a decision by the

Committee of Ministers, composed of representatives of all 46 member states, which establishes the text of a proposed treaty. A convention usually requires ratification at national level. An agreement can be signed by a member state without having to seek national ratification. The ECHR established the European Court of Human Rights in Strasbourg (not to be confused with the ECJ in Luxembourg).

The European Commission on Human Rights was established to monitor implementation of the Convention (the ECHR). In 1958 it noted that:

> a state which signs and ratifies the ECHR must be understood as agreeing to restrict the free exercise of its rights under general international law, including the right to control the entry and exit of foreigners to the extent and within the limits of the obligations which it has accepted under that Convention. (Quoted in Plender, 1988: 227)

There is, though, a key difference with EC law, because the ECHR is international law and depends for its effect on national ratification. This means that national legal contexts are central to an evaluation of impact. When seeking to account for the impact of international legal standards on EU member states, a distinction has been made between 'monist', 'quasi-dualist' and 'dualist' legal systems (Baldwin-Edwards, 1991: 203–4). Monist systems, like those in Belgium, France, Greece, Luxembourg, the Netherlands, Portugal and Spain, incorporate treaties automatically after approval by the competent state bodies. International laws can be invoked in national courts if the treaty is 'self-executing' and does not require national legislation. Quasi-dualist systems, like those of Germany and Italy, require a transforming legislative act prior to incorporation into national law. In dualist systems, like those in the UK, Ireland and Denmark, implementation depends upon separate national legislation. The result is that international conventions and treaties have different effects in different EU member states, depending on national legal systems.

Article 1 of the ECHR provides that contracting states have to secure the Convention's rights and freedoms to 'everyone within the jurisdiction', not just to nationals of that state. This means that the rights granted by the ECHR are available to TCNs in EU member states. All EU member states have ratified the Convention, have allowed the right of individual complaint, and recognised the jurisdiction of the European Court of Human Rights. Article F of the Maastricht Treaty stated that: 'The Union shall respect fundamental rights, as guaranteed by the ECHR ... and as a result from the constitutional traditions common to the Member States, as general principles of Community law', but this is a non-justiciable declaration and does not constitute accession by the EU to the ECHR. There was some discussion during the negotiation of the Amsterdam Treaty about whether the EU should accede to the ECHR. Even though most member states favoured accession, the view of the ECJ was that accession would be problematic within the existing legal framework of the EU and without an explicit Treaty commitment to accession (Hix and Niessen, 1996).

The ECHR does not apply specifically to immigration. If challenges to national immigration laws have been made which draw from its provisions, then the foundation for these claims has tended to be derived from one of six Convention articles:

- Article 3, prohibiting inhuman or degrading treatment;
- Articles 5 and 6, protecting the liberty of the person and ensuring the right to a fair hearing;
- Article 8, providing for respect of family and private life;
- Article 12, covering the right to marry;
- Article 14, establishing the principle of non-discrimination (on grounds that include race, colour, language, religion and national origin). A 1996 judgement of the European Court of Human Rights (*Gaygusuz* v. *Austria*) established that Article 14 of the ECHR prohibited discrimination against resident TCNs on grounds of nationality for access to social security entitlements.[27] This demonstrated the potential for the ECHR to tackle discrimination on grounds of nationality that the EU currently does not.

Other Council of Europe conventions have implications for migrants, but these usually apply only to persons who are nationals of a signatory state.[28] For instance, the European Convention on Establishment (1955) deals with admission, expulsion and the legal status of persons who are nationals of one signatory state in the territory of another. The European Social Charter (1961) protects a wide range of social and economic rights and, in certain circumstances, applies to foreigners so long as they are nationals of another signatory state. This means that the European Social Charter applies to TCNs working in an EU member state, so long as they are nationals of a member state of the Council of Europe. For instance, Turks working in an EU member state are covered. The European Convention on Social Security (1972) makes provision in Article 73 for social security for migrants, for aliens to secure their acquired rights and for the principle of equality of treatment. The European Convention on the Legal Status of Migrant Workers (1977) protects migrant workers in their migration to work in another country and covers such things as recruitment, travel to and establishment in that country. The 1992 European Convention on the Participation of Foreigners in Public Life at Local Level noted in its preamble that 'the residence of foreigners on the national territory is now a permanent feature of European societies'. The Convention deals with such issues as the right of association. The most ambitious part of the Convention is Article C, which provides for the right of foreigners to vote and stand in local elections. Denmark, Finland, Ireland, the Netherlands and Sweden are the only EU member states to have granted local voting rights to all non-citizens meeting residence requirements. The Convention aimed to improve the participation of foreigners in their local communities. By April 2008 the Convention had entered into force in eight Council of Europe members (including the EU members Denmark, Finland, Italy, the Netherlands and Sweden, which have extended voting rights to foreigners).

In 1997 the European Convention on Nationality was opened for signatures. The Convention made it very clear that each state had the right to determine under its own law who its nationals are (Article 3). It then proceeded to lay down a series of principles on non-discrimination, acquisition of nationality, loss and recovery of nationality, procedures relating to nationality, multiple nationality, state succession and nationality, and military service. By April 2008, 16 of the 46 Council of Europe's member states had ratified the Convention.

Given the absence of direct effect, what impact have international legal standards had on migrants' rights in EU member states? Guiraudon (1998: 12) is sceptical and prefers to focus on national-level political–institutional structures as facilitating or militating against the extension of rights to migrants. Writing in the late 1990s, she noted that since the European Court of Human Rights began operating in 1959, 'less than half a dozen decisions have involved the civil rights of foreigners (2.5 per cent of the decisions) and they were all issued in the preceding ten years', that is, between 1987 and 1997. Ireland (1995: 247) is equally sceptical when he describes international standards as 'soft law ... vaguely worded and with no real enforcement mechanisms, their goal is really to pressure governments to change their policies'. Niessen (1994: 5) acknowledged the difficulties faced by individuals or groups seeking to draw from international legal standards when he wrote that:

> conventions are often too much a compromise and offer too little. States also often undermine the significance of conventions ... by frequently using the possibility offered in conventions to make reservations with respect to certain parts. In addition, states tend not to recognise supervisory mechanisms such as, for example, the right of individual complaint.

The effect is that the usefulness of these conventions may be diminished in the eyes of the people whose rights are supposed to be protected. However, Niessen goes on to argue that conventions do offer significant resources to individuals and NGOs:

> They offer protection in addition to national laws and practices, provide for friendly settlements and remedies for victims, oblige states to adapt their legislation to international norms, have a preventative effect on state's behaviour and offer possibilities of having public and parliamentary debates on the efforts of states to comply with international human rights standards.

While EU member states have acknowledged their obligations under international treaties, it remains the case that they can legitimately discriminate on behalf of their own nationals and the nationals of other EU member states. Discrimination against TCNs is in accord with the principle of international law that it is for a state to decide who can or cannot become its citizens and obtain access to associated rights and obligations. The strong connection between nationality and the right of free movement within the EU means that international legal standards have been largely tangential to the operationalisation of the EU's free movement framework. A discourse of universal entitlement does provide political conviction, a lobbying resource and moral force to the arguments of pro-migrant NGOs, but the political sensitivities associated with immigration and asylum policy, coupled with moral equivocation by member states, have militated against expanded rights for TCNs within the EU.

Conclusion

This chapter has explained the origins in the period between 1957 and 1986 of a strongly institutionally structured (in terms of supranational legal and political competencies) EC-level free movement framework and virtually non-existent extra-EC migration policies. There was substantial encroachment upon national prerogatives by supranational legal and political authority to promote and protect the rights of EC nationals moving for purposes of work, establishment and to provide services. There was no legal basis for the development of supranational legal and political authority to deal with immigration and asylum issues. Even when immigration became more salient and its relationship to free movement more clearly evident, member states were still reluctant to extend the competencies of EC institutions, as is shown in the next chapter.

The chapter has identified the ontological status of free movement in the European project as indicative of the EU's identity as a regional actor with core economic purposes but with links between these economic purposes and changed notions of territoriality in Europe arising from European integration. It was shown, too, that a supranational/intergovernmental dichotomy may not capture the development of particular forms of legal, social and political power centred on free movement and with some relation to migration and mobility.

Free movement within a common market was a central aspiration of the Treaty of Rome and it was highly unlikely that the EC's economic purposes could be attained without it. Immigration and asylum policy were not associated with this economic imperative. Instead, they were associated with state sovereignty and bedevilled by the difficulties of securing positive integration.[29] When immigration became more salient from the mid-1970s, member states displayed determination to maintain national jurisdiction.

Livi-Bacci (1993) captures this disjunction by referring to a 'positive ideology' of European integration and a 'negative ideology' of immigration. Despite the vital contribution made by migrant workers to European economic reconstruction, by the 1970s there was a drive towards restrictive immigration legislation. The 'problem' of immigration (as defined) was to be 'solved' by restrictive immigration policies adopted and enforced at national level, coupled with immigrant integration policies embedded within national traditions of citizenship and nationhood.

Despite this apparent disjunction between intra- and extra-EU migration, it is not possible to separate free movement entirely from immigration and asylum policy. Freer movement for EC nationals within the common market raised questions associated with entry, movement and residence by TCNs, and these questions became even more salient in the aftermath of the SEA (1986). This could be characterised as some kind of generic spillover effect, but member state opposition to supranationalisation draws attention to the difficulties of securing policy integration. It does, though, suggest that low and high politics cannot be neatly separated, because the pursuit of market development and free movement drew immigration and asylum closer to European integration. While intergovernmental deals were central to progress in this area, these 'history-making decisions' (Peterson, 1995) did create scope for day-to-day processes of European economic and political integration that allowed interventions by the Commission and the ECJ. The next chapter takes forward the analysis of free movement, migration and asylum by exploring the impact of economic liberalisation in the 1980s through the SEA.

Notes

1   There are three founding treaties of what is now known as the European Union: the Treaty of Paris (1951), which created the European Coal and Steel Community; the Treaty of Rome (1957) that established the European Economic Community; and the Treaty of Rome that established the European Atomic Energy Community (1957). Our attention is mainly focused on the Treaty of Rome establishing the European Economic Community.
2   *Official Journal*, L56/850, 1964.
3   Case 30/77, *Bouchereau* [1977] European Court Report (ECR) 199.
4   A famous ECJ decision established the supremacy of EC law by stating that 'The Community constitutes a new legal order of international law for the benefit of which states have limited their sovereign rights, albeit within limited fields, and the subjects of which comprise not only Member States, but also their nationals'. *Costa v. ENEL* [1964] ECR 585.
5   *Official Journal*, L257/13, 1968.
6   *Official Journal*, L257/13, 1968.
7   *Official Journal*, L172/14, 1973.
8   Directive 2004/38/EC of the EP and the Council of 29 April 2004 on the rights of citizens of the Union and their family members to move and reside

freely within the territory of the member states, amending Regulation 1612/68 and repealing Directives 64/221/EEC, 68/360/EEC, 72/194/EEC, 73/148/EEC, 75/34/EEC, 90/364/EEC and 93/96/EEC. See *Official Journal*, L158, 30 April 2004, p. 77.

9 Case 12/86, *Demirel* [1987] ECR 3719.

10 Case C-192/89, *Sevince* [1990] ECR I-3641.

11 Case C-237/91, *Kus* [1992] ECR I-6781.

12 Council Resolutions 2210/78 (Algeria), 2211/78 (Morocco) and 2212/78 (Tunisia), all 27 September 1978.

13 Case C-18/90, *Kziber* [1990] ECR I-199.

14 New Association Agreements were signed with Morocco (1996), Algeria (2001) and Tunisia (1998) in the context of the Barcelona process of EU–Mediterranean relations (Bicchi, 2007).

15 Case C-113/89, *Rush Portugesa* [1990] ECR I-1417.

16 Case C-43/93, *Vander Elst* [1994] ECR I-3803.

17 Directive 96/71/EC of the EP and the Council of 16 December 1996 concerning the posting of workers in the framework of the provision of services, *Official Journal*, L018, 21 January 1997, pp. 1–6.

18 *Official Journal*, C277/2, 1976.

19 *Official Journal*, C103, 1977.

20 *Official Journal*, C13/1, 1974.

21 'Towards European citizenship', *Bulletin of the European Communities*, Supplement 7/75, 1975.

22 EP Document 481/75, pp. 39–43.

23 *Official Journal*, C296/26, 1977.

24 The *ad hoc* committee produced what is known as the Adonnino report, after its chair, published in *Bulletin of the European Communities*, Supplement, 7/85, 1985.

25 *Official Journal*, C246/3, 1988, superseded by discussions within the pre-Maastricht intergovernmental conference on EU citizenship. It was, in fact, Directive 93/109 of 6 December 1993 and Directive 94/80 of 31 December 1994 that extended voting rights for local and European elections to citizens of the EU, as provided for by Article 8 of the Maastricht Treaty.

26 Europe Document 1653, 2 October 1990.

27 *Gaygusuz* v. *Austria*, European Court of Human Rights. Report of Judgements and Decisions, 16 September 1996 – IV.

28 The texts of Council of Europe agreements are available at www.coe.int.

29 Positive integration refers to the difficulty of creating new structures at supranational level (see Pinder, 1968).

4

Migration, freedom and security after the Single European Act

Introduction

This chapter examines the free movement, migration and security implications of the SEA (1986), which was widely seen as relaunching European integration through its plan to create a single European market. Particular impetus was given to the creation of economic space, but this brought with it greater efforts to develop European-level forms of co-operation on migration and asylum from outside the EU. The result was that freedom and security became more closely bound in the late 1980s. This chapter explores the profound effects of these developments on the conceptualisation of Europe's borders and on population control evident at them. It maintains the focus of the previous chapters, to explore the major effects on Europe's territorial, organisational and conceptual borders of the SEA's definition of the European single market as an area without internal frontiers, within which the free movement of people, services, goods and capital would be ensured. This chapter analyses the period 1986 to 1993 (i.e. up to Maastricht, which is the subject of the next chapter) to demonstrate the important implications for European strategies of border management and population control of efforts to strengthen and enhance economic integration. Indeed, these efforts to develop new patterns of European integration and co-operation provided a powerful impetus to the European framing of migration and asylum as security issues requiring some form of collective, European response, particularly to address the external frontiers of those member states deemed most vulnerable to migration flows. The chapter identifies the factors that drove co-operation and integration in the areas of free movement, migration and asylum, examines the forms of integration and co-operation that developed, asks whether this represented a genuinely 'European' response (as opposed to a new forum for the attainment of national policy objectives) and assesses the extent to which the SEA reframed the relationship between Europe's territorial, organisational and conceptual borders.

The resurgence of European integration

Capax imperii nisi imperasset – it seemed capable of power until it tried to wield it – was the epitaph provided for the EC by *The Economist* in its edition of 20 March 1982.[1] The EC appeared moribund at best, yet within four years a remarkable resurgence in European integration occurred, which stemmed from the challenges addressed by the SEA and the view among key member states that deeper European economic and political integration was an essential element of an effective response to these challenges. The SEA placed at the core of European integration the plan to create a single market, within which people, services, goods and capital would be able to move freely. Once attained, the single market would contribute to an economic renaissance and help close the gap that had emerged between EC economies and their principal rivals, or so it was claimed (Cecchini, 1988).

Free movement for EC nationals within the single market did bring with it pressure for closer co-operation on immigration and asylum from outside the EC. Questions of external frontier control were transplanted to those member states on the edge of the single market, particularly the new member states in southern Europe. Greece joined in 1981, while Portugal and Spain joined in 1986. These were becoming immigration countries and are proximate to major sending countries/regions. There was, however, no explicit Treaty competence for immigration and asylum policy; there was actually a marked reluctance on the part of some national governments, such as the British, Danish and Greek governments, to extend the remit of supranational institutions into these areas.

Despite this reluctance, there was evidence of integrative intent among a smaller group of member states, which resolved to move more quickly towards a frontier-free Europe within which people could move freely. In 1985 five EC governments (those of Belgium, France, Germany, the Netherlands and Luxembourg) signed the Schengen Agreement in the eponymous Luxembourg town. Even though this was outside of the EC Treaty framework, it embodied a resolution by the signatories to move more quickly towards the abolition of border controls, so as to secure free movement for people between the participating states. Schengen is crucially important, because the Schengen framework has made its way into the EU, particularly since the Amsterdam Treaty (1997). Guiraudon (2001) has argued that the Schengen Agreement demonstrates the strong intergovernmental push behind the quest for closer European co-operation and integration. She sees this as closely linked to the desire of member state governments to circumvent domestic constraints on their immigration control capacity and to seek new, European-level venues for collaboration. While this argument possesses a great deal of force and utility, core Schengen states were pro-integration countries prepared to countenance a common EC migration policy but realising, too, that such action was unlikely to be agreed by more reluctant member states. Schengen became a 'laboratory' (Monar, 2001) where practices developed that were to fuse freedom and security. Schengen was also an early instance of 'flexible integration' or a sign of 'variable geometry', which was to become an important feature of the EU free movement, migration and asylum framework.

The SEA also implicitly addressed the 'who are we' question, by re-affirming the distinction between free movement for EC citizens and that for TCNs. Free movement for EC nationals derived from prior possession of the nationality of a member state, but was a supranationalised competence, with Commission and ECJ competencies. The SEA provided new impetus to the free movement framework and put in place decision-making processes – principally qualified majority voting (QMV) – that aimed at speeding implementation of many single market issues, although not free movement of people, which remained subject to unanimity. In contrast, immigration and asylum policies remained outside the Treaty framework. They were dealt with by *ad hoc* intergovernmental co-operation. The Commission was only loosely associated with this work, while the ECJ and EP were excluded. Executive authority was strengthened, while judicial and legislative authority were weak. Interior and justice ministries were the particular focus for this co-operation and for the development of a 'political field' at EU level, with a strong focus on the meaning of security (Favell, 1998; Wacquant, 2005; Huysmans, 2006).

Free movement in the SEA

The SEA arose, as do all revisions of the Treaty of Rome, from an inter-governmental conference (IGC) of member state governments, convened in this instance by the summit meeting of the European Council held in Milan in June 1985. Within the IGC, decisions upon substantive change had to be agreed unanimously. The distinction between negative and positive integration is apposite: the legal basis as well as the economic, political and ideological impetus behind the market-making project and associated removal of obstacles to trade were far stronger than pressure for the kinds of 'positive integration' necessary to develop new immigration and asylum policy structures at EU level (Sandholtz and Zysman, 1989; Fligstein and Mara-Drita, 1996).

The need for unanimity raised particular problems because of the general reluctance of the British, Danish and Greek governments, all of which had even opposed the convening of the IGC in the first place. The basic divergence was not so much about the desirability of the single market programme (the British, for instance, were keen advocates, because it chimed with domestic policy preferences, and were prepared to see some use of QMV in the Council), but about the level and the extent of supranationalisation that would be associated with it. More enthusiastic member states raised the possibility – probably as a bargaining device – that a 'two-speed' Europe could emerge, within which the reluctant member states would find themselves in a marginalised 'slow lane'.

Once again, while delving into the specificities of the SEA, it is important to bear in mind both the links between free movement, immigration and asylum and the continued exclusion of TCNs from EC provisions. The SEA defined a single market in Article 8a as: 'an area without internal frontiers in which the free movement of goods, persons, services and capital is ensured within the provisions of this Treaty'. The SEA gave a decisive boost to the free movement impulse put in place by the Treaty of Rome and consolidated by the creation of the common market in 1968. Moreover, it established a deadline of 31 December 1992 for attainment of these targets. Although the deadline had debatable legal standing and was not wholly met, it imparted a degree of urgency and gave the Commission an argument to use against member states that tried to block proposals. Equally importantly, the introduction of QMV for key aspects of the single market programme – but not free movement of people – reduced the ability of individual member states to block Commission initiatives.

The Commission's June 1985 White Paper contained nearly 300 legislative proposals for the creation of a single market, including proposals on refugees, asylum, visas and the status of TCNs, but these were not included in the final legislation (CEC, 1985a; Callovi, 1992). The Commission envisaged EC action on immigration and asylum policy – not intergovernmental co-operation – because the single market was viewed as analogous to existing national markets. The Commission's view was that the free movement provisions and the abolition of internal controls applied to all people, regardless of their nationality. This seemed both logical and practical, as it would be impossible for states to dismantle controls on movement by nationals of EC member states and retain them for TCNs. The White Paper's plans for the co-ordination of national rules on residence, entry and employment of TCNs, an EC visa policy, and common rules on extradition were all seen as necessary if checks at internal frontiers were to be abolished. The integrative 'logic' expounded by the Commission was not politically feasible, however, because there was not the will among all member states to cede competence for immigration and asylum policies to the EC.

The constraints on the Commission's role demonstrate the limits of neo-functional approaches to European integration that emphasise Commission leadership and the generation of spillover effects whereby small steps towards closer economic and political integration beget further steps in that direction (Rosamond, 2000: ch. 3). There can be no doubt that member states were in the driving seat on immigration and asylum policy. That said, some of these member states did favour a stronger supranational response. Moreover, as has already been discussed, it was difficult to neatly disentangle free movement, migration and asylum, which gave scope for unintended consequences that could draw migration and asylum closer to the Community method of decision-making.

The intergovernmental/supranational distinction neglects the ways in which a political field was constituted at EU level comprising particular sets of institutions operating within more informal European-level structures, but drawing from very powerful and well established national resources because, of course, many of these European actors were based in national interior ministries or security agencies (Favell, 1998; Guiraudon, 2003). The post-SEA period saw the development of forms of what has been called 'intensive transgovernmentalism', where the intensity and dense structuring of co-operation between member states has not been accompanied by a willingness to accept the Community method of decision-making, with all its legal and political implications (Wallace, 2005: 87). Networks link more informal modes of social action to more formal, institutionalised forms of action and can serve as a venue for the exchange of ideas and information and policy learning. They are not necessarily a route to supranational integration, but could be the basis for the development of a more inclusive, EU-level security community, with shared understanding of common problems. Huysmans (2006) provides a Foucauldian view of spillover based on political speech acts, discourses and the development of technologies of population control that he sees as binding freedom and security. He does not, however, ascribe a specific leadership role to the Commission. Instead, securitisation practices are embedded within the technologies of modern government and operated through various kinds of networks that transcend the boundaries of national politics. These particular forms of network constitute a security field populated by government officials, people from security agencies and private companies providing new technologies of surveillance and population control. A narrow focus on Commission-led action could then miss dynamics that lie at the heart of the free movement framework and that have come to define the relationship between freedom, security and justice in the EU.

The rejection by some member states of any explicit notion of Commission-driven 'spillover' of the White Paper's plans for immigration and asylum integration illustrates the ability of member states to resist attempts to drive European action in the direction of institutional forms that do not command the support of all member states. If integration were to occur, then it would require unanimity. Some member states were not prepared to countenance measures impinging upon national immigration and asylum policies. Member states were, though, prepared to seek closer co-operation on immigration and asylum policy. The dynamics were thus largely intergovernmental, but the underlying changes in the conceptualisation of Europe's borders that were necessarily linked to economic integration did provide a new frame for the conceptualisation of migration as a 'European' issue in the sense of some interdependencies rather than necessarily requiring a common EC policy.

The negative response from member states to EC immigration and asylum policy also meant a negative answer to a central question posed by the SEA. Would free movement for people become a generalised right applying to all people permanently resident in the EC? Article 8a of the SEA – as Article 48 of the Treaty of Rome had done before it – left scope for an expansive interpretation, because it did not specify that free movement was a right to be restricted to nationals of EC member states. O'Keeffe (1992: 16–17) wrote that: 'If the Community is to have an area without internal frontiers, it becomes progressively absurd that non-Community nationals established in the Community should not be afforded the protection of Community law'. The key issue with regard to the rights of legally resident TCNs was neither entry nor residence nor movement, but equal treatment, which was already a principle of Community law with regard to gender.[2] Member states, however, sustained a less expansive interpretation of the SEA's provisions and the distinction was maintained between EC nationals and TCNs. Unequal treatment persisted and was sanctioned by EC law.

The decision-making procedures put in place by the SEA facilitated attainment of ambitious single market objectives in an EC that had grown in membership from 9 to 12 between 1981 and 1986. The SEA added a new Article 100a to the Treaty of Rome, to give institutional backing to the policy objectives, by shifting towards QMV for issues related to the single market, but this did not apply to free movement of persons, which continued to depend on unanimity. This did not mean that the EC lacked competence to act for free movement of people; rather, it derived competence from Treaty articles other than the new Article 100a. The Treaty articles that were particularly relevant for free movement of people were Articles 100 and 235 of the Treaty of Rome, both of which required unanimity.

The member states rejected immigration and asylum policy integration and, as shown below, preferred forms of intergovernmental co-operation outside of the Treaty framework. This presented the Commission with a dilemma. Its preference, outlined in the 1985 White Paper, was for a supranational policy, but this was infeasible. What stance should the Commission adopt in response to forms of co-operation on immigration and asylum that related to key aspects of Community competence for free movement but that were not governed by the EC's institutions? The Commission adopted a pragmatic stance: it was prepared to forswear the moral high ground of opposition to informal co-operation, and to participate, when able, in forms of co-operation between member states that occurred outside of the Treaty framework. The Commission moderated its stance to secure a seat at the intergovernmental bargaining table when immigration and asylum policy co-operation was undertaken (Monar, 1994). It was seen as better to observe and thereby attempt to exert some influence on co-operation rather than shun nascent co-operation because it fell short of more ambitious targets. The Commission adopted a similar stance on Schengen.

A paradox of liberalisation?

Freer movement for EC nationals within the single market brought with it attempts to establish tighter controls on movement by TCNs. Liberalisation within the single market was primarily bounded by the prior possession of the nationality of a member state. It was not free movement for all – it was essentially an extension of the common market's functional right of free movement for workers. Freer movement for EC nationals prompted nascent co-operation on migration, asylum and borders. This apparent paradox of liberalisation replicated those within EU member states, which combine free movement within their own national markets with controls on entry, movement and residence by non-nationals.

In practical terms, the maintenance of free movement as a functional right related to attainment of labour market purposes meant that free movement was not for everyone. Moreover, plans to abolish border controls between participating states in a single market would not mean un-impeded or unmonitored movement, because internal security checks were the focus of Schengen co-operation. It was never the corollary for those member states that were prepared to remove their external frontiers that free movement was a route to abolition of controls on population. Rather, co-operation between member states was a way of attempting to reinforce existing national controls while raising the possibility of pan-European controls exercised through co-operation between national agencies and EC institutions. Aspects of these internal security arrangements – such as the form that identity checks at the internal frontiers of the single market could take – fell within the ECJ's jurisdiction. To be in accord with the principles of Community law, the ECJ decided that controls needed to be sporadic and unsystematic and not 'systematic, arbitrary or unnecessarily restrictive'.[3] Also, only identity controls were to be allowed. Questioning that went beyond attempts to ascertain identity breached Community law. More detailed questions could be asked only when non-nationals sought the right of residence.[4]

Ad hoc co-operation

Despite opposition to the immigration and asylum policy proposals of the Commission's 1985 White Paper laying out plans for the single market, the member states realised that the supranationalisation of free movement within a single market raised immigration and asylum issues. The chosen form of action was *ad hoc* and intergovernmental in character. In a politi-cal declaration attached to the SEA, the member states noted that, in order to promote free movement of persons, they were to co-operate without prejudice to the powers of the Community, in particular as regards entry, movement and residence of TCNs (CEC, 1985a). At the same time, the member states also declared that nothing contained within the SEA affected the rights of member states to introduce measures they saw as necessary to control immigration from third countries. The SEA was a recipe for blurred competence. The Commission's 1988 communication on the abolition of border controls illustrated its pragmatic desire to keep a seat at the intergovernmental negotiating table (CEC, 1988b). Once again, the link between removal of internal frontier controls and European competence for external controls was stressed, but the Commission directed attention towards practical effectiveness rather than legal doctrine.

Co-operation on internal security policy did not just emerge in response to the SEA – it built on previous patterns of co-operation. Before the SEA, EC member states had already put in place some mechanisms for co-operation on internal security issues. The 1967 Naples Convention dealt with mutual co-operation between the customs authorities of the six EC member states. Judicial co-operation occurred within the framework of the European political co-operation (EPC) form of working, established in 1970. This co-operation was outside the Treaty framework, unencumbered by the jurisdiction of supranational institutions, and almost impossible to subject to political or judicial scrutiny at either national or European level. Democracy and accountability fell through the net of intergovernmental internal security co-operation between EC member states, although these policy areas could hardly be characterised as being particularly open or accountable at national level either.

Interior policy co-operation took a stronger organisational form following a European Council meeting in Rome in 1975 that set up a special working group called Trevi, which operated within the framework of EPC and had particular responsibility for dealing with problems posed by terrorist groups. Trevi met twice a year under the chair of the minister for home affairs from the country holding the EC presidency. In practice, its management mimicked that of the Council and it was presided over by a *troika* comprising the country holding the EC presidency and the two countries that had either just held or were about to assume the presidency. These ministerial meetings were supported by the work of national officials. Trevi's working groups, composed of national officials, dealt with terrorism, equipment, public order, training, drugs, serious crime and, later on in its existence, the internal security implications of '1992' (with completion of the single market). Trevi helped instigate a 'wining and dining' culture of co-operation among interior ministry officials, which was strengthened during the 1980s and 1990s (den Boer, 1996). European integration was beginning to have an impact on policy areas, such as interior policy, that had hitherto been quintessentially national.

As noted in the previous chapter, Commission attempts during the 1970s to bring aspects of immigration and asylum policy under EC control – such as action against clandestine migration – had been firmly rebuffed by the Council. The Commission took further tentative steps towards the establishment of EC competence in 1985, when it proposed *Guidelines for a Community Policy on Migration* (CEC, 1985b). This document stressed the importance of free movement for EC nationals, while also emphasising the importance of 'equality of treatment in living and working conditions for all migrants, whatever their origin' (p. 8). With regard to TCNs, the *Guidelines* used terms such as 'consultation', 'experimentation' and 'information' rather than 'legislation' (Handoll, 1995: 355). In July 1985, on the basis of its *Guidelines*, the Commission proposed a decision establishing prior consultation and communication procedures on migration policy, aimed at 'achieving progress towards a harmonisation of national legislation on foreigners'.[5] The decision required member states to give advance notice of measures they intended to take that affected TCNs and their families. Denmark, France, Germany, the Netherlands and the UK challenged the use of Article 118 of the Treaty of Rome for such a decision and argued that it exceeded Commission competence. In July 1987, the ECJ annulled certain aspects of the decision,[6] but a consultation procedure was established and the ECJ ruling did not completely block the Commission's first tentative steps towards institutionalisation of an extra-EC migration policy context (Papademetriou, 1996: 21). Even so, there was no evidence that the guidelines were ever operationalised (EP, 1991).

The British Conservative government was a champion of informal, intergovernmental co-operation and during the British Council presidency tenure of the second six months of 1986 the *Ad Hoc* Group on Immigration was established, following a meeting of immigration ministers of the member states and the Commission Vice-President, Martin Bangemann. The *Ad Hoc* Group on Immigration was composed of high-level immigration policy officials from the member states and was divided into six subgroups dealing with asylum, external frontiers, forged papers, admissions, deportations and information exchange. The Commission was represented on the Group when EC powers were involved, but had no power of initiative. Bureaucratic support for the *Ad Hoc* Group was provided by the Council Secretariat. This meant a loose association between *ad hoc* intergovernmental co-operation and the Commission, but no room for involvement by the ECJ or EP.

The member states still faced the problem of trying to ensure co-ordination between the free movement objectives of the single market programme and the internal security issues raised by its creation. The Rhodes meeting of the European Council in December 1988 established a Group of Co-ordinators charged with seeking the co-ordination of activities occurring within and outside of the Treaty framework. The groups it sought to co-ordinate included Trevi and the *Ad Hoc* Group on Immigration. The Group of Co-ordinators was composed of representatives of the member states and reported regularly to the European Council on progress, or lack of it. The Rhodes Council also grandly declared that: 'The internal market will not close in on itself. 1992 Europe will be a partner and not a "fortress Europe"' (quoted in Handoll, 1995: 357).

Within six months the 'Palma document' was presented to the European Council, at its meeting in Madrid in June 1989 (Statewatch, 1997: 12–16). A senior Commission official (Fortescue, 1995) viewed the Palma document as a realistic attempt to plot a politically manageable course through the thorny issues associated with free movement, by dividing them between those seen as 'essential' and those deemed 'desirable'. Deemed 'essential' were the harmonisation of external frontier controls, a common visa policy and the right of TCNs residing in a member state to move without a visa to another member state.

> The result was a comprehensive and responsible programme which, if completed on schedule, should make it possible to confront governments with this stark but essential question: since the programme you agreed to be necessary is now complete, how can you any longer justify the maintenance of controls at the frontiers between you? (Fortescue, 1995: 30)

But such developments still relied to a large extent on unanimity among member states within informal structures for co-operation that were outside the Treaty framework. Co-operation also exacerbated the democratic and information deficits of the EC, because of the increased powers in the hands of largely unaccountable officials and confusion about whether the Palma document was confidential or could be made public. This reflected a more general confusion about the new internal security mechanisms that were being created. The Palma document entered the public domain when scrutinised by the British House of Lords in July 1989, but when the Dutch government distributed it to MPs, some of them treated it as confidential. As well as these difficulties, the Group of Co-ordinators also faced practical problems justifying its title, because of the diverse forums within which the issues it was concerned with were discussed.

Asylum and external frontiers

Following the Madrid Council's acceptance in 1989 of the Palma document, the *Ad Hoc* Group on Immigration turned its attention to two of the most pressing issues: asylum policy and external frontier control. The tail end of these discussions occurred during a period when asylum issues increased greatly in salience following the end of the Cold War and when there were large increases in intra-European movement as a result of the conflict in Yugoslavia. The German government, in particular, pressed for a European response to what it saw as a European problem. Other member states were less willing to embrace this conceptualisation of a European problem if it meant sharing responsibility for asylum-seekers with Germany. However, during the 1980s and 1990s it was noticeable that European-level co-operation was allowing member states to circumvent domestic legal and political constraints and elaborate a European policy framework that emphasised restriction (Lavenex, 1998a). Lip service may be paid to international legal standards, but aspects of European asylum policy could bear dubious relation to these standards.

The initial asylum efforts of the member states came to fruition at Dublin on 15 June 1990, when the member states (except for Denmark, which signed on 13 June 1991) signed the Convention Determining the State Responsible for Examining Applications for Asylum Lodged in One of the Member States of the European Communities, or the Dublin Convention as it was rather more conveniently known (Handoll, 1995: 419–25; Statewatch, 1997: 49–54). The Convention sought to remove the possibility of asylum-seekers making applications in more than one member state, so-called 'asylum shopping'. The Convention did not attempt to harmonise the rules for examining applications; rather, it aimed to ensure that, in a frontier-free Europe, only one member state would be responsible for judging any one particular asylum application. The principle underpinning the Convention was that an application for asylum would be made in the member state in which the applicant had arrived, unless he or she was joining a spouse or dependant in another member state. This meant that not all asylum applications would be investigated, because if the applicant had arrived from another EC member state then he or she would be returned to that member state. The Convention also effectively pushed the problems of asylum to member states bordering third countries or those with large air and seaports. The Dublin Convention also offloaded responsibility for asylum to non-EC 'third countries' deemed 'safe' in relation to their compliance with the Geneva Convention. Guild and Niessen (1996: 120) note that:

> The Dublin system began as a logical development of the internal market. The difficulty is that what might have been a solution providing some security to asylum applicants in an integrated Europe is now being used to move asylum-seekers out of the Union altogether.

Readmission agreements signed in the 1990s with third countries in central and eastern Europe deemed 'safe' reduced the administrative and financial burdens of asylum-seeking on EU member states and offloaded substantial costs on to 'safe' countries that were less likely to be able to meet them, with deleterious effects on the standards of treatment received by asylum-seekers (Abell, 1999; Schieffer, 2003). The complex web of readmission agreements that were signed between EU member states and central and

eastern European countries then formed part of the context for incorporation of these countries into the EU's migration control framework during
their pre-accession process (Lavenex, 1998b). These aspiring member states
were thus obliged to participate in the EU's restrictive immigration and
asylum policies before joining (see Chapter 8).

Other asylum-related developments were linked to the Dublin Convention. A meeting of immigration ministers held in London between 30
November and 1 December 1992 adopted a resolution on 'manifestly
unfounded applications for asylum'.[7] An application was to be deemed
manifestly unfounded if it raised no issues under the terms of either the
Geneva Convention or the New York Protocol. This could be because
there was no fear of persecution in the applicant's own country, or because
the claim was based on deception or an abuse of procedures. Applications
suspected of being manifestly unfounded would be fast-tracked, leading
to speedier resolution and more often than not rejection. Paragraph 1(a)
of the resolution on manifestly unfounded applications made reference to
countries where there was deemed to be no serious risk of persecution. A
set of conclusions drafted by the immigration ministers at their London
meeting explained the criteria by which countries were to be deemed safe:

> This concept means that it is a country which can be clearly shown, in an
> objective and verifiable way, normally not to generate refugees, or where it
> can be clearly shown, in an objective and verifiable way, that circumstances
> which might in the past have justified recourse to the 1951 Geneva Conven-
> tion have ceased to exist. (Quoted in Statewatch, 1997: 66)

There was outcry from human rights groups when a draft version of the
criteria judged states by the human rights standards they had signed rather
than by whether or not they respected them. The final version went some
way to assuage these concerns when it referred to both criteria. The basic
purpose of the procedures as a mechanism to reduce the numbers of asylum-
seekers was noted by Guild and Niessen (1996: 181), who wrote that they
were 'clearly designed to fit a numbers game' because 'an assessment of a
state will only be relevant where substantial numbers of people from that
state apply for asylum in the member states. Therefore the assessment of a
country is a tool for the rapid refusal of asylum applications.' If a country
was deemed to meet the criteria for being 'safe', then all applications from
that country could be assumed to be unfounded, unless individuals could
overcome massive odds and prove otherwise in their own particular case.
The elaboration of an asylum policy framework within the EU was giving
its member states increased powers to expel those deemed to be abusing
the asylum system.

A resolution on a harmonised approach to questions concerning host
third countries (i.e. countries migrants move to before moving on to the
EU) was also agreed at the London meeting. Its preamble outlined the

intention to return refugees and asylum-seekers to third countries deemed safe if they had unlawfully left those countries. With a degree of understatement, Guild and Niessen (1996: 168) refer to this as a 'somewhat unreal document' because: 'It is somewhat irregular in international law that one state or group of states should seek to impose obligations unilaterally or through an agreement *inter alia* on other states which have not participated in or accepted the obligation'. An information clearing house, the Centre for Information, Discussion and Exchange on Asylum (which in French produces the acronym CIREA) was established by a meeting of immigration ministers in Lisbon in June 1992 for the deposit and exchange of information to assist member states in their harmonisation of asylum determination procedures. Sharing the same staff was an immigration information clearing house called the Centre for Information, Discussion and Exchange on the Crossing of Borders and Immigration (in French, CIREFI).

The intention to exert tight controls on asylum-seekers was evident in the Eurodac Convention, which sought to give effect to Article 15 of the Dublin Convention. The draft Eurodac proposed the compulsory fingerprinting of asylum-seekers over 14 years of age. Once the member states had taken the fingerprints, then the images were to be promptly transmitted to the Eurodac database. Former British Home Secretary Michael Howard illustrated the motivations for this kind of action designed to speed up assessment of asylum applications. He hoped it would:

> Serve to identify asylum applications made on entry at UK ports to which the UK was not obliged to give substantive consideration and which offered the possibility of effecting a swift return to the Member State having responsibility. There would in any such instance, be potential savings in benefit. (Quoted in *Statewatch*, July–August 1996: 1)

The entry into force of the Amsterdam Treaty in 1999 changed the legal basis for Eurodac, and so the Council had already decided in December 1998 to use a Community legal instrument. The resultant Eurodac regulation of December 2000 allows member states to use fingerprints as well as data on the member state of origin and the place and date of an asylum application to identify asylum applicants and people who have been apprehended while unlawfully crossing a member state's external frontier.[8]

In 1990, two reports on immigration policy were submitted to the Rome meeting of the European Council. The first was prepared by a group of independent experts and discussed immigrant integration (CEC, 1990). The report made the connection between immigration control and immigrant integration, and argued for legal residence, equal opportunities in jobs, education, vocational training and housing, and easier access to naturalisation for TCNs. The experts' report also called for the building of greater tolerance between communities through the establishment of 'structures for dialogue'. The Commission's basic problem was that, whether or not it agreed with these objectives, it did not possess the capacity to act in these areas. Competence for such measures did not exist in the Treaty of Rome, nor was there the political will among member states to put it in place at that time. In addition to this, national frameworks to deal with these issues were highly diverse. There was no sense of a common European way of responding to these questions.

The second report was prepared by the *Ad Hoc* Group on Immigration and paid particular attention to migration from southern, central and eastern Europe. The report advocated a 'root causes' approach to try to stem migration pressures by, for instance, aid programmes designed to stimulate economic development. The report noted that control of immigration was an important component of any policy that sought to integrate settled migrants (Papademetriou, 1996: 45). A problem with root causes approaches is that the dislocation caused by attempts to promote economic and social development in emigration countries may actually prompt increased short-term migration. A root causes approach is a policy for the medium to long term (Martin, 1993).

An attempt to elaborate an external frontiers policy was also a key task for the *Ad Hoc* Group. The immediate outcome in June 1991 was the draft – and ultimately abortive – External Frontiers Convention (EFC). The EFC's travails illustrate both the difficulties associated with co-operation between member states with disparate histories and policies on immigration issues and the limitations of the chosen form of intergovernmental co-operation, which relied on enacting conventions in international law. Such conventions needed to be signed by all member states and then ratified at national level. The path towards ratification for the Dublin Convention was tortuous: ratification in all the member states was not achieved until September 1997. The draft EFC was concerned with the conditions for access to the territory of EC member states by TCNs. In June 1991 agreement was secured on the general principles with regard to the crossing of external frontiers, and surveillance and the nature of the controls at these frontiers, as well as surveillance at airports. The EFC foundered because of a dispute between the Spanish and British about the status of Gibraltar that dated back to the 1713 Treaty of Utrecht, which ended the Spanish War of Succession. The EFC could not come into effect if it was not signed by all member states.

Schengen

Alongside the development of *ad hoc* co-operation between EC member states on immigration and asylum policy, five pro-integration member states (Belgium, France, Germany, Luxembourg and the Netherlands) resolved to move more quickly towards free movement for people and the abolition of internal border controls between their own territories. Schengen's importance to the development of EU immigration and asylum policy should not be underestimated. It has been seen as serving as a 'testing ground for the Community, from the standpoint of completion of the internal market, and as a driving force for those member states which are not signatories to the Schengen Agreements'.[9] This became even clearer when the 1997 Amsterdam Treaty moved the Schengen framework into the EU, although with a strong intergovernmental basis.

A 'mini-Schengen' had been established among the Benelux countries as far back as 1970, but the more immediate impetus behind the Schengen Agreement arose from protests in 1984 by lorry drivers angered by delays at the Franco-German border. This prompted an intergovernmental agreement between the two countries signed at Saarbrucken on 13 July 1984. The Schengen Agreement of 14 June 1985 brought the Benelux countries on board and constituted a more far-reaching attempt to abolish border controls. At this stage, Schengen was an agreement among signatory states and the hard work of putting it into effect remained to be done. A convention to implement the agreement was signed in June 1990. The removal of internal frontier controls between participating states then took a further six years.

Articles 2–38 of the 1990 implementing convention provide for: the removal of checks at the crossing of internal frontiers; the crossing of external borders; visas for short- and long-term visits; the movement of aliens; the residence and reporting of people not to be permitted entry; carrier liability; and asylum policy. Schengen's ambitious goals are evident in Article 17 of the 1985 Agreement, which stated that:

> In regard to the free movement of persons, the Parties shall endeavour to abolish the controls at the common frontiers and transfer them to their external frontiers. To that end they shall first endeavour to harmonise, where necessary, the laws and administrative provisions concerning prohibitions and restrictions which form the basis for the controls and to take complementary measures to safeguard security and combat illegal immigration by nationals of States that are not members of the European Communities.

Articles 131–3 established the Schengen Executive Committee, which was composed of national officials whose responsibility it was to secure implementation of the convention. When the Schengen framework was incorporated into the EU by the Amsterdam Treaty, the decisions were incorporated, with some becoming part of Community law. Schengen is of central importance to the development of EU measures on migration, asylum and border security. It contributed to the securitisation of migration, but also created rather insulated 'Eurocratic structures' or, as Schmidt (2006) puts it, policy without politics (see also Kelemen, 2002). That said, the creation of such structures is a political decision and not some artefact of the integration process.

The Schengen Agreement foreshadowed the free movement objectives of Article 8a of the SEA. It allowed the signatories to maintain tight control over development of 'Schengenland's' free movement framework. They could exclude EC institutions from involvement, although the Commission viewed Schengen positively and was an observer at meetings. Creation of the Schengen – as opposed to a pan-EC – framework also obviated potential difficulties from EC member states that might be hostile or not well equipped in terms of their own national policies to take part in such an arrangement. For instance, the British government was hostile and never joined, while pro-European Italian governments were rather upset that they were excluded from the original group of members and had to observe from the sidelines. Other Schengen states doubted Italy's capacity to implement the Agreement, although Italy has since become a full participating member.

Schengen's immigration and asylum implications are clear. The removal of internal frontiers between participating states meant the introduction of 'compensating' immigration and asylum policies, including harmonisation of visa policies and conditions for entry, and improved co-operation and harmonisation of asylum laws. Schengen's work was to be supported by the SIS, a computerised resource that has now developed to include more than 15 million entries linked to border security and population control. The capacity of EU member states to store and share data has grown exponentially, as has the desire to do so. The terror attacks of the 2000s influenced but did not impel this co-operation, because the origins of this action can be traced back to at least the early 1980s. Those attacks created new and additional rationales for such action, alongside longer-standing arguments for such data-gathering in relation to, for example, TCNs who should be denied entry to a Schengen state.[10] The SIS began operations in 1995 and now applies to all 15 Schengen states (13 'old' EU member states, minus the UK and Ireland, plus Norway and Iceland). The Commission is now developing plans for SIS II (initially planned for the end of 2006, but since put back to the end of 2008). Seven member states (Belgium, Germany, Spain, France, Luxembourg, the Netherlands and Austria) agreed the Prüm Convention[11] (outside the formal Treaty structure, but analogous to Schengen) to share information on terror suspects, cross-border crime and illegal immigration (House of Lords European Union Committee, 2007). The main aim is to speed up the transfer of information in an areas where there are already existing provisions for sharing of information and proposals to extend this principle of availability. EU member states gather a vast amount of data, are exploring new ways of sharing this data and also making data available to other countries, particularly the USA, and thus raising concerns about civil liberties.

The main problem with the Schengen Agreement as initially developed during the 1980s and 1990s was that it would not enter into effect until the conditions for its attainment had been met in each signatory state. This caused delay and the Schengen Convention implementing the earlier Agreement was not signed until 19 June 1990. One reason for the delay was German reunification, which meant that Schengen's provisions needed to be extended to cover the ex-German Democratic Republic, so that East Germans would be exempt from visa requirements when entering the territory of the other signatories.

Schengen provided more formalised institutional resources as a basis for the consolidation of networks of 'transgovernmental' action largely centred on security. In this way, it contributed to the operationalisation of free movement while affirming the strong links between freedom and security and the notions of population control and territorial management that would become integral components of EU action. There was very limited scope for democratic and judicial oversight, which becomes important when bearing in mind arguments about rights-based politics and the role of courts in opening social and political spaces for migrants at national level (Hollifield, 1992). Article 135 did state that the Convention was subject to the provisions of the 1951 Geneva Convention and the 1967 New York Protocol on refugees. But it would have been more of a surprise if these ritual declarations had not been made and even more surprising if judicial authorities had been given the teeth to interpret Schengen arrangements in the light of these international standards. There was no judicial body able to interpret the Convention or to adjudicate if disputes arose. The relationship of Schengen with EC law was outlined in Article 134 of the 1990 Convention. This stated that the Convention's articles were to apply only insofar as they were compatible with Community law. The Commission tended to see the Schengen arrangements as necessary for eventual attainment of Article 8a of the SEA, on free movement within the single market. Therefore, it sought to ensure via its role as an observer at Schengen meetings that there was no discrimination between nationals of Schengen member states and nationals of other EC member states, and that Schengen did not jeopardise attainment of Article 8a.

Article 2 of the 1990 Convention had established the principle that internal borders could be crossed without checks on persons, although there is the derogation from this principle that member states may carry out checks for a limited period for public policy or national security reasons. The Schengen Agreement had been supposed to come into operation on 26 March 1995. Passport controls were dropped, but on 1 July 1995, when it was intended to drop checks at land border controls, the French government insisted on maintaining them after terrorist attacks on the Paris metro and the invocation of the 'safeguard clause' (Article 2(2)). At the Schengen Executive Committee meeting of 18 April 1996, the French government announced that it would maintain controls on the borders with Belgium and Luxembourg, because they were seen as being transit countries for drugs leaving the Netherlands. France also promoted a Council of Europe resolution that sought prohibition of the production of, and trading in, all drugs. The Dutch refuted the suggestion that they were 'soft' on drugs, and noted that Schengen made no mention of a harmonised drugs policy. The French stance was perceived as an opportunistic move by the right-wing government to offset opposition to immigration and European integration. Thus, the French government had initially reinstated border controls to combat terrorist attacks and when these had ended had maintained controls because they said they were needed because of the problems caused by Dutch drugs policy (*Statewatch*, May–June 1996).

Even though it rested on intergovernmental foundations, Schengen was not the product of intergovernmentalism as some kind of defence of the nation state. Rather, it is emblematic of the ways in which freedom and security were conjoined within the new economic space that was being constructed at European level. It is illustrative, too, of 'boundary build-up', whereby liberalisation of certain types of flows of goods, capital and services also generates concerns about security and promotes new forms of build-up designed to reinforce borders against those population flows deemed most threatening (Nevins, 2002). Schengen is also linked to 'boundary shift' to new migration countries and new member states. Schengen facilitated the attainment of participating states' objectives with regard to economic liberalisation and population control within a frontier-free European space. It also established policies and decision-making structures that demonstrated both a deeper integrative intent on the part of some key EC member states and their willingness to embrace more 'flexible' forms of co-operation and integration if these would allow them to reach their ambitious objectives.

In his famous statement of the neo-realist position, Hoffmann (1966: 882) argued that states would shy away from integration in areas of high politics because 'Russian roulette is fine only as long as the gun is filled with blanks'. The functional method of integration with its spillover dynamics would, Hoffmann argued, be confounded by the opposition to political union because 'Functional integration's gamble could be won only if the method had sufficient potency to promise an excess of gains over losses, and of hopes over frustrations. Theoretically, this may be true of economic integration. It is not true of political integration.' The SEA blurred this distinction between political and economic integration. Rather than embarking on some kind of death pact, the Schengen signatories were developing forms of co-operation intended to lead to deeper integration in key areas of state sovereignty, but by doing so they were changing the meaning and practice of sovereignty. Market-making and population control could not be separated once the single market programme was operationalised. The Schengen signatories were pursuing fundamental EC objectives, albeit beyond the 'constraints' imposed by the EC's legal and political order, as well as excluding those member states that were opposed to supranationalisation of these policy areas or unable to fulfil external and internal security requirements.

Conclusion

This chapter has shown that there were expanding spheres of primarily intergovernmental co-operation after the SEA, but this co-operation was very much focused on a security 'field' that drew from Trevi, Schengen and new modes of working together. This chapter has addressed three main questions. First, it has explored the drive underlying European economic and political integration as it related to free movement, migration and asylum in the 1980s. The chapter has shown that free movement was never intended for everyone. Instead, what we see is consolidation of a European-level relationship between economic freedoms and security that has since become one of the EU's core defining features. Mechanistic notions of neo-functionalism have little analytical purchase in issue areas where national interests are so much to the fore. To think about these issues in such stark intergovernmental versus supranational terms would miss some underlying dynamics linked to the emergence of intensive networks of transgovernmental action in the European internal security field. These networks drew from resources created through existing patterns of co-operation and began to develop 'European solutions' which could then be applied to 'problems' such as economic integration, enlargement and post-Cold War European politics (Cohen et al., 1972; Kingdon, 1984).

The chapter has also addressed the question of the extent to which these developments were *European* in the sense of being more than just a convenient device for member states to attain their domestic objectives. To focus on the underlying dynamics in terms of a supranational versus intergovernmental dichotomy would miss developments linked to the 'transgovernmental' action in the nascent European internal security field. The SEA provided scope for a profound restructuring of European economic space that recast state sovereignty and its meaning. Consequently, while the developments in free movement, migration and asylum cannot be understood in isolation from the strong intergovernmental impetus that underpinned much action in these areas, it is also the case that we begin to see the emergence of certain forms of European action and forms of co-operation linked to security networks. Debates about migrants' rights were almost entirely national at this time.

The third question addressed by this chapter was the extent to which European developments at the time of the SEA represented a reframing of Europe's border relationships. In a certain sense, it was self-evident that this is precisely what they did, because the single market was defined as an area without internal frontiers. These developments began to initiate a

European reframing of debates about territorial management and access to key organisational borders of work and welfare, and of the 'who are we' issues integral to conceptual borders of belonging, entitlement and identity. As the next chapter shows, these debates became more profound in the 1990s and also began to shape quite strongly the relationships between EC/EU states and neighbouring states, through accession, as members of Europe's neighbourhood, or as countries from which security threats were deemed to emanate. The next chapter examines how the Maastricht Treaty and its aftermath placed EU action in the area of Justice and Home Affairs on a more formal footing and began to impart real significance to debate about common European migration and asylum policies, to such an extent that they became feasible topics for debate rather than bold aspirations.

Notes

1 In its edition of 16 March 2007, *The Economist* lamented the EU's mid-life crisis, so maybe this, too, augurs a dramatic relaunch of European integration?
2 Council Directive 76/207, 9 February 1976, on the implementation of the principle of equal treatment for men and women as regards access to employment, vocational training and promotion, and working conditions, *Official Journal*, 39, 14 February 1976, pp. 40–2.
3 *Commission v. Belgium*, Case 321/87 [1989] ECR 997.
4 *Commission v. Netherlands*, Case C-68/89 [1991] ECR I-2637.
5 *Official Journal*, L217/25, 1985.
6 Joined cases 281, 283–5, 287/87, *Germany, France, Netherlands, Denmark and UK v. Commission* [1987] ECR 3245.
7 Council press release 10518/92.
8 Council Regulation (EC) 2725/2000, of 11 December 2000, concerning the establishment of 'Eurodac' for the comparison of fingerprints for the effective application of the Dublin Convention. *Official Journal*, L316, 15 December 2000, pp. 1–10.
9 Commission answer to Written Parliamentary Question 3044/90, *Official Journal*, C214/12, 1991.
10 This is one 'alert' in the Schengen system, the others being persons wanted for extradition (Article 95), missing persons (Article 97), persons wanted as witnesses, for prosecution or for the enforcement of sentences (Article 98), persons to be placed under surveillance or subjected to specific checks (Article 99) and objects sought for seizure or use in criminal proceedings (Article 100).
11 Council Secretariat, Prüm Convention, 10900/05, LIMITE, CRIMORG 65, ENFOPOL 85, MIGR 30, 7 July 2005.

5

Maastricht's Justice and Home Affairs pillar

Introduction

The Treaty on European Union, or Maastricht Treaty as it is more commonly known, which came into force in 1993, formalised, but did not supranationalise, co-operation on immigration and asylum policy. It confirmed executive dominance of this policy area and a limited role for legislative and judicial involvement and oversight. This chapter explains how these developments came about, through analysis of the background to the Maastricht Treaty, its negotiation, the components of the Treaty itself, and its effects on migration and asylum issues. The chapter demonstrates that the formalisation of co-operation and collaboration centred, in particular, on a security-driven response to migration that drew from co-operation in the Trevi group and Schengen to address questions of territorial management arising from the end of the Cold War and the prospect of a wider Europe. We see, too, the parameters of an EU response focused on visas, asylum and external frontier controls.

The Maastricht Treaty is important because it drew co-operation that had been outside the Treaty into an intergovernmental 'pillar' of the newly created EU. Aside from its immigration and asylum policy implications, if the famous – or perhaps infamous – Maastricht Treaty had but one virtue, it was that it drew debates about European integration from the realm of élite discussion, where they had tended to dwell, and placed them more squarely in the spotlight of broader public debate in the member states. This is not to suggest that the minutiae of inter-state negotiations and the riveting detail of Treaty articles transfixed the peoples of Europe: it was probably only the lawyers who truly rubbed their hands with glee. Rather, the deals and compromises struck by national governments, as well as their implications, were subject to more critical scrutiny than had previously been the case. The discussion of the implications of the creation of the EU by the Maastricht Treaty even caused 'Euroscepticism' – conflated with domestic political factors such as the unpopularity of national governments – to advance beyond its traditional territorial confines in 'awkward partners' such as Denmark and the UK, as the French people's *petit oui* in their September 1992 referendum on Maastricht ratification demonstrated (Franklin et al., 1994).

Three sets of issues are central to this book's analysis and are developed in this chapter. First, the underlying dynamics of co-operation on migration and asylum – with movement from post-SEA *ad hoc* co-operation outside a Treaty framework to more formal intergovernmental co-operation – could be construed as indicative of a creeping supranationalisation, as immigration and asylum moved closer to political integration. A weakness of this line of argument is its concession to integrative inevitability and neglect of state motivations underpinning co-operation on migration and asylum. What this chapter shows is the development and consolidation of networks of co-operation and collaboration, centred largely on internal security and drawing in representatives – often at official level – of member state governments. This connects with the powerful interpretation of these events that argues that member states sought European co-operation on migration and asylum to release themselves from domestic (national) judicial and political constraints on policy development, as they preferred secretive, executive-dominated action, but were reluctant to allow scope for supranational constitutionalisation and institutionalisation of immigration and asylum competencies (Freeman, 1998; Guiraudon, 2001, 2003). During the Maastricht negotiations, it was also the case that the more sceptical national governments, such as the British and Danish, were able to put a brake on ambitious plans for the development of EU immigration and asylum policy.

The second issue is the distinct 'European' content of this action. This chapter shows that the development and consolidation of networks of action around migration and asylum helped establish a European framework for these issues, but that, at same time, the predominant structures of power, authority and capacity in the areas of migration and asylum remained largely national and centred around security. European developments cannot be understood separately from these national developments. It does, though, become increasingly relevant through the 1990s to examine the ways in which EU action began to affect member states, potential member states and other neighbouring states. This has now become a very clearly defined component of EU action and represents an external face of European integration (Olsen, 2002).

The third set of issues concerns the impact of these developments on territorial, organisational and conceptual borders. European integration since the 1980s had begun to reconfigure territory and strategies of territorial management as a consequence of the single market programme, but without necessarily presaging either the end of territory or the end of the nation state. What we do see are changes in both understandings and management of territory and in understandings and practices of sovereignty.

Clear links became evident at EU level between territory, organisational borders of work and welfare, and conceptual borders of belonging and entitlement, for example through debate about EU citizenship. We thus begin to see EU-level resonance of the two core dimensions of migration policy: the regulation of international population movement and – to a more limited extent – the integration of migrants.

The negotiations

The perceived inadequacies of post-SEA *ad hoc* intergovernmental co-operation on immigration and asylum policy, coupled with a desire on the part of some member states to seek deeper political integration, prompted Maastricht's re-evaluation of immigration and asylum policy co-operation. This was for three reasons. First, the end of the Cold War and the geo-political shake-up that resulted from it had a major effect on understandings of internal security. The distinction between external and internal security was blurred, as internal security issues such as migration and asylum also became seen as external security challenges. The demarcation between domestic and international challenges to security was breaking down. Migration and asylum were salient components of a new security agenda and became integral both to the discursive framing of 'security' beyond its traditional Cold War frame of reference and also to the emergence of new technologies of population control (Wæver et al., 1993; Bigo, 2001; Huysmans, 2006). It has been argued that the end of the Cold War 'unleashed a flood of immigrants from the east and seemed to open the door to criminal organisations' (Turnbull and Sandholtz, 2001: 195). In fact, although there was increased migration – with much of it in the early 1990s focused on Germany – actual numbers of migrants nowhere near matched apocalyptic forecasts of 'floods' (Codagnone, 1999). It was not so much the reality of floods of migrants or some kind of invasion by unwanted immigrants that fuelled the EU response, but the *fear* of such events occurring and thus a perceived need to guard against them. Second, decision-making procedures to deal with these new security challenges were viewed as inadequate, as evidenced by the difficulties experienced by the Dublin Convention on asylum and the EFC (discussed in Chapter 4). Third, *ad hoc* co-operation exacerbated a perceived 'democratic deficit', because there existed at best a tenuous relationship between, on the one side, internal security co-operation and, on the other, civil liberties, human rights and accountability. Secretive intergovernmental forums insulated EU action from legislative and judicial oversight at either national or supranational level (Spencer, 1990, 1995; Bunyan, 1991). This shielded executive forum may actually have been the intention of the actors most central to the development of EU action on migration and asylum, not some sort of unfortunate and unanticipated side-effect.

In its 1991 communication on immigration policy, the Commission noted that the intergovernmental method had failed to produce any meaningful results. The Commission was prepared to be pragmatic because of the difficulties of securing more ambitious forms of immigration and asylum policy integration. It emphasised the importance of dialogue between the EC member states through the General Affairs Council and through meetings of immigration ministers (CEC, 1991). It sought to participate in what was essentially an attempt to develop EU-level co-operation on immigration and asylum, with the emphasis heavily on restriction. The EP felt marginalised by the Commission's pragmatic stance. It adopted a highly critical tone, condemned *ad hoc* intergovernmentalism and urged that immigration and asylum policies be brought within the EC framework and that action be taken at Community level to tackle racism and xenophobia.[1]

Despite the views of supranational institutions, it was the policy preferences of the member states that mattered. Ultimately, the Maastricht Treaty gave legal effect to a compromise between integrative 'maximalists', who favoured deeper integration, and 'minimalists', who were opposed. As is often the case, maximalists outnumbered minimalists, but negotiations proceeded on the basis of unanimity, with the effect that the preferences of more reluctant member states had a decisive and limiting effect on the range of possible outcomes. This did not mean that the outcome mirrored the policy preferences of the minimalists, but that they were able to put a brake on more ambitious integrative objectives by limiting the range of outcomes. Effectively precluded from the outset was communitarisation of immigration and asylum policy, meaning a common EU policy.

The immigration and asylum policy compromise between maximalists and minimalists was reflected in the creation of the 'third pillar' of the Maastricht Treaty, which dealt with Justice and Home Affairs (JHA). The JHA pillar made a clear connection between immigration and asylum and other internal security issues. It was a tangible manifestation of the difficulties associated with securing agreement on the content of such a policy, given the widely divergent policy paradigms in member states and the need for unanimity if an EU context were to be established. There was far less divergence on the need for tighter immigration controls; indeed, there was a detectable convergence of policy preferences on this issue. This provided all the necessary ingredients for a 'lowest common denominator' immigration and asylum policy, emphasising restriction. It also laid the foundations for blurred competence, derived from the cautious ceding to the Council and its Secretariat of competencies, which in turn left questions concerning competence, discretion and the location of capacity to act.

The intention of Maastricht's drafters was for the JHA pillar to stand alongside the 'first pillar' (the Community pillar) and the 'second pillar' (dealing with a common foreign and security policy, CFSP). Co-operation on CFSP had occurred outside the framework of the Treaty of Rome

since 1970, when EPC had been established (see Chapter 4). Inter-state
dynamics during the Maastricht negotiations and the political sensitivity of
immigration and asylum issues precluded supranational integration, despite
the hopes of integrative maximalists, such as the Dutch government, which
drafted the Maastricht Treaty. The Maastricht negotiations, the Treaty itself
and its aftermath also illustrate how freedom and security became more
closely bound in the 1990s. Economic freedoms linked to the single market
were closely linked to new EU mechanisms of population control in this
new European space. Freer movement for EU citizens prompted closer co-
operation on entry, residence and movement of TCNs, but did not dictate
that these areas had to be supranationalised. Free movement by EU citizens
and non-EU nationals also raised concerns about the impact of liberalisation and its effect on national welfare states. This was evident, for example,
in the debate about posted workers (Hunger, 2000).

The Dublin meeting of the European Council in June 1990 had agreed
to convene two IGCs composed of national ministers to consider Treaty
reform. One dealt with EMU, the other with political union. The two IGCs
were formally opened at the Rome summit in December 1990. The EMU
IGC was rather more straightforward, because the groundwork for the
discussion had been laid in the Delors report, which had investigated the
prospects for EMU and suggested a plan of action (Delors et al., 1989). The
agenda for the political union IGC was far less certain and there was greater
scope for conflict between member states over objectives. Immigration and
asylum aroused particular controversy within the discussions. There was a
basic measure of agreement that the *ad hoc* structures put in place after the
SEA were problematic, for a number of reasons, including the effectiveness of the response to new security challenges, democratic scrutiny and
accountability. Two basic questions configured discussion of future policy
development. Would immigration and asylum be incorporated within
the existing EC structure, meaning powers for the Commission, ECJ and
perhaps even the EP? Or would new structures be established which would
place immigration and asylum in a separate intergovernmental pillar? The
former option would mark a significant encroachment of supranational
authority into policy areas strongly associated with state sovereignty. The
latter would bring immigration and asylum within the structure of the EU,
but restrict the extent of communitarisation of the policy because of the
reliance on intergovernmental co-operation.

The Luxembourg government held responsibility for management of the
IGC process when it assumed the Council presidency for the six months
between January and June 1991. In January 1991 it made four immigration
and asylum policy suggestions, between which member states were invited
to express a preference:

• that the existing *ad hoc* arrangements be maintained;

- that reference be made in the Maastricht Treaty to co-operation but that the Council be left to sort out the details;
- that more elaborate Treaty provisions be made, outlining areas of co-operation;
- most ambitiously, that immigration and asylum policies be fully incor-porated into the Treaty framework, with the use EC decision-making methods for those policies.

Opinions among member states were divided.[2] The Danish government favoured the first option. The British, Irish and Greek governments pre-ferred the second. France, Germany and Portugal expressed a preference for the third option (for the French and German governments as a short-term measure before full communitarisation). The Netherlands, Belgium, Italy and Spain favoured the fourth option. The majority of member states leaned towards closer integration but there was a requirement to proceed by unanimity. The balance of intergovernmental preferences meant that the fourth option was unattainable. The range of possible alternatives suggested some kind of compromise secured through maintenance of inter-governmentalism, but with a closer association with the legal framework of the Treaty of Rome and EC institutions.

In April 1991 the Luxembourg government produced a 'non-paper' containing draft Treaty amendments. This proposed the creation of an EU within which would be created separate CFSP and JHA pillars. Because of its long-standing preference for intergovernmentalism, the British Con-servative government led by Prime Minister John Major favoured this pillared approach. The French, Germans, Belgians and Spanish saw it as too minimalist in its ambitions. The Commission and EP also reacted un-favourably to what they saw as a consolidation of intergovernmentalism, which would minimise their role in policy development and decision-making. Despite the satisfaction of the British government, the Luxembourg presidency's suggestions were not *in toto* an intergovernmentalists' charter, because they contained ambitious proposals for deeper integration, such as plans to extend local and European election voting rights to permanently resident non-EC nationals (ultimately, not to be realised). It was, though, the Luxembourg proposals that were to be the basis of the Maastricht deal, because they were acceptable to the minimalists while they were also seen as opening the possibility for communitarisation in the future.

On immigration and asylum policy integration, the German, Belgian, Italian, Greek, Dutch, Spanish and Irish governments, plus the Commission, could broadly be classed as maximalists. All preferred that immigration and asylum be placed within EC decision-making procedures. The Danish and British governments wanted a separate intergovernmental pillar. Luxem-bourg and France suggested a compromise: the creation of a pillar but with the presumption of temporariness and the likelihood of closer integration in the future. The German government strongly favoured Europeanisation of asylum policy because of the salience of the asylum issue in German politics. The German government thought that a common European effort might help establish a more equal distribution of asylum-seekers. This was a reason why other member states were decidedly less enthusiastic than the Germans about common asylum policies.

On 1 July 1991 the Dutch government assumed the Council presidency. It faced the difficult task of reconciling divergent views within the political union IGC. The Dutch also held their own long-standing preference for deeper economic and political integration, embodying some kind of explicitly stated 'federal vocation'. There were also other pressing issues for the Dutch presidency to deal with, particularly the civil war in Yugo-slavia, which dominated the political agenda and generated large refugee flows, particularly to Germany. The Dutch government took a maximalist approach and sought a statement in the Treaty expressing support for federal objectives. This was reflected in proposals that resulted in a black day for Dutch diplomacy, 30 September 1991, when an ambitious draft Treaty proposed, among other things, communitarisation of immigration and asylum. The Dutch proposals likened the EU to a tree, with immigra-tion and asylum as one of its branches, subject to the Community method of decision-making. Only the Belgian government and the Commission rallied to the Dutch proposals. Other member states strongly criticised the Dutch draft, refused to negotiate on the basis of it, and expressed a clear preference for the Luxembourg version (with its plan for a pillared struc-ture). The Dutch government had to swallow its pride and the eventual basis for negotiation at the Maastricht summit was far closer to the Luxem-bourg proposals than the more overtly federalist Dutch plans.

In October 1991, as part of its contribution to the IGC process, the Commission issued a communication covering immigration and asylum (CEC, 1991). The document called not only for the control of migration to become an integral element of EC policy, but also for the strengthening of European-level measures aimed at the integration of settled migrants and their descendants. The Commission contended that European-level co-operation was skewed in the direction of control, with few countervailing measures designed to promote migrant integration. The non-binding Social Charter of 1989 had indicated some of the problems that were faced when its outline of a strengthened EC social dimension made no commitment to the fundamental social rights of TCNs. As had become very clear when the free movement policy was enacted, the rights of TCNs who were not dependants of an EC national or covered by an Association Agreement were matters for the member states, not the EC. The communication maintained the Commission's pragmatic stance towards policy development, while re-flecting the constraints imposed by the limited legal basis for EC action. It did, however, also propose laying the foundations for a comprehensive EC migration policy, encompassing a threefold strategy combining immigration control with immigrant integration and measures to tackle the root causes of migration. The EP criticised the Commission communication for being compliant with the restrictionist drift of policy.[3]

The work of national ministers responsible for immigration and asylum continued in the run-up to Maastricht and fed into the IGC process. The immigration ministers presented a report to the Maastricht European Council that set out an immigration and asylum work programme.[4] This concentrated on the harmonisation of admission policies for family reunion, work, study or humanitarian reasons. It also sought the development of a common approach to illegal immigration, labour migration policies and the status of TCNs, including labour market access. The work programme also spelt out priorities for asylum policy related to the implementation of the Dublin Convention. Asylum policy harmonisation would include attempts to define the principle of first host country, as well as a common interpretation of the definition of a refugee. The report outlining the work programme expressed no opinion on the institutional structures within which the work should be conducted, because this would have been too controversial. It did, though, express a commitment to policy development based on social justice and human rights, with implications for refugee policy and family reunion, as well as for anti-discrimination and migrant integration policies. This work programme formed the basis for the subsequent co-operation within the JHA pillar discussed later in this chapter.

Maastricht's pillars

The Maastricht Treaty was negotiated on 9–10 December 1991 and signed in Lisbon in February 1992, but then hobbled through a ratification process that was not completed until November 1993, when the German articles of ratification were deposited following the defeat of challenges made in the German constitutional court. The Treaty created a pillared structure incorporating JHA and CFSP into the framework of the EU, but maintaining intergovernmental co-operation for decision-making and a severely constrained role for supranational institutions in these two areas. This led to the Treaty structure being likened to a Greek temple, the roof of which was supported by three pillars.

- *Pillar 1.* The central and largest pillar was the 'Community', with significant supranationalisation across a range of policy sectors. Within these sectors, the core elements of a supranational community were evident: EC law had direct effect, the ECJ held jurisdiction, QMV applied to more policy areas, the Commission was closely associated with policy development and the EP was, to varying degrees, involved in policy development. Visa policy was located within this pillar.

- *Pillars 2 and 3.* The intergovernmental CFSP pillar built on EPC structures put in place in 1970, while the JHA pillar formalised prior patterns of *ad hoc* co-operation on migration, asylum policing and judicial co-operation (Monar and Morgan, 1994).

How appropriate was this temple analogy? Handoll (1995: 32) suggests that it was not particularly useful, because the pillared structure did not create 'classical harmony', but an unbalanced and lopsided structure that was part of a process by which the two new intergovernmental elements would be gradually subsumed by the Community element (the central pillar). As well as the absence of architectural symmetry, the rather strange constitutional design of the pillared structure – the product of compromise, not of clear intent – also raised the issue of the legal foundations of the EU. What legal status did the pillars possess? Clearly, they were not EC laws as typically understood, because they were neither supreme nor possessed of direct effect. Müller-Graff (1994) described the Maastricht framework as 'legal sandstone' not 'legal granite'; the pillars were not amendments to the Treaty of Rome and so were not part of EC law, but were likely to be eroded as a consequence of gradual encroachment by the Community pillar. This meant that the legal foundations of the Maastricht Treaty were public international law. Snyder (1994: 89) agreed that the JHA pillar was not EC law as usually understood, but argued that the connections were close because the third pillar was an integral part of the EU and subject to its single institutional structure: 'The EC and the EU are thus distinct but intimately related'.

Relations between the three pillars arose from procedural, institutional and functional connections (Müller-Graff, 1994: 24–30). Procedural connections derived from the incorporation of interior policy within the EU's single institutional framework. Institutional connections arose from the fact that even though they relied on unanimity, EU institutions were empowered to act upon immigration and asylum issues (with significant limitations). Functional connections derived from links between the attainment of single market objectives and interior policy issues drawn into the realm of EU competence, which included immigration and asylum. It was not possible, for instance, to demarcate clearly between free movement ('communitarised') and immigration and asylum ('intergovernmental') and deal with them entirely separately: functional connections meant that the issues were linked. This is a key point and an important factor underpinning pressure for supranationalisation of immigration and asylum policies. Legal and institutional connections created a web of linkages between intra- and extra-EU migration policy and meant that the two could not be treated as though they were wholly distinct. The economic logic of market-making had political consequences that drew issues of high politics into the EU's remit. Free movement had become communitarised, while immigration and asylum remained largely beyond the remit of national and supranational institutions. Links were the basis for the further consolidation and intensi-fication of co-operation, which drew from both the formal institutional resources created by Maastricht and patterns of co-operation dating back to Trevi, in the 1970s.

There is also a cross-cutting issue dimension to the analysis of this pillared structure. Free movement, migration and asylum cut across all three pillars. This became clearer as the 1990s progressed. It was not possible to neatly separate free movement as a pillar 1 concern from immi-gration and asylum as pillar 3 issues. Visa policy was the best example of this, discussed later in this chapter. The blurring of the distinction between external and internal security that arose as a consequence of the post-Cold War security agenda also meant that the functional and organisational distinction between pillars 2 and 3 was not easy to sustain.

The JHA pillar

Title VI of the Maastricht Treaty dealt with JHA co-operation. Article K1 listed the issues that were to be regarded as matters of 'common interest', that is, not 'common policies'. The distinction is important. Indeed, for the British Conservative government, the JHA pillar was a diplomatic triumph, or 'game, set and match' as John Major put it when speaking to the press outside the Maastricht negotiating rooms (perhaps unwisely in the light of the calamities that would befall his government as a result of the European issue). Major stated that:

> At Maastricht we developed a new way, and one much more amenable to the institutions of this country – co-operation by agreement between govern-ments, but not under the Treaty of Rome. It covers interior and justice matters, foreign affairs and security, and the option is available for it to cover wider matters in the future. (Quoted in Duff, 1994: 20)

Was Major right? Was this a new way of co-operating on immigration and asylum issues that could be sustained in the long term and, perhaps, broadened to cover other policy areas? Major was mistaken. Other member states did not share his vision of enlarging spheres of intergovernmental co-operation. Indeed, even a cursory analysis of the negotiations preceding the Maastricht summit would show that most member states saw the pillars as a compromise and not as a model for future development – as 'sandstone', not 'granite'. For maximalists, the pillared structure was also part of what they saw as a slow and incremental movement towards immigration and asylum policy integration. The JHA pillar was likely to set the ground rules for debate about further extension of EU competence for immigration and asylum in the future. Bieber (1994: 38) noted of the third pillar arrange-ments that: 'their intrinsic evolutionary and provisional quality is framed by the first pillar, which hence establishes the long-term centre of gravity of this complex system'.

From this perspective, Maastricht's JHA pillar was a compromise, but a 'bridge' existed between the third and first pillar which could lead to greater supranationalisation of immigration and asylum issues in the future. This bridge was provided for by Article K9, which created a procedure for a *passerelle* from the JHA pillar to the Community pillar, albeit this was a procedure that lawyers liked to analyse but that member states preferred not to follow (Bieber, 1994). To restate a by now familiar point about the difficulties of 'positive integration': crossing the bridge from the third pillar to the first required unanimity among member states, which was unlikely to be forthcoming.

Maastricht's JHA provisions were seen as widening the 'democratic deficit' (Geddes, 1995). Patterns of democratic control and accountability at both national and supranational level were weak. While the preference of most member states was for greater supranationalisation of immigration and asylum policy, with an extended role for the Commission, ECJ and EP, there was also readiness to accept structures that favoured executive-dominated forms of action. The democratic deficit was not necessarily widened because of a malevolent disregard for democracy exacerbated by European integration (a conspiracy theory of European integration) but because of difficulties in securing agreement between maximalist and minimalist states during intergovernmental negotiations (the problems of positive integration). The majority of member states would have preferred more 'democracy', as measured by increased power for the EP and ECJ, albeit within a more secretive institutional framework than for other inte-grated policy areas and thus analogous to national policy settings. However, an insufficient number of member states preferred this option and, in a system reliant on unanimity, the minimalists were able to hold sway. The UK and Denmark, in particular, were reluctant to see communitarisation of immigration and asylum issues, with increased power for the EP, Com-mission and ECJ, despite other member states being prepared to see these issues brought within the framework of the EU. The point is not that the preferences of Denmark and the UK prevailed exactly (they had to make some concessions on these and other issues), but that they decisively affected the possible outcomes in a negotiating environment reliant on una-nimity. If supranationalisation rather than intergovernmentalism had been the chosen path, then the problems of democratic accountability at national and supranational level might not have been so marked; but this route was patently unacceptable to a minority of member states, which were able to decisively influence the treaty outcome.

JHA provisions
Maastricht recognised the following as matters of 'common interest':

- asylum policy;
- rules governing the crossing by persons of the external borders of the member states and the exercise of controls thereon;
- immigration policy and policy regarding TCNs –
  (a) their conditions of entry to and movement within the territory of member states;
  (b) their conditions of residence on the territory of member states, including family reunion and access to employment;
  (c) combating their unauthorised immigration, residence and work on the territory of member states.

Article K1 also listed other issues that were to be covered by inter-governmental co-operation, such as combating drug trafficking and addiction, international fraud, terrorism, police co-operation (via Europol) and judicial co-operation in civil and criminal matters. Immigration and asylum were placed alongside internal security issues. Parallel immigrant integration measures were limited and did not possess a sure footing in the Treaty. A declaration added to the Treaty at the instigation of the German government did, however, declare that co-operation on asylum policy would be a priority.

Article K2 stated that these matters of common interest would be dealt with in compliance with the ECHR and the Geneva Convention. This was an easy declaration to make but more difficult to enforce, because the provision was not justiciable by the ECJ. Third pillar issues would be subject to ECJ review in the light of international obligations only if arrangements were made to extend ECJ jurisdiction to cover these matters. This indicated superficial regard for the symbolic importance of these international obligations and scant regard for ensuring effective compliance. Twomey (1994: 56–63) points out that states cannot ignore their international obligations by simply stating that breaches of them are due to the creation of the third pillar and that this somehow excuses the breach. Declarations by EU member states of their collective respect for international law may not tally with practice. For instance, the assumption by non-state agents, such as airlines, of responsibility for aspects of migration control can compromise the very standards that the member states have pledged to uphold. The result of the imposition of carrier sanctions on airlines carrying undocumented migrants has been that inadequately trained airline personnel have to deal with complex immigration questions, as they know that the threat of large fines hangs over the heads of their employers if the 'wrong' people are allowed to travel (Lahav, 1998).

Article K3 of the Maastricht Treaty confirmed unanimity in the Council of Ministers as the basis for decision-making. Except for the visa provisions of Article 100c of the Community pillar (see below), there was to be no QMV. The Commission's powers were also watered down, in that it would have to share its right of initiative with the member states. Indeed, the Commission proved to be so sensitive about national policy preferences in the third pillar that most initiatives actually came from the member states. The ECJ was deprived of jurisdiction unless it was specifically allocated under the terms of an international convention. Moreover, the legal basis of the JHA pillar was also weakened, because the issuance of regulations or directives – the mainstays of the Community legal system – were not options. Instead, three far less substantive courses of action were available to the member states:

- *joint positions*, which did not have binding effect;
- *joint actions*, which could have binding effects in relation to the kinds of action agreed upon and could be implemented by use of QMV, if member states agreed unanimously to do so (the unanimity problem again);
- adoption of *conventions* in international law, which would need to be ratified at national level and could be interpreted by national courts in accordance with the characteristics of national systems (but remember the travails of the Dublin Convention, which took seven years to enter into effect, and the EFC, which in 1999 had still not even been signed by all the member states and which was superseded by the Amsterdam Treaty).

There were also the tasks associated with bureaucratic support for the operation of Councils of Ministers dealing with JHA issues. This role was assumed by the 'K4 Committee' (the name was derived from the Treaty article), composed of senior officials, which assumed the responsibilities previously performed within groups such as Trevi and the *Ad Hoc* Group on Immigration (see Chapter 4). The K4 Committee preferred similar levels of secrecy and helped propagate an information deficit arising from the absence of publicly available documentation on its activities. Article K5 committed the member states to defending common positions adopted under the third pillar provisions.

The Commission and, particularly, the EP and ECJ were marginal to decision-making. There was a precedent within the framework of EPC (on foreign policy) which developed during the 1970s for exclusion of the Commission and EP (Monar, 1994). It was difficult to justify exclusion of supranational institutions from immigration and asylum policy issues, as these related so strongly to the fundamental objectives of the EU associated with attainment of the single market's free movement objectives. The *passerelle* clause, Article K9, established a potential bridge from the JHA pillar to the EU. It provided that the Council, acting unanimously on the initiative of the Commission or a member state, could decide to apply Article 100c of the EC Treaty to areas covered by Articles K1–6 and determine the relevant voting conditions, that is, unanimity or QMV. In theory this could have prompted the supranationalisation of immigration and asylum issues, but in reality it did not. The declaration on asylum attached to the final act of the Maastricht Treaty required the Council to consider, by the end of 1993, the possibility of applying Article K9 to asylum policy. Such a move would involve amendment of the Treaty, so there was also the requirement that any decision to use the *passerelle* would need to be ratified by member states in accordance with their respective constitutional requirements. A November 1994 Commission report on the possibility of applying Article K9 to asylum policy identified certain advantages, but argued that it was too soon to take such a step (CEC, 1994a). This was a realistic assessment of the position by the Commission, as there was little prospect that the member states would all agree.

A revised draft of the EFC was drawn up to take account of Maastricht's JHA pillar. The proposal was for a Council decision based on Article K3 of the Maastricht Treaty (CEC, 1993; O'Keeffe, 1994). The reformulated proposal sought to maintain the political consensus that had existed on the previous draft EFC, brought forward within the post-SEA *ad hoc* procedures. The disagreement between the Spanish and British governments about the status of Gibraltar continued to prevent agreement being reached on the draft EFC, however. In the absence of such agreement, the Commission pushed ahead in July 1997 with a joint action on co-operation between national immigration officials and the EU through the 'Odysseus' programme, which between 1998 and 2002 provided 12 million ecus (euros) to support the development of border controls (CEC, 1997b).[5]

The focus so far has been on the emergence of an EU approach to territorial management and border control, which have been central to EU action since at least the 1980s. This should not distract us from the implications for organisational and conceptual borders. The Maastricht Treaty contained social policy provisions in its Social Chapter that had some effect on the rights of TCNs. The Social Chapter, signed by 11 member states, with the UK opting out (and opting back in after the election of a Labour government in May 1997), included among the objectives of EU social policy: improved living and working conditions, proper social protection and the combating of exclusion. It has been noted that 'All these objectives naturally concern the position of all workers, irrespective of nationality (and arguably residence status)' (Handoll, 1995: 392) and thus applied to TCNs. The Social Chapter was utilised by pro-migrant lobby groups as they pressed for a 'Resident's Charter' to extend to permanently settled TCNs many of the rights held by EU citizens. The social dimension is particularly important in this respect: migrants who are legally resident in EU member states acquire social entitlements as a result of their residence but, at EU level, social entitlements derive from prior possession of the nationality of a member state.

The balance of institutional power

Thus far, much of the focus has been on the underlying dynamics of EU action and their relation to state and supranational power. There are equally relevant concerns about the relationship between executive, legislative and judicial power within this emergent EU policy field. The JHA provisions stated that the Commission was to be 'fully associated' with JHA issues. The Commission did not hold the same power in the third pillar that it was able to exercise in communitarised areas. For instance, Articles 155 and 163 of the EC Treaty, which allowed Commission monitoring of compliance with Treaty obligations by member states and other actors, did not apply in the JHA pillar. The Commission continued to face the dilemma it had encountered in the aftermath of the SEA. Advocating supranational integration could risk distancing the Commission from day-to-day co-operation between member states on JHA policy that had significant free movement implications. Participation could offend maximalist sensibilities but would offer the practical advantage of allowing the Commission to continue to develop its immigration and asylum policy role in a piecemeal and pragmatic way, with communitarisation as the eventual objective. To the chagrin of the EP, which was hostile to intergovernmental co-operation that excluded it from participation, the Commission continued to choose the pragmatic course of action. Even though the Commission's own 1985 White Paper on the single market (CEC, 1985a) had staked out an ambitious immigration and asylum policy role for supranational institutions, the Commission was prepared to compromise ambitious objectives to secure a role in discussions about immigration and asylum. It took the view that some member states were not prepared to countenance the kind of deeper integration it had envisaged in 1985. To this end, the internal market Commissioner, Martin Bangemann, stated that: 'where the best prospects for progress lie in going down the road of intergovernmental conventions rather than Community legal instruments, the Commission has opted for making progress rather than fighting time-consuming battles for competence' (quoted in Monar, 1994: 71).

The EP was marginal to the work of the third pillar. It had only the right to be informed after the fact of third pillar developments. In formal terms, the Council presidency and the Commission were obliged to 'regularly inform' the EP of their discussions, 'consult' it on 'principal aspects of activities' and take its views 'into consideration'. The EP was determined to express its opposition to what it saw as the deficiencies of intergovernmental co-operation with regard to its implications for human rights, democracy and accountability. The main vehicle for its attempts to examine third pillar provisions was its Civil Liberties and Internal Affairs Committee, which showed the eagerness of a watchdog, but without the necessary teeth. The effect was that parliamentary scrutiny was rather like being barked at by a puppy. The EP was also hampered by the absence of information on JHA activities. National parliaments were not much better placed to monitor European decisions, which were often made behind closed doors before they were opened to any form of public scrutiny.[6] The EP did bring forward an ambitious – and at the time unrealistic – draft inter-institutional agreement that formalised EP involvement in JHA issues and gave the EP quite substantial powers of consultation over action taken within the third pillar.[7] For instance, before adopting joint positions, joint actions or conventions, the Council would first have to consult the EP. But the Council was under no compulsion to negotiate on the issues covered by the draft agreement and in February 1994 made it clear that it had no intention of doing so. There was nothing the EP could do about this and it was forced to continue to state its case from the sidelines for closer involvement in immigration and asylum policy and EU action against racism and xenophobia.

Not all immigration and asylum issues were placed in the JHA pillar. Article 100c of the Community pillar covered visa policies and created a problem of blurred competence (which was also to be a theme within the reflections on the Maastricht Treaty during the IGC leading up to the 1997 Amsterdam Treaty). The German government had favoured more extensive supranationalisation of immigration and asylum policy within the Community's framework, not a separate pillar. Article 100c provided that the Council, acting unanimously, would draw up a list of third countries whose nationals needed visas to cross the external borders of the member states. The issuance of visas is a highly sensitive issue because they are 'a symbol of the State's right to control entry of aliens; an instrument of foreign policy; and an instrument which gives expression to internal policy objectives on the preservation of external links and on internal security' (Meloni, 2005: 1359). The Council was given power to act by QMV in emergencies. It was also given power, acting by QMV, to draw up a uniform format for visas. The K4 Committee was also to be involved in this work on the visa list and uniform visa format. As well as imparting an element of supranationalisation into immigration and asylum policy, Article 100c added some confusion because visa policy was now also to be dealt with by Article K1(2,3), in the third pillar.

Two regulations covering visas were introduced on the basis of Article 100c. Regulation 1683/95 established a uniform visa format and Regulation 2317/95 listed the 101 countries whose nationals needed visas to enter the EU. There were some problems of co-ordination, as evidenced by the fact that the separate Schengen visa list named 129 countries, while nationals of a further 28 countries required visas to enter certain EU member states (Baldwin-Edwards, 1997: 499). However, the ECJ annulled Regulation 2317/95 in June 1997, after a challenge from the EP arising from a lack of proper consultation with it.[8] The Commission was forced to bring forward new proposals that reintroduced the visa list.[9]

The EU has also sought to develop the VIS as a tool for sharing information between member states on visas and, for example, diminishing the scope for 'visa shopping'. The Seville European Council in June 2002 called for the introduction of a common identification system for visa data as a top priority. The Thessaloniki European Council in June 2003 then called for planning for the VIS and the identification of the necessary financial resources within the EU budget. A June 2004 Council decision established the legal basis and financial resources for the creation of the VIS.[10] The VIS shares a 'technical platform' with the Schengen Information System (or so-called SIS II), with both containing extensive personal information that has been supplied in an estimated 20 million visa applications to the EU. Both SIS II and VIS will contain biometric identifiers, including photographs and fingerprints.

EU citizenship

Another innovation contained within the Maastricht Treaty was the introduction of EU citizenship. The 'democratic deficit' and the creation of a 'people's Europe' began to be cast as problems to which European citizenship was a possible solution. The Spanish government's influential memorandum proposed the establishment of EU citizenship as a complement to national citizenship and as a 'qualitative step' from 'privileged foreigner' to 'European citizens' and, as such, associated with the creation of a political union.[11] EU citizenship was to be a derived right, that is, derived from holding the citizenship of a member state and thereby complementing, not replacing, national citizenship. The effect of it being a derived right was that legally resident TCNs who were not citizens of the member state in which they resided were not entitled to become EU citizens. Although the creation of EU citizenship could be construed as evidence of the deterritorialisation of citizenship, which has been discussed in terms of 'post-national membership' (of the international community), this view needs to be qualified by the exclusion of TCNs. It also remained a clear principle enunciated in the Treaty (and in international law) that it was for states to determine who could or could not become a national (and, thereby, a citizen of the EU). A declaration attached to the final act of the Maastricht Treaty stated that: 'the question whether an individual possesses the nationality of a Member State shall be settled solely by reference to the national law of the Member State concerned'.

The creation of citizenship of the EU did, however, draw the nationality criteria of member states into question. For example, the establishment of EU citizenship could be seen as creating some anomalies arising from, for instance, ease of access to national citizenship in different member states and subsequent entitlement to rights accruing from EU citizenship. Descendants of immigrants born in France, for example, could relatively straightforwardly acquire French nationality at the age of 18 and thereby automatically become EU citizens. They could then move freely within the EU and exercise the rights of EU citizens, such as voting and standing in local and European elections. Immigrants and their descendants in Germany, on the other hand, found it far more difficult to acquire citizenship because of the emphasis on blood descent (*jus sanguinis*) in German nationality law at that time. Consequently, a French person of immigrant origin who had acquired French nationality could, at the age of 18, move to Germany and stand and vote in local elections, while a person of Turkish origin born in Germany who had lived there her whole life could not. Such anomilies were the consequence of the transposition of a derived right of EU citizenship on divergent criteria for allocation of nationality (Weil, 1996).

In terms of formal provisions, citizenship of the EU as created by Maastricht has been described as of rather limited value, although others have emphasised its constructive potential (Martiniello, 1994; Wiener, 1997). Article B of the Maastricht Treaty stated that one of the objectives of the EU was 'to strengthen the protection of the rights and interests of the nationals of its member states' through the introduction of a citizenship of the Union'. Article 8 provided that every person holding the citizenship of a member state was to be a citizen of the EU. To some extent, the rights associated with EU citizenship actually bundled many pre-existing rights which had been scattered across the framework of the Treaty of Rome and the SEA. As a result of Maastricht, nationals of member states, as EU citizens, would be entitled:

- to move freely and reside within the EU;
- to vote and stand in municipal and European elections;
- to acquire rights of diplomatic protection;
- to petition the EP and the newly created ombudsman.

In addition to this, newly created EU citizens also possessed entitlements within the Union's social dimension. Chapter 7 analyses the ways in which migrant integration is now dealt with at EU level and the ways in which, to some extent, they draw from a citizenship frame.

The parameters of policy

Following Maastricht's ratification, the member states and EU institutions began to develop an immigration and asylum framework via a morass of non-binding recommendations and declarations that would render weary even the most ardent student of European integration. The limitations of the Treaty framework led to a fragmented system of decision-making, without clear ascription of competence to EU level for even those areas where co-operation was deemed desirable. What emerged was a complicated and secretive four-level immigration and asylum policy decision-making structure, although to characterise it as a decision-making structure could be to exaggerate its effectiveness. At the top was the Council, supported by the Committee of Permanent Representatives, beneath which was the K4 Committee, comprising senior interior ministry officials; the work of the K4 Committee was then conducted through steering groups and working parties.

Immigration and asylum policy in the post-Maastricht period was not supranationalised. The Commission had to share its power of initiative with member states and preferred to state its position by way of communications to the Council and EP. For instance, the Commission's 1994 communication called for: the harmonisation of the legal status of permanently resident TCNs; attention to the residence status of relatives of TCNs; the realisation of the objective of free movement within the EU for legally resident TCNs; the removal of nationality criteria for access to rights or benefits when not objectively justified; the monitoring of agreements between EU member states and third countries; and the ratification of the UN's 1990 International Convention on the Protection of the Rights of All Migrant Workers and Members of Their Families (CEC, 1994a). Such plans had little chance of success, because of opposition from more sceptical member states and the requirement for unanimity. Participation by the Commission in policies affecting immigration control (the JHA pillar) and immigrant integration (through the Migrant Integration Unit within the Commission's Social Affairs Directorate-General, DGV, for instance) is evidence of the potential for 'separate universes of discourse' and 'orders of comprehension' that can develop within administrative organisations (Dunsire, 1978). The co-operation that developed in the post-SEA period showed how this form of European integration presented opportunities to circumvent domestic constraints on immigration and asylum. The Commission was drawn into these forms of co-operation and integration while espousing increased EU-level rights for migrants and their descendants.

The difficulties faced by the Commission in developing a JHA role stemmed in part from limitations derived from member states' sensitivities to its activism in these areas. In addition, the Commission's own resources in terms of staff and political leadership were limited. A five-person JHA taskforce was established within the Commission's General Secretariat, but JHA co-operation was not perceived as a high priority, particularly when compared with the resources devoted to promoting the EU's external political profile through the CFSP. The Commission's caution could be construed as a lack of dynamism, but also indicated how prevailing inter- and intra-institutional dynamics at both national and supranational level tempered ambitious plans for integration.

Between 1993 and 1998 the Council adopted more than 70 immigration and asylum measures.[12] The immigration ministers meeting in the Council preferred to use non-binding recommendations, resolutions and conclusions. This meant that the efficacy of the policy output was questionable and that it was difficult to monitor, because many agreements were not actually published. There were also effects of EU action on non-member states, both through enlargement and through concern about countries from which 'unwanted' migrants were arriving in Europe. A joint action plan agreed in April 1998 was illustrative of the external dimension of the EU's developing immigration and asylum framework. This was adopted on the basis of Article K3 of the Maastricht Treaty, to provide finance for the 'voluntary repatriation of displaced persons who have found temporary protection in the Member States and asylum seekers' in the EU. A Council press release of 27 April 1998 stated that the joint action plan gave 'a legal and financial basis to the implementation of the Action Plan on the influx of migrants from Iraq and the neighbouring regions'. The General Affairs Council adopted this 46-point action plan on 26 January 1998. Although its title referred to the influx of migrants from Iraq and neighbouring countries, the intentions were broader: 'the initiative is primarily concerned with plugging the gaps in the operation of existing policies (for example, the Dublin Convention and Eurodac) and second, and specifically, to deal with migrants coming through Turkey' (*Statewatch*, May–August 1998: 1). Seven Council working parties – asylum, Eurodac, immigration, visas, Europol, CIREA and CIREFI – were circulated with copies of the plan and each was assigned tasks. In March 1998 a high-level group of EU officials visited Ankara and Istanbul to seek Turkish co-operation over migrants passing through Turkey from Iraq, Iran, Egypt, Sri Lanka, Pakistan and Bangladesh (*Statewatch*, May–August 1998). The title of a press release issued by the British Refugee Council on 18 May 1998 gave a good indication of the views of pro-migrant NGOs: 'EU Asylum Policy – help Turkey to keep people out'. The Turkish government said that it would create 'reception houses', for which the Commission and presidency offered the prospect of EU expertise and funding. The Turkish government was not interested in seeking readmission agreements with neighbouring states, but did state that it would be content to allow the EU to take the lead and negotiate readmission agreements with Bangladesh and Pakistan on Turkey's behalf. The action plan marked Turkey's incorporation within the EU's buffer zone, created by the complex web of agreements already existing with neighbouring states to the east and south of the Union, and which formed part of pre-accession and other agreements for the 2004, 2007 and subsequent enlargements.

The action plan also marked a movement towards elaboration of the EU's emphasis on developing schemes for temporary protection. A 1996 Council resolution noted the need for a separation between the problems of temporary protection and the examination of forms of protection for *de facto* refugees and those with humanitarian residence permits.[13] The European Council on Refugees and Exiles (ECRE) argued that 'temporary protection should be implemented in situations of emergency and should extend for a period, between six months and two years, only to deal with the consequences of that emergency' (ECRE, 1997a: 1). ECRE opposed any further extension of such schemes because they would deny security of status to refugees and create the objective risk of a state enforcing an order for premature return without any individual legal remedy. ECRE broadly welcomed the Commission's 1997 proposals for a joint action on temporary protection but argued that its main failing was that it did not specify a maximum duration for temporary protection schemes after which persons would be allowed to regularise their status (CEC, 1997c; ECRE, 1997b). The suspicions of those who saw temporary protection as a way of reneging on international obligations and seeking to circumvent constraints on immigration control were heightened in July 1998, when the Austrian government presented a strategy paper on migration. The Austrian paper suggested a re-evaluation of EU asylum policy via the development of a system of temporary protection. The Austrian plan contained a critique of the Geneva Convention, which was viewed as both outmoded and encouraging permanent settlement (Travis, 1998; *Statewatch*, October 1998).

During the post-Maastricht period EU immigration and asylum policy can, to use Lowi's (1972) term, be characterised as a 'constituent' rather than a 'regulated' policy sector, because the parameters of the policy were still in the process of being negotiated, although there were strong control and security policy 'frames'. The post-Maastricht period saw policies skewed towards control, with restrictions moving 'out' from core EU member states to those on the periphery, as well as to non-state agencies, such as airlines, which acquired increased responsibility for monitoring the status of people who travelled with them. A key dilemma for EU member states is that movement of control to other EU member states and to non-state actors need not guarantee effective implementation, because of diffuse lines of command, multiple actors and the difficulty of imposing sanctions on non-compliers. The policy also needed to be based on a valid theory of cause and effect. If restrictions lead to increased migratory pressure (exploited by criminal gangs and unscrupulous employers seeking illegal immigrants), then these circles of control can do little else but increase the sum of human misery in states surrounding the EU, to which the problems of immigration control are being transplanted.

Conclusion

The aftermath of the Maastricht Treaty was a confused and confusing immigration and asylum policy picture. The absence of effective structures of scrutiny and accountability allowed for the elaboration of the development of networks of co-operation centred on internal security that drew from Trevi and Schengen. This period also allows us to sketch the parameters of an emergent EU immigration policy framework. Primarily, we see that EU action focused on some but not all immigration and asylum issues. The main focus was on borders, visas, asylum and irregular migration.

In terms of the three issues raised at the start of this chapter, we see the consolidation of networks of co-operation largely centred on national officials drawn from interior ministries, who worked together more intensively on migration and asylum issues. A 'European' frame began to emerge that was to serve as the basis for future collaboration and co-operation, comprising decision-making structures within which there was a marked reluctance to cede power and competence to supranational institutions and to compromise executive action with legislative and judicial oversight at either national or supranational level. Maastricht and its aftermath also demonstrated a focus on the consolidation of the EU's territorial borders and the emergence of a differentiated strategy of territorial management. There were, however, clear links between territory and organisational borders of work and welfare and conceptual borders of belonging and entitlements. EU action in these areas was under-developed, but through EU citizenship and EU social policy we begin to see the emerging parameters of an EU migrant integration agenda, which was to become far more prominent after 1999 (see Chapter 6).

The legacy of Maastricht was a three-pillar structure but with procedural, functional, institutional and issue-based linkages between them. The question that Europe's political leaders had to deal with when they reconsidered the Treaty structure in the mid-1990s was whether free movement, immigration and asylum would remain separated by the 'pillared' institutional architecture. Would future Treaty reform bring them closer together and, perhaps, create scope for legal and political processes at supranational level? It fell to the drafters of the Amsterdam Treaty to seek clarification of the structure put in place by Maastricht. Amsterdam did indeed draw free movement, immigration and asylum into the main body of the Treaty, but maintained the intergovernmental constraints on policy development, which, initially at least, hindered clear definition of competencies and offered limited scope for judicial and political oversight.

Notes

1 See, for instance, the following EP resolutions: on the harmonisation of policies on entry to the territories of the member states, *Official Journal*, C72/213, 1991; on the abolition of border controls at internal frontiers and the free movement of persons within the EU, *Official Journal*, C337/211, 1991; on migrant workers from third countries, *Official Journal*, C175/180, 1990; on racism and xenophobia, *Official Journal*, C69/43, 1989; and on European immigration policy, *Official Journal*, C337/94, 1992.
2 This section draws from *Statewatch* and *Migration Newssheet* (various issues) and interviews conducted by the author in Brussels in 1995–6.

3 See, for instance, the EP's resolutions on the European Council meeting in Luxembourg on 28 and 29 June 1991, *Official Journal*, C240/132, 1991, and on the IGCs, *Official Journal*, C125/81, 1992.

4 *Ad Hoc* Group on Immigration, *Report from the Ministers Responsible for Immigration*, SN 4038/91 (WGI 930). A summary of this report is contained in the 1992 *Report on Community Migration Policy of the House of Lords Select Committee on the European Communities*, Session 1992–93, 10th Report, HL Paper 35.

5 Joint action of 19 March 1998, adopted by the Council on the basis of Article K3 of the Treaty on European Union, introducing a programme of training, exchanges and co-operation in the field of asylum, immigration and crossing of external borders (Odysseus programme) (98/244/JHA).

6 These problems were identified in the Robles Piqeur report, EP Document A3-0215/93.

7 EP Document 207.086.

8 Case C-392/95, 10 June 1997, I-3213.

9 Council Regulation (EC) 539/2001, of 15 March 2001, listing the third countries whose nationals must be in possession of a visa when crossing the external borders and those whose nationals are exempt from that requirement, *Official Journal*, L81, 21 March 2001.

10 Council Decision 2004/512/EC, of 8 June 2004, establishing the Visa Information System (VIS), *Official Journal*, L213, 15 June 2004, pp. 5–7.

11 Europe Document 1653, 2 October 1990.

12 Authors own calculation compiled from various official sources, primarily Commission documentation and from *Statewatch* and *Migration Newssheet* (various editions).

13 Council resolution laying down the priorities for co-operation in the field of Justice and Home Affairs for the period July 1 1996 to June 30 1998, *Official Journal*, C319/1, 1996.

6

The Amsterdam Treaty and beyond

Introduction

Following Amsterdam's entry into force on 1 May 1999 it became meaningful to analyse common EU migration and asylum policies. These were not comprehensive, because key elements, such as labour migration, have thus far been omitted, but common policies regarding visas, asylum, illegal immigration, border security and co-operation with non-EU states were further developed. These policies and approaches did not spring fully formed from the Amsterdam negotiations. The chronological approach adopted in this book so far has demonstrated the development of an EC/EU response to migration and asylum over a longer period of time, with linkages to Trevi, Schengen and Maastricht's 'third pillar'. To comprehend the underlying conceptualisation of policy problems and the 'solutions' that became attached to them requires factoring into the analysis earlier patterns of co-operation. The referent for co-operation on migration and asylum in the 1980s and 1990s was the management of territory in the light of economic integration and geo-political changes, particularly the end of the Cold War. Developing EU linkages between territory, organisational borders of work and welfare, and conceptual borders of entitlement, belonging and identity are integral to this chapter's analysis of the Amsterdam Treaty and subsequent developments through the Nice and Lisbon Treaties. So, too, are new security challenges arising from the terror attacks of the 2000s, which have contributed to a renewed intensification of debate about immigration to Europe. In this context, boundary build-up and boundary shift are explored as challenges to EU enlargement, challenges that had important effects on responses to migration, asylum and border management.

This chapter identifies the main elements of common EU migration and asylum policies that have developed since 1999. It asks why certain areas (border security, asylum, illegal immigration) and not others (TCN labour migration) were main areas of focus, explores whether or not these measures provide evidence of policy convergence between EU member states, and examines the implications of Amsterdam, Nice and Lisbon for territorial, organisational and conceptual borders. To begin with, the focus is on the Amsterdam Treaty.

The origins of the Amsterdam Treaty

When compared with the Maastricht Treaty, Amsterdam appeared an un-ambitious document in many of its key elements. Its centrepiece was the definition of the EU as an 'area of freedom, security and justice', which is the main focus of this chapter. Proponents of European integration and advo-cates of legal clarity professed to be horrified. Allott, an academic lawyer, wrote that: 'The Amsterdam Treaty will mean the coexistence of dozens of different legal and economic sub-systems over the next ten years, a sort of nightmare resurrection of the Holy Roman Empire' (cited in Moravcsik and Nicolaïdis, 1998: 14). Others argued that the outcome was dangerous for the EU because it went against the 'bicycle theory' of European integra-tion – if momentum was lost it could never be regained. Moravcsik and Nicolaïdis (1998: 16–17) dispute this assessment by arguing that:

> The teleological ideal – a United States of Europe characterized by central-ized, uniform, universal and undifferentiated institutions is no longer an appropriate standard (if it ever was one) by which to judge further steps towards integration.... Governments continue to move forward towards centralized federal institutions in some areas – notably EMU – but seek pragmatic, flexible solutions in areas where the lack of negative externalities renders decentralized policy-making a workable solution.

This chapter shows that migration and asylum policy fits with these 'pragmatic, flexible solutions' because, by focusing not just on the 'high politics' of inter-state negotiation but also on the elaboration of an EU migration and asylum policy, we can see how key actors in this policy area from interior ministries and various security agencies worked together to resolve dilemmas that they thought could not be resolved by member states acting alone. In the area of free movement, migration and asylum, these officials and security professionals with an interest in migration, asylum and borders were the 'busy bees in the third pillar factory', as den Boer (1998: 73) put it. They formed an important link in a 'transmission system' connecting the member states and the emerging EU internal security field (Johansson, 1999). These 'securocrats' were not the only actors. This chapter also shows the development and consolidation of an EU-level migrant rights agenda, with proposals for anti-discrimination legislation and some kind of 'resident's charter' to extend to legally resident TCNs rights equivalent to those of EU citizens. But here, too, we need to explore particular linkages between domestic and EU politics and the types of actors and forms of social and political action enabled at EU level.

To communitarise or to fudge?

The member states faced a similar question when drafting the Amsterdam Treaty to that confronted at Maastricht: should immigration and asylum be supranationalised by being brought within the first pillar? This question was answered in the negative at Maastricht. At Amsterdam, the member states did bring free movement, immigration and asylum into the first pillar, but brought with them Council dominance and unanimity. Moreover, because Amsterdam sought to supranationalise immigration and asylum policy, a whole series of other questions had to be addressed. In particular, how could British government opposition be overcome? Was 'flexible integration' inevitable, with pro-integration member states forming a hard core at the cost of a fragmentation of the legal basis? After all, Schengen had already provided a model for such an approach, while more recent developments such the Prüm Convention suggest the continued power of integration 'laboratories' outside the Treaty framework. There was also the question of whether the issue agenda could be broadened by, for instance, extending the Treaty's anti-discrimination provisions (focused on gender and nationality) to cover racial and ethnic discrimination.

During the pre-Amsterdam IGC, a core group of member states declared that they favoured supranationalisation of immigration and asylum policy, combined with tougher Treaty articles against racism and xenophobia, the protection of fundamental human rights via accession to the ECHR and incorporation into the EU of the Schengen *acquis*. A smaller group of member states were opposed to such rapid integration, with the British Conservative government once again holding fast to the banner of minimalism and a refusal to countenance loss of external frontier controls (with a future Labour government waiting in the wings that shared these policy preferences). A diverse range of national policy preferences therefore needed to be accommodated during the IGC. On immigration there was a broad measure of agreement on the 'control' dimensions of policy, but there was disagreement about the form that EU-level co-operation/integration should take and the extent to which the EU should develop responsibilities affecting the rights of migrants.

It seems implausible to attribute a leadership role to the European Commission in this area, as it more often followed member state agendas. This could then leave us with a focus on member state interests and their accommodation at EU level, but this would be too broad. Rather, there were particular forms of co-operation linked to a security 'field', with patterns of co-operation that were increasingly able to draw from formal, institutionalised resources at EU level and to contribute to the further development of transgovernmental action (Wallace, 2005). These networks were driven by a series of concerns arising from the changed meaning of territory in post-Cold War, post-single market and pre-enlargement Europe, of which some of the most pressing related to migration and asylum.

In terms of the approach that was adopted to migration and asylum by Amsterdam – and drawing from the policy studies and organisational sociology literature – Guiraudon (2001) argues that it would be wrong to see the underlying motive for co-operation and policy development as some kind of logical progression from the identification of 'problems' to the specification of 'European solutions' (*pace* Cohen et al., 1972). Instead, solutions may be looking for problems to which they can attach themselves, with the EU migration and asylum 'field' an organised anarchy, characterised as 'a collection of choices looking for problems, issues and feelings looking for decision situations in which they might be aired, solutions looking for issues to which they might be the answer, and decision-makers looking for work' (Cohen et al., 1972: 2). It is the organisational context itself that allows individuals to arrive at an understanding or interpretation of what they are doing. A 'choice decision' can then be understood as 'an outcome or interpretation of several relatively independent streams within an organization', the three streams being: *problems* requiring attention; *solutions* in search of problems; and *participants* who come and go. The analytical issue is to identify the different rates and patterns of flow in these problem, solution and participation streams. The resultant '"garbage can" does allow choices to be made and problems to be resolved, even when the organisation is plagued with goal ambiguity and conflict, with poorly understood problems that wander in and out of the system, with a variable environment, and with decision-makers who may have other things on their mind' (Cohen et al., 1972: 3). Guiraudon's point is that the solutions stream at EU level had been heavily populated by security professionals since the 1970s, as had Trevi and then Schengen since the 1980s; the problems stream included the implications of the single market, the end of the Cold War and EU enlargement; and the participants stream included EU institutions such as the Commission, which was trying to carve out a role for itself, a plethora of national officials who had been working in 'the third pillar factory' (as den Boer, 1998, put it) and some pro-migrant NGOs that were also trying to carve out a role for themselves. On top of this were the formal, inter-state negotiations that were central to the Amsterdam deal and that created more formal institutional structures from which these networks of co-operation and collaboration could draw.

During the Amsterdam negotiations the laggards were the British and Irish governments, although the UK had been to the fore in developing intergovernmental forums for co-operation on migration and asylum post-SEA. The point was, however, that neither was a Schengen member. Although Denmark was a Schengen signatory, it opposed supranationalisation of immigration and asylum. The UK had long opposed the relaxation of internal frontier controls that would jeopardise its own border controls.

Ireland was tied to the UK through their Common Travel Area. Irish participation in Schengen with the UK outside would raise the politically unpalatable prospect of the border between the Irish Republic and Northern Ireland becoming an external frontier at which Irish citizens would be required to show their passports. France sought to limit any extended jurisdiction of the ECJ to internal security matters. The Dutch government sought limitations on ECJ involvement on asylum applications. The Germans maintained their preference for greater sharing of responsibility for migrants between the member states (Monar, 1998: 138).

The Amsterdam Treaty was, as were its predecessors, the product of compromises rather than of a design capable of imparting clear structure to the issues of free movement, immigration and asylum. It did, though, make more explicit the close relation between free movement, immigration and asylum policy, by moving immigration and asylum issues from the third pillar to a newly created Title IV of the Community pillar. If, however, the Amsterdam Treaty did constitute movement towards supranationalisation – erosion of the 'legal sandstone' of the third pillar – then movement in this direction was rather tentative, because the Council retained the upper hand in decision-making, with unanimity as the decisional *modus operandi*. EU institutions were constrained. The Commission continued to share the right of initiative with member states for at least five years after ratification, while the EP and ECJ found their roles limited by the emphasis on intergovernmentalism. Amsterdam also specified a timescale of five years for the adoption of many immigration and asylum measures. This could be difficult to reconcile with the need for unanimity: how could targets be attained if member states opposed them and, what is more, possessed the voting power to give teeth to their opposition? Provisions for 'closer co-operation' removed the more obvious recalcitrance of the British government, but drew into the spotlight the intentions of other member states that had previously been able to hide behind British 'awkwardness'.

The negotiations

Article N of the Maastricht Treaty had stated that 'A conference of the representatives of the Member States shall be convened in 1996 to examine those provisions of the Treaty for which revision is provided'. Three general considerations with immigration and asylum implications contextualised these IGC discussions (Moravcsik and Nicolaïdis, 1998: 14). First, the price of the Maastricht compromise had been a pledge to the more federally inclined member states to reconsider political union soon. A key area of unfinished business was the JHA pillar. Second, the problems encountered over the ratification of the Maastricht Treaty prompted greater attention to be paid to closing the 'democratic deficit' and bringing the EU closer to its citizens. Third, there was pressure on member states to reform the policy-making and institutional structures of the EU in readiness for the accession of central, eastern and southern European countries.

During the pre-Amsterdam IGC, the EU's institutions expressed eagerness to take account of the views of a wide range of NGOs, as a way of reducing the potential for a hostile reaction like that engendered by the Maastricht Treaty. Pro-migrant lobby groups were active in the run-up to the Treaty, but expressed disappointment with the outcome. In the words of ECRE, Amsterdam's asylum provisions constituted a technical transfer of competence without a substantive role for the ECJ and Commission (ECRE, 1997c). For these groups, supranationalisation with attendant EU legal and political effects was viewed as desirable in order to ensure an EU immigration and asylum policy that was more open to legislative and judicial influence.

The IGC was launched at the Corfu European Council in December 1994. A Reflection Group chaired by the Spaniard Carlos Westendorp was established, with one of its purposes being to evaluate the role of the EU in seeking to 'provide a better response to modern demands as regards internal security and the fields of Justice and Home Affairs more generally'. The Reflection Group was composed of one representative from each of the member states, plus Commissioner Marcelino Oreja, and two MEPs, the French Socialist Elisabeth Guigou and German Christian Democrat Elmar Brok. The Group concerned itself with the creation of a 'people's Europe', a 'Union closer to its citizens', while also thinking about the role of the EU's institutions in a 'more democratic and efficient Union' (Reflection Group, 1995).

Much of the agenda for the pre-Amsterdam IGC developed by the Reflection Group and at meetings of EU leaders had direct relevance to migration issues. The Corfu meeting of the European Council in December 1994 listed six issues as priorities for discussion, of which five were especially relevant to immigration and asylum policy. The first priority was to address the new challenges facing the EU, one of which was new sources of migration. Second was a consideration of the JHA pillar and whether it should be 'communitarised' by being moved to the first pillar or whether mainly intergovernmental co-operation should remain in place. Third was the need for greater openness and decision-making efficiency. Fourth was an attempt to build a Europe closer to its citizens, with reinforced human rights, which included discussion of the incorporation of the ECHR into Community law. A fifth priority for discussion was the issue of subsidiarity. Immigration and asylum policy had been nationally based and closely linked to national sovereignty, but EU action was now deemed appropriate.

The Reflection Group's basic headings for discussion were then boiled down within the IGC to three immigration and asylum policy issues:

• the possible supranationalisation of immigration and asylum policy via incorporation of all or some parts of the JHA pillar provisions into the

main body of the Treaty, with a concomitant increase in competence for supranational institutions;
- strengthened Treaty provisions for EU action against racism and xenophobia;
- the possible incorporation of the ECHR into the Treaty.

As the discussions progressed, member states and EU institutions produced documents outlining their positions on the key issues.

As had been the case before the Maastricht Treaty, it was the Dutch government that held the Council presidency and it assumed a leading role in drafting the proposed Treaty changes. The Dutch were keen to avoid the diplomatic calamity that accompanied their June 1991 draft version of the Maastricht Treaty (see Chapter 5), which had united virtually all the other member states in opposition to it. The Dutch presidency proposed a strengthened immigration and asylum role for the ECJ, Commission and EP, as well as increased scope for an EU approach to immigration and asylum policy, and incorporation into the EU of the Schengen *acquis*. In February 1997, a Dutch government 'non-paper' on the incorporation of Schengen also recognised the possibility of some form of flexible integration, because Ireland and the UK were not Schengen members.

The key IGC players were, as usual, the French and German governments. In December 1995, a joint declaration by Chancellor Kohl of Germany and President Chirac of France listed a series of objectives for the ongoing IGC. JHA was identified as one of four key priorities for reform. Both governments favoured supranationalisation of immigration and asylum policy, the strengthening of anti-racism and xenophobia provisions and accession to the ECHR. As had been the case during the Maastricht negotiations, Germany seemed keen to ensure supranationalisation and a transfer from the third to the first pillar because of the disproportionately large number of asylum-seekers Germany attracted compared with other EU member states. France also favoured the creation of legal instruments at EU level to combat racism and xenophobia, while Germany favoured police co-operation to counter the cross-border dissemination of racist material and also advocated an EU-wide ban on the offence of holocaust denial (Hix and Niessen, 1996). A Franco-German initiative at the 1994 Corfu Council saw the creation of a Consultative Commission on Racism and Xenophobia, chaired by the Frenchman Jean Kahn. The Kahn Commission's work was divided between three sub-committees: the first dealt with communication and information; the second with education and training; and the third with policing and justice. In April 1995 the Kahn Commission proposed the creation of a European Observatory on Racism and Xenophobia, which, after some opposition from the UK, was established in 1997 and based in Vienna.[1]

Of particular importance during the IGC were Franco-German positions on 'flexible integration' (Stubb, 1996) that could allow the hard core of pro-integration member states to bypass the more reluctant member states. The Kohl–Chirac declaration of December 1995 contained the following statement:

> Where one of the partners faces temporary difficulties in keeping up with the pace of progress in the Union, it would be desirable and feasible to introduce a general clause in the Treaties enabling those Member States which have the will and the capacity to do so to develop closer co-operation among themselves within the institutional framework of the Union. (Quoted in Hix and Niessen, 1996: 49)

The key problem was, of course, not so much that partners faced 'temporary difficulties in keeping up', but that the British Conservative government was opposed to supranationalisation of immigration and asylum. This did not mean that the British government opposed European-level action *per se*, as it had, in fact, been a key player in the late 1980s. Rather, British governments opposed the supranationalisation of policies that would threaten UK border controls. Moreover, the change of government from Conservative to Labour in May 1997 did not change this stance. Other countries also expressed reservations about flexible integration. Greece and Ireland favoured supranationalisation of immigration and asylum policy, but expressed opposition to 'flexibilities' that relegated them to the EU's 'outer core'. A slightly more flexible British approach was evident when the Labour Party came to power in 1997. During the 1997 general election campaign, Labour had been keen to mimic Conservative Euroscepticism, for fear of being outflanked on these issues. At EU level since 1997, however, the UK has been prepared to lead on some migration issues for which European-level solutions seem appropriate, such as British proposals for the offshore processing of asylum applicants, although it has refused to countenance the removal of the right of the British immigration authorities to maintain border controls on all those entering the country. While this preference has been consistently applied, the UK has actually engaged with around half the measures introduced as a result of the Amsterdam Treaty.

A further joint declaration, this time by the French and German foreign ministers, de Charette and Kinkel, of 17 October 1996, spoke of 'intensified co-operation in the light of the further deepening of European integration'. It advocated the placing of a new flexibility clause within the Treaty allowing for 'closer co-operation' between more integration-minded member states (quoted in Ehlermann, 1998: 6). The declaration then contained specific proposals for a new article of principle covering all three pillars and three special articles dealing with each of the pillars in more detail. The Dutch presidency took up these proposals and – except for the CFSP provisions, which were omitted – inserted into the proposed Amsterdam Treaty a Title dealing with 'Provisions on Closer Co-operation'. The main target of the Franco-German statement on flexible integration was the

British government. In a White Paper in March 1996, revealingly entitled *A Partnership Among Nations*, the British Conservative government stated that co-operation on JHA issues should continue to be dealt with on a 'multi-national basis' (Foreign and Commonwealth Office, 1996). This meant continuation within the existing intergovernmental pillar, with unanimity for decision-making and no increased role for the Commission, ECJ or EP. The British government adopted the most minimalist position in the IGC negotiations and argued that the JHA pillar had worked better than either the Commission or EP was prepared to admit. The British government was, though, prepared to accept that what it called 'variable geometry' might be the solution to the impasse between maximalist and minimalist member states. It also opposed the extension of Treaty competence to cover action against racism and xenophobia, by arguing that British race relations policy already made adequate provision in these respects and that national action should remain the basis of the response (Hix and Niessen, 1996: 57–8).

The British government was not alone in opposing supranationalisation of immigration and asylum policy. The Danish government admitted that some transfer of competence was 'conceivable', but expressed the opinion that decision-making should remain mainly intergovernmental and based in the Council, with the role of the Commission, ECJ and EP kept to a minimum. The Danes, reflecting the importance of the Common Market Relations Committee in their own parliament, called for a strengthening of the role of national parliaments as the guardians of citizens' rights, but did concede a role for the EU in the fight against racism and xenophobia. The Swedish government also argued that JHA issues were closely linked to national sovereignty and should remain largely the responsibility of national governments, although the role of supranational institutions could be in-creased if it enhanced the effectiveness of policy co-operation. The Finnish government was quite specific in its proposals when it called for measures that would improve the security of groups of people excluded from the Treaty provisions for free movement and social entitlement, such as TCNs, asylum-seekers and refugees. Of the other member states, the Benelux countries issued a joint memorandum in which they adopted the strongest pro-integration stance and called for common immigration and asylum poli-cies, the incorporation of Schengen into the Treaty, and provisions on the protection of civil, social and political rights, regardless of 'racial' origins. Austria, Italy, Portugal and Spain also supported greater supranationalisation, accession to the ECHR and the strengthening of provisions on racism and xenophobia, as did Greece and Ireland, with reservations about flexibility.

A particularly decisive event during the negotiations was the change in Germany's stance. Domestic political considerations led Chancellor Kohl to oppose the extension of QMV to immigration and asylum. Kohl's change in approach was driven by the more flexible approach to negotiation on the part of the incoming British Labour government, which then forced the

German government to reveal that it had been 'slipstreaming' the British position because both the Länder and the interior ministry were less integrationist (Green, 2004). German opposition put an end to any lingering hopes that the Amsterdam Treaty could secure fully supranationalised immigration and asylum policy, albeit with provisions for opt-outs for those, such as the British and Danes, who were unwilling to participate.

The main EU institutions also issued position documents before the IGC. The Council presented a report to the Reflection Group that reviewed the operation of existing procedures but that did not contain proposals for reform (Reflection Group, 1995; Hix and Niessen, 1996). The Council expressed the view that JHA provisions were inadequate with regard to the use of legal instruments, because in the first 18 months of operation following ratification of the Maastricht Treaty in November 1993, only two joint actions had been adopted. Ministers preferred non-binding recommendations and resolutions. The Council also expressed dissatisfaction with blurred competence, because of the absence of a clear demarcation between what were first-pillar matters and what were concerns of the third pillar. It was also noted that many of the provisions of the third pillar, such as the ability to extend jurisdiction to the ECJ or to act by QMV, had not been used. The Council also expressed dissatisfaction with the overly complicated decision-making structures resulting from the four-level framework with the Council, Committee of Permanent Representatives, the K4 Committee, plus various steering groups and working parties.

The ECJ also prepared a report on possible Treaty revisions but did not include concrete proposals for reform because this was not seen as a proper role for the Court (Reflection Group, 1995; Hix and Niessen, 1996). Instead, the ECJ pointed out some difficulties with its role caused by the operation of a third pillar from which it was excluded, while being obliged to protect the rights of individuals affected by EU activities in the first pillar. This was seen as particularly important in relation to JHA activities, because they were likely to impinge quite significantly on citizens' rights. The ECJ stated that:

> Judicial protection ... especially in the context of co-operation in the fields of Justice and Home Affairs, must be guaranteed and structured in such a way as to ensure consistent interpretation and application of both Community law and of the provisions adopted within the framework of such co-operation. (Quoted in Hix and Niessen, 1996: 38)

The ECJ's view was that the EU could not accede to the ECHR because the Treaty basis for this (Article 235 of the Treaty of Rome) was deemed insufficient. Moreover, there were other complicated questions that would be raised by accession for which there existed little guidance, such as the relation between the ECJ and the European Court of Human Rights. Accession would also involve a fundamental change in the EU's human rights protection regime, by integrating the EU into a different international legal community, with associated implications for member states' legal systems. The ECJ's view was that, if accession were to occur, then it would require a change to the Treaty, one which made this an explicit objective and provided a clearer basis for it.

The Commission issued two reports as its contribution to the IGC process. The first, in May 1995, was to the Reflection Group, on the operation of the Maastricht Treaty. The second, in February 1996, focused on political union and preparations for enlargement (CEC, 1995a, 1996). In its May 1995 report the Commission strongly criticised the operation of the JHA pillar. It was characterised as ineffectual, because the instruments available were inappropriate and the cumbersome decision-making process and lack of openness compounded problems. As an example of this, the Commission noted that there was disagreement among member states about whether or not common positions or joint actions were mandatory, except in circumstances where they contained explicit obligations. It also criticised the reliance on unanimity, which was portrayed as a brake on decision-making. For instance, the October 1993 meeting of the European Council in Brussels had called for a joint action on minimal procedural guarantees for granting asylum, but member states could then only agree on a far weaker non-binding resolution. For other adopted texts, on family reunification and admission for employment, the Commission noted that 'it was more an exercise of reproducing the existing rights in the member states than of bringing them into line' (*Migration Newssheet*, 147/95-06, June 1995: 1). This could be a motto for much of the subsequent asylum and family reunion legislation.

The Commission went on to argue that the basic challenges facing the EU concerned democracy and effectiveness, and that deeper European integration was the solution to both. This would involve more QMV, with increased use of co-decision-making, to strengthen the role of the EP. The Commission expressed opposition to 'lowest common denominator' decision-making arising from the emphasis on unanimity in the JHA pillar. It also noted that it felt constrained in its own role within the JHA pillar, because of the politically sensitive nature of immigration and asylum policy, and wanted the right of initiative in all JHA matters. The Commission was reluctant to antagonise member states that were sensitive about supranational encroachment into immigration and asylum policy. Most JHA pillar initiatives emanated from the country holding the presidency, with the Commission preferring to state its views via communications, such as that issued on immigration and asylum policy in 1994 (CEC, 1994a).

The Commission referred to the same problems of blurred demarcation between the first and third pillars that had also been addressed by the Council. For instance, the list of countries whose nationals required a visa to enter the EU was a first pillar matter, while conditions for issuing a visa were in the JHA pillar.[2] 'Hence,' the Commission argued, 'in determining whether a policy is adopted under the first or third pillar, the legal provisions of the Treaty are less important than the level of political commitment for common action' (quoted in Hix and Niessen, 1996: 33). The Commission proposed that JHA objectives be summarised into 'main themes'. It also proposed that more effective legal instruments, such as directives, be used and not just non-binding joint actions or common positions. Finally, it was deemed essential that decisions be subject to ECJ review. In short, the Commission proposed a greater role for EU legislative and judicial authority, as well as a more clearly defined role for itself. This involved supranationalisation of immigration and asylum policy, with accession to the ECHR (or a clearer statement on human rights in the Treaty) and the introduction of Treaty provisions against racism and xenophobia.

Not surprisingly, the EP also adopted a maximalist position in its two reports and expressed strong opposition to the JHA arrangements (see Hix and Niessen, 1996). It called for supranationalisation and the strengthening of legal instruments, accession to the ECHR and tougher Treaty articles on anti-racism, xenophobia and holocaust denial. It did, though, argue that the transfer of competencies associated with supranationalisation should be achieved 'progressively' and be associated with strengthening of the roles of the Council (via majority voting), the ECJ and the EP.

Amsterdam's provisions

The Amsterdam Treaty[3] amended Article 2 of the Maastricht Treaty, which stated general policy objectives. These were extended to state that: 'the Union shall set itself the objective to maintain and develop an area of freedom, justice and security in which the free movement of persons is assured in conjunction with appropriate measures with respect to external borders, asylum, immigration and the prevention and combating of crime'. Amsterdam's tentative movement in the direction of supranationalisation was marked by the incorporation of immigration and asylum, with free movement, in a new Title IV. Unanimity was to be the basis of decision-making for at least five years after ratification. The recast third pillar remained, but was slimmed down to deal with judicial co-operation in criminal matters and police co-operation.

The most relevant migration and asylum provisions of the Amsterdam Treaty were the following:

Article 61 dealt with the introduction of free movement provisions within a five-year time period following the Treaty entering into force and 'directly related flanking measures' on external border controls, asylum and immigration.

Article 62 provided that within a five-year time period internal border controls would be abolished and measures on the crossing of external frontiers would be introduced. These measures included standards and procedures on border checks, visa rules, a list of countries whose nationals must be in possession of visas when crossing the external borders and those nationals exempt from such a list (so-called 'black' and 'white' lists), procedures for issuing visas, a uniform visa and measures on the status of TCNs.

Article 63 provided that within a five-year time period measures on asylum would be adopted that respected international standards and covered the mechanisms determining the state responsible for assessing a claim, minimum standards on reception of asylum-seekers, minimum standards on procedures for granting refugee status, measures on refugees and displaced persons, measures on temporary protection, and measures to 'ensure a balance of effort' between member states. Article 63 was thus concerned with further development of the framework put in place by the Dublin Convention. Although the creation of minimum standards could have provided a basis upon which applicants could challenge decisions, there were no thresholds established in the Treaty below which minimum standards must not fall. A protocol was also added to the Amsterdam Treaty that covered asylum for nationals of EU member states. This forbade the making of an asylum application by an EU citizen in another EU member state, although Belgium reserved the right to judge all applications on their merits. The protocol arose as a result of Spanish pressure derived from the domestic problems with Basque separatism (particularly ETA). The assumption underpinning the protocol was that all EU member states respect human rights and are, therefore, assumed to be safe. It was argued that the protocol could place the EU in contravention of the Geneva Convention. Dennis McNamara, the Director of the Division of International Protection at the UNHCR, stated that the protocol 'in our considered view (supported by the Office of the Legal Counsel in New York) violates the object and purposes and some of the basic provisions of the Refugee Convention' (ECRE, 1997d: 8; see also Bank, 1998).

Article 63 also included immigration provisions covering conditions of entry and residence, issuance of visas and residence permits, including for family reunion, but these were not within the five-year time period. Measures on illegal immigration and residence, including repatriation, were within the five-year time period. Article 63 also allowed for measures defining the rights and conditions under which legally resident TCNs could reside in another member state.

Article 64 stated that Title IV measures would not affect the ability of member states to maintain law and order and safeguard internal security. However, in the event of an emergency, such as a sudden inflow of TCNs, then the Council could act by QMV, on a proposal from the Commission, to adopt measures lasting no longer than six months for the benefit of the member state(s) concerned.

Articles 65 and 66 covered judicial co-operation in civil matters.

Article 67 provided that, for a transitional period of five years following the entry into force of the Treaty of Amsterdam (in the event, until 30 April 2004), the Council could act unanimously on a proposal from the Commission or on the initiative of a member state (i.e. a shared right of initiative) and after consulting the EP. At the end of the five-year period, the Council, acting unanimously but after consulting the EP, could determine that all or some of the areas covered by Title IV were to be covered by QMV, with co-decision for the EP.[4]

Article 68 limited the power of the ECJ by specifying that legal avenues must first be exhausted in the relevant member state, to the level at which a court or tribunal is reached against which there is no judicial remedy under national law. This covered both the interpretation of Title IV and rulings on the validity or interpretation of acts of the institutions of the EU when a case was raised before a court of final instance against whose decision there is no remedy in that member state. These final instance national courts or tribunals can request a ruling from the ECJ. This differs from the powers of the ECJ in other areas, where any court or tribunal is able to ask the ECJ to clarify Community law and courts of final instance are required to do so if there is ambiguity. The result of this, it was argued, would be that 'coherence will be much slower dependent first on the adoption of measures which will regulate TCNs in the Community and it will take much longer for interpretative questions to reach the Luxembourg Court' (Guild, 1998: 619). The Amsterdam Treaty excluded from ECJ jurisdiction measures regarding controls on persons at internal frontiers if these related to the 'maintenance of law and order and the safeguarding of internal security', as well as excluding judgements of national courts that have become *res judicata* from the application of the ECJ's rulings (Monar, 1998: 141).

Article 69 dealt with the British, Irish and Danish opt-outs. Amsterdam formalised the possibility of a two-speed EU. The Treaty's flexibility provisions were particularly important with regard to the free movement, immigration and asylum provisions. A key feature of the Treaty was its provision for 'closer co-operation'. Ehlermann (1998: 1) noted that:

> For the first time, the Amsterdam Treaty regulates in general terms the objectives, procedures and legal consequences bound up with closer co-operation of one group of member states within the EC/EU institutional framework and with its instruments. It thus goes far beyond what was hitherto possible as regards differentiation and flexibility in EC/EU law.

The British and Irish governments opted out of Title IV completely. The UK affirmed the right to exercise its own external frontier controls with other member states, while the British and Irish governments secured the right to maintain the Common Travel Area between the two countries. Denmark was granted a similar opt-out from Title IV to the British and Irish, but because Denmark is a Schengen member it was given six months to decide whether it would implement any Council decision that is binding on the Schengen *acquis* (Monar, 1998: 142). The UK has since opted in to almost all measures on asylum and illegal immigration and out of almost all measures on visas, border controls and immigration (Geddes, 2005b).

Responsibility for the co-ordination of EU activity on Articles 62, 63 and 64 was given to SCIFA, which is composed of senior officials positioned between a plethora of working parties and the Committee of Permanent Representatives. SCIFA issues strategic guidelines in matters relating to immigration, borders and asylum and provides substantive input to the discussions of that Committee.[5] Its initial mandate ran until 2004; this has since been extended, because of the key role it has come to play as a basis for intensive collaboration on migration, asylum and borders in the shielded executive forums that have become the hallmark of EU action on migration and asylum.[6]

The issues of voting and decision-making were revisited in December 2004. The 'Hague Programme' committed the member states to change decision-making systems on most immigration and asylum measures by 1 April 2005 and to increase the use of QMV and co-decision. The Treaty of Nice, which came into force in 2003, had already re-weighted QMV to give more voting power to medium-sized and larger member states. A December 2004 Council decision[7] then implemented the decision to leave the situation as follows (Peers, 2004):

- Decisions on a uniform visa format had been decided by QMV since the Maastricht Treaty entered into force in November 1993 and rules on visa lists since January 1996. The EP has the right only to be consulted on these issues.
- Rules on uniform short-term visas and the conditions and procedures for obtaining short-term visas had been covered by QMV since May 2004. The EP has the right of co-decision on these issues.
- The Nice Treaty provided that most asylum issues would be covered by QMV as soon as EC legislation set out 'common rules and basic principles' on these issues, which happened in December 2005, when the asylum 'procedures' directive was agreed (see Table 6.1, p. 132). Co-decision with the EP then applied.
- The bulk of immigration measures remained subject to unanimity, with the EP consulted on: conditions of entry and residence, issuance of long-term visas and residence permits, illegal immigration and illegal residence, measures defining the rights and conditions for legally resident TCNs, and asylum 'burden sharing'.

The result was therefore QMV and co-decision on much of the asylum framework, but immigration remained subject to more intergovernmental procedures, with the EP having the right only to be consulted on these measures.

Amsterdam also strengthened the EU's anti-discrimination provisions with a new Article 13 added to the EC Treaty, which conferred on the Commission the power to bring forward proposals seeking to counter discrimination based on race, ethnic origin, religion, disability or sexual orientation. These proposals would then have to be agreed unanimously by the Council. Following post-Amsterdam consultations, the Commission's 1998–2000 Social Action Plan envisaged three areas of action in relation to Article 13:

- a 'horizontal' directive covering direct and indirect discrimination in employment and occupation, and applying to all the forms of discrimination mentioned in Article 13;
- a 'vertical' directive dealing with direct and indirect discrimination on grounds of race or ethnic origin, which would lay down minimum standards enabling member states to introduce provisions more favourable to the protection of the principle of equal treatment and, as in the case of equal treatment, would permit positive action to overcome existing inequalities;
- an action programme to support and complement these proposals.

Chapter 7 analyses how these proposals were put into effect through two directives issued in June and November 2000.

In what post-Amsterdam became a Judicial and Police Co-operation pillar (i.e. the JHA pillar with the immigration and asylum bits taken out), the scope for joint actions was removed and two new decision-making instruments were introduced:

- *framework decisions* seek approximation of laws and are binding on member states with regard to the purposes to be achieved but leave the method of implementation to the member states;
- *binding decisions* are used for other purposes.

It was also decided to make it easier for conventions in international law to come into effect, by providing for ratification procedures to begin within a time limit specified by the Council and for a convention to enter into force when at least half the member states had adopted it.

The Amsterdam Treaty was seen as doing little to satisfy a requirement for greater transparency: 'the proliferation of protocols and declarations at the end of the Treaty stamp it indelibly with a bazaar-like bargaining character' (Crossick et al., 1997: 3). It has been written that: 'communitarisation hardly merits the term, and Amsterdam set a highly questionable precedent for the import of intergovernmental procedures into the Community framework' (Monar, 1998: 139). Much of the disappointment with the outcome of the Treaty is linked to the desire for clarity, but is also grounded in a normative supposition implying some kind of teleological perspective on European integration. Amsterdam, in fact, demonstrates – as previous Treaty revisions did – the contingent nature of European integration and the difficulties of securing 'positive integration' (Pinder, 1968). It also showed that inter-state negotiation was based on more intensive patterns of co-operation and action that had been in place for more than 30 years and that played an important role in configuring or constituting the migration and asylum policy field. These patterns of interaction and co-operation were centred on internal security and populated largely by interior ministry officials and security professionals drawn from the executive branch of national governments. Many of the 'solutions' to 'European problems' of migration and asylum had been developing for a considerable period of time, through Trevi, Schengen and the third pillar. A 'supply side' of the market for security had developed, ready and waiting for demand-side impetus such as large-scale asylum-seeking, increased irregular migration flows and, in the early years of the twenty-first century, terror attacks. The scope for legislative and judicial involvement in these areas was minimal, but this may well have been the intention of those actors who were most dominant in this process. If we follow the 'venue shopping' argument developed by Guiraudon (2001), then, in terms of institutional design, member states would resist empowering supranational institutions and, in terms of policy outcomes, focus on stemming flows of 'unwanted' migrants, such as irregular migrants and asylum-seekers. Trevi, Schengen and the 'third pillar factory' were testing grounds for ideas that were to enter the EU framework through the Amsterdam Treaty (Monar, 2001).

Incorporation of Schengen

Amsterdam incorporated the Schengen *acquis* into the EU. This included the Schengen Agreement of 1985 and the Implementing Accord of 1990, the various accession protocols and agreements with member states, and the decisions and declarations adopted by the Schengen Executive Committee. This inclusion meant that the primary, intergovernmental treaty law of Schengen 'in one fell swoop' became secondary Community law (Kuijper, 2000: 346). The flexibility/opt-out protocols that were added to the Amsterdam Treaty covered the positions of Ireland and the UK, which were not members of Schengen. They also covered Denmark, which was in Schengen but which did not want to participate in Amsterdam's Title IV provisions on free movement, migration and asylum.

A major task post-Amsterdam for interior ministers and officials was to incorporate around 3,000 pages of the Schengen framework into either the new Title IV or into the Judicial and Police Co-operation pillar. The Danish government released the full list of documents comprising the *acquis* in September 1996 and the Norwegian government, which had non-member 'observer' status, followed suit a couple of weeks later. The list of documents itself was 18 pages long and referred to 172 documents, covering all aspects of the 142 articles of the Agreement.[8]

The incorporation of Schengen meant that decisions made by Schengen's Executive Committee would, immediately after Amsterdam's ratification in May 1999, become Community law if placed within the free movement, immigration and asylum provisions of Title IV. In turn, this raised a series of questions about how the Schengen framework, with its rather shadowy and secretive elements, could accord with EU principles concerning the accountability and transparency of decision-making (Thym, 2002). The Council was given responsibility, acting by unanimity, to determine Schengen's location, that is, either in Title IV or in the Judicial and Police Co-operation pillar. The ECJ was declared competent to act according to the provisions of the Treaties (i.e. whether provisions were to be located in the first or third pillars). The EP was to be consulted about measures included in Title IV.

Article 2 of Amsterdam's protocol incorporating the Schengen *acquis* states that, from the date of entry into force of the Amsterdam Treaty, the Schengen *acquis* would immediately apply to the 13 signatories of the Schengen Agreement. Article 4 allows the UK and Ireland to opt into measures of which they approve, though this is dependent upon unanimity among the 13 signatories. Article 8 stated that the Schengen *acquis* and associated measures must be accepted in full by all new member states. This is unprecedented, because neither of the other areas of closer co-operation – monetary and social policy – contained such provisions for new members (Ehlermann, 1998: 22). This means that prospective member states in central, eastern and southern Europe were expected to be wholehearted participants in the EU's internal security arrangements and to translate EU migration policies into their own national systems. The EU framework also spilled over into relations with non-EU member states, as an external dimension of EU migration policy became more important.

The Vienna action plan and Tampere agreement

The Commission then had to think about how it planned to give legal effect to the Amsterdam arrangements. The European Council, meeting in Cardiff in June 1998, called on the Commission to submit, with the Council, an action plan to the forthcoming Vienna European Council in December 1998 on how best to implement the Title IV provisions. The Council and Commission 'action plan' presented, on implementation of the area of freedom, justice and security,[9] contained a critique of the 'soft law' of the post-Maastricht period, when non-binding recommendations and resolutions had characterised policy development, with inadequate monitoring arrangements, and specified measures to be implemented or adopted within two years of Amsterdam's ratification (and so by summer

2001), which had a strong focus on asylum, visas, borders and illegal immigration, and those within five years (by summer 2004), with a stronger focus on immigration.

The heads of government demonstrated how seriously they took these issues by agreeing to hold a special European Council meeting in Tampere, Finland, in October 1999. Again, the name of a European city came to signify a programme of activity. In this case, 'Tampere' signified a commitment to some kind of common EU migration and asylum policy. The Laeken summit in December 2001 then renewed the call for what was called 'a true' common migration and asylum policy.[10]

The Tampere meeting of the European Council was extremely important because it addressed four separate but closely related issues of asylum and migration and called for the development of a common EU policy.[11] These four issues were as follows:

1 Partnership was to be sought with countries of origin, with a 'comprehensive approach' addressing political, human rights and development issues.
2 A common European asylum system was to be established, 'based on the full and inclusive application of the Geneva Convention', with measures to cover the state responsible for the examination of an asylum application, common standards on asylum procedures, common minimum reception conditions, the approximation of rules on the recognition and content of refugee status, and measures on subsidiary forms of protection. The longer-term aim was a common asylum procedure and a uniform status throughout the EU for those granted asylum. The Eurodac system would be developed as a shared EU data source with information on asylum applicants.
3 Fair treatment of TCNs would require 'a more vigorous integration policy', aimed at 'granting them rights and obligations comparable to those of EU citizens' and measures to combat racism and xenophobia.[12] A particularly important commitment was to 'approximate' the rights of legally resident TCNs to those of EU citizens, with the right to reside, receive education and work as an employee or self-employed person and with application of the principle of non-discrimination relative to member state nationals.
4 Management of migration flows placed a strong emphasis on the external dimension of policy-making and the externalisation of EU action. This externalisation was to be based on 'close co-operation with countries of origin and transit, information campaigns on the actual possibilities for legal immigration, and for the prevention of all forms of trafficking in human beings'. This would also require a strengthening of EU visa policy as well as making resources available to EU and non-EU states in order to improve border controls.

Elements 3 and 4 are the focus of Chapter 7 and 8, respectively. In the remainder of this chapter we look at asylum and migration management. The Tampere agenda set the direction for migration and asylum policy for the next five years and marked an approach centred on the management of territory, but with recognition that this impinged on relations with non-EU member states and had an 'internal' organisational and conceptual dimension, related to the status and rights of TCNs. Asylum, for example, was understood to raise particular issues at organisational borders of work and welfare, because of the 'burdens' of 'bogus' asylum-seekers. Moreover, the 'bogusness' of these claims undermined claims for entitlement and entry into the legitimate community of welfare state beneficiaries, as it has been put (Bommes and Geddes, 2000). EU action to control territory and population against this particular form of unwanted migration was predicated upon a close relation between the regulation of territory and the maintenance of organisational and conceptual boundaries. The complicating factor was that, at the time of the Tampere meeting, EU governments were beginning to think about the migration implications of labour market and population change, with some acceptance that new migration would be necessary to fill labour market gaps and so on.

The politics of all this is important and can get lost in discussions of meetings, decisions, directives and the like. It is, however, worth bearing in mind that the backdrop for the analysis in this chapter (and the two that follow) was an intensification of debate at national and European level about immigration. In line with arguments sketched elsewhere in this book, European integration can be understood as a way of seeking new means of addressing domestic political problems, but, as has also been argued, it does so in ways that reconfigure notions and practices of state power, authority and capacity and also raise the possibility of outcomes that were not intended at the time decisions were made.

Reinforcing and moving borders

If the shift to EU-level venues can be understood to be the result of a calculation by the executive branches of national governments, then developments would be expected to have occurred in those areas that were most troubling to those national actors. This section explores whether or not this has been the case since the Amsterdam Treaty. It shows that there has been a strong focus on 'unwanted' forms of migration and that this allows us to see some of the dynamics underpinning boundary build-up in a wider Europe.

The EU's strategies of territorial management focused in particular on the external frontiers of the member states and relations with non-EU member states. This necessarily brings into view the relationship between asylum and irregular/illegal migration. The EU now devotes great effort to what it calls the 'fight against illegal immigration', and has particular concerns about trafficking, smuggling and facilitation, but if the 'end game' in European migration policy is ever tighter controls on external borders, then this could have the effect of denying territorial access to asylum-seekers and thus creating *de facto* the 'illegal asylum-seeker' (Morrison and Crosland, 2000). In terms of categorisation and the power of state thinking and state institutions, illegal immigration is epiphenomenal: it is the definition of certain types of migration as legal and regular that creates forms of movement that are illegal or irregular. The boundaries between legality and illegality are not as clear cut as sometimes seems to be the case. People may move for a 'legal' purpose, such as short-term work or to study, and then stay on beyond the period of their visa and thus become 'illegal'. There are also significant pull factors in informal and/or hard-to-regulate sectors of European labour markets that provide spaces for irregular migrants (Baldwin-Edwards and Arango, 1999). Continued demand for migrant workers may produce new control-defying strategies. There are also epistemological uncertainties, because the scale, extent and effects of irregular forms of migration remain unclear, which creates a challenging backdrop for the formulation of an EU policy response.[13]

Asylum

Initially, we explore the development of a common EU response to asylum, which has largely centred on the development of the 'Dublin' approach based on the principle of the 'one stop' asylum procedure. The level of activism can be seen from the fact that agreement was reached on the variety of measures presented in Table 6.1.

The agreement on the asylum 'procedures' directive in December 2005 (see Table 6.1) put in place the main element of the first phase of an EU asylum policy, with the main elements of the common approach specified at Tampere and the reinforcement of budget lines to provide support and assistance for states to develop their capacity to manage asylum systems. Agreement thus signifies 'progress' in terms of the attainment of Tampere's objectives, but others have questioned whether these developments constitute progress in relation to international human rights commitments. The content of these measures largely centres on the creation of minimum EU-wide standards that replicate existing national provisions and create what has been called a 'Common Market of deflection' (Noll, 2000), as the asylum system was 'exported' to accession states and has been the context for co-operation with non-EU member states on border controls (see also Byrne et al., 2003; Byrne, 2003; Hailbronner, 2004). International protection could fall through the cracks of EU action concerned to reduce the numbers of asylum-seekers. During the January–June 2003 Greek presidency the UK government initiated a debate (inspired by the Australian 'Pacific solution') about the future of the international refugee protection

Table 6.1 Development of a common EU response to asylum

Area of activism	Council response	Document	Date
The asylum process	Minimum standards for temporary protection in the event of a mass influx of displaced persons and on measures promoting a balance of efforts between member states in receiving such persons and bearing the consequences thereof	Council Directive 2001/55/EC	20 July 2001
	Establishment of criteria and mechanisms for determining the member state responsible for examining an asylum application lodged in one of the member states by a third-country national	Council Regulation (EC) No. 343/2003	18 February 2003
	Establishment of minimum standards for the qualification and status of TCNs or stateless persons as refugees or as persons who otherwise need international protection and the content of the protection granted	Council Directive 2004/83/EC	29 April 2004
	Establishment of minimum standards on procedures in member states for granting and withdrawing refugee status	Council Directive 2005/85/EC	1 December 2005
Resettlement and integration	Establishment of the European Refugee Fund for the period 2005–10	Council Decision 2004/904/EC	2 December 2004
EU financial and technical assistance with development of asylum systems	Adoption of an action programme for administrative co-operation in the fields of external borders, visas, asylum and immigration (ARGO programme)	Council Decision 2002/463/EC	13 June 2002
	Establishment of a programme for financial and technical assistance to third countries in the areas of migration and asylum (AENEAS)	Council Regulation (EC) No. 491/2004 of EP and Council	10 March 2004
Eurodac	Establishment of 'Eurodac' for the comparison of fingerprints for the effective application of the Dublin Convention	Council Regulation (EC) No. 2725/2000	11 December 2000

system. This was intended to externalise the response to asylum as a way of reducing refugee flows to EU member states.

The broader political debate on asylum coalesced around positions staked, on the one hand, by the British government and, on the other, by the UNHCR. The British government's 'new vision' paper proposed the creation of regional and transit processing centres outside EU territory. The UK plan was that asylum-seekers would be kept closer to their countries of origin in 'regional processing centres'. Apparently, camps were envisaged in Turkey, Iran and Iraqi Kurdistan for Iraqis, in northern Somalia for southern Somalis and in Morocco for Algerians. In March 2003 a letter from British Prime Minister Tony Blair to Greek Prime Minister Costas Simitis outlined the British 'new vision', which was coupled with a strong condemnation of the failings of the existing system.[14] The British government also proposed the creation of 'transit processing centres' in states bordering the EU (Albania, Bulgaria and Romania were mentioned). The idea was that applicants entering the EU would be sent back to regional or transit processing centres while their claim was assessed. In May 2003, the British government representative on the Convention on the Future of Europe, which prepared the aborted Constitutional Treaty, proposed altering Article 11 of the draft of that Treaty so as to place more emphasis on processing and protecting asylum-seekers and refugees in their regions of origin.

A flaw in the British proposal was identified by Noll (2003: 304) when he argued that 'The injustice of the global refugee regime, so vigorously decried in the UK vision paper, is addressed by locating the refugee beyond the domain of justice', that is, outside the destination state and outside the established mechanism for assessing the claim. Noll (2003) went on to say that the British proposal would 'liberate an exercise of discretionary sovereignty which we believed to be fettered in international refugee law since 1951'. Loescher and Milner (2003) called for comprehensive engagement by the EU in regions of origin and, on this basis, they then argued that the British government proposal did not conform to international human rights and refugee protection standards, and would place asylum-seekers at risk.

The UNHCR responded with a 'three pronged' approach that emphasised the principle of state responsibility: burden and responsibility sharing; the better working of national asylum systems; and the strengthening of capacity in asylum countries at the point where asylum-seekers first seek protection. The EU elements of this would include: the closing of reception centres and the listing of safe countries of origin (a concession to the British position); speedier determination of claims; rapid return of persons not in need of protection; and strengthened 'protection capacity' (i.e. to look after asylum-seekers), with EU support in countries of origin.

In a June 2003 communication, the Commission distanced itself from British proposal and seemed more inclined to support the UNHCR 'three pronged' solution. The Commission outlined 10 premises on accessible, equitable and managed asylum systems, including resettlement schemes (that share responsibility between member states) and protected entry procedures (that allow access for those who apply for asylum outside the EU), as well as a new legal basis for co-operation with third countries, to build their capacity. These ideas were taken forward by the Commission in plans for regional protection as a 'durable solution' to asylum ('durable solutions' being repatriation, local integration or resettlement in a third country). The Ukraine, Belarus and Moldova were envisaged as transit countries for the first such programme, which would draw from budget lines to facilitate capacity building, such as the AENEAS programme (CEC, 2003b).

With the first phase of EU asylum policy completed with the 2005 procedures directive, the Commission began to think about phase 2 and the realisation of the objective, contained in the Hague Programme, of creating a common asylum area within the EU. Again, a place signifies a programme of activity. In this case, 'the Hague' signifies EU action on freedom, security and justice for the period 2005–10.[15] A common asylum area would mean a single asylum procedure and a uniform status for those granted asylum or subsidiary protection, with shared data on countries of origin (CEC, 2003c, 2003d, 2006a).

'The fight against illegal immigration'

There are clear links between asylum and what the EU calls its 'fight against illegal immigration' (CEC, 2006a). Asylum has been primarily an issue for older immigration countries, in northern Europe, although asylum applicants may well pass through newer immigration countries, in southern and eastern Europe. Southern European countries have had very small numbers of asylum applicants, perhaps in part because of the availability of spaces in the informal economy for migrant workers. The Commission links action on illegal immigration to measures on legal migration, migration and development, and the Commission's 'Common Agenda for Integration'.

Legal migration has been a major gap in EU migration and asylum policy development. The Commission's 2005 policy plan on legal migration sketched out a programme of discussion, consultation and research, for the purposes of consultation over the introduction of a series of measures, including on entry by high-skilled workers (CEC, 2005c). There have been openings to new migration flows in member states, but these have been predicated on national concerns about work and welfare rather than indicating any common EU approach. Indeed, there are highly diverse European migration systems, ranging from quotas in countries such as Italy to a points system in the UK. A central element of the developing EU approach is co-operation with third countries, a key Tampere objective reaffirmed by the Hague Programme. This shifts analytical attention to boundary shift and the external dimension of EU action, which is analysed more closely in Chapter 8. It is relevant to note that the EU's 'fight against illegal immigration' is projected into the future, in the sense that the aim of policy is, so far as possible, to ensure that people do not get the opportunity to enter EU territory. Thus, the 'fight' is against the *potential* illegal immigrant, who, by definition, is not on EU territory. There is an additional ambivalence, because irregular migration flows have played an important role in the European labour market, particularly in southern Europe. The 'fight' as it has been constructed focuses on external borders of territory and action against illegal employment. A core relationship here is between the 'internal' borders of work and welfare and external borders of territory (both their location and their meaning).

The Reform Treaty

In the early to mid-2000s, the EU embarked on a process of constitutional reform which, ultimately, led to the failed attempt to create an EU Constitutional Treaty. Despite ratification in most member states, the Treaty was irreparably damaged by referendum rejections in France and the Netherlands on 29 May and 1 June 2005, respectively. The substantive content of the Constitutional Treaty was then effectively resuscitated through the Reform Treaty, also known as the Lisbon Treaty (signed in December 2007). The substantive difference between the Constitutional and Reform Treaties was that the former was supposed to mark some kind of new constitutional order while the Reform Treaty was 'merely' an amendment to the current EC and EU Treaties. The key point, however, is that the content of the two specifically in relation to migration and asylum was largely the same. The Reform Treaty is thus consistent with the direction of travel established by the Amsterdam Treaty and its predecessors, and by subsequent developments, as already charted in this book.

As always, the specific content of EU treaties such as the Reform Treaty can be rather baffling, as they amend existing texts rather than providing some crisp and clear statement of purpose. In terms of content, the Reform Treaty renames Title IV (which, under Amsterdam, dealt with free movement, asylum and visa policy) the 'area of freedom, security and justice'. This marks the final erosion of the legal distinction between the 'Community' and the old JHA pillar created by Maastricht. Title IV then contains five chapters:

1 General provisions;
2 Policies on border checks, asylum and immigration;
3 Judicial cooperation in civil matters;
4 Judicial cooperation in criminal matters;
5 Police cooperation.

Carrera and Geyer (2007: 1–2) note that the Greek temple analogy that emerged as a result of the Maastricht Treaty has lost its resonance, but then wonder whether the complexity of the Reform Treaty – with its talk of 'emergency brakes', 'flexibility', 'enhanced co-operation', 'opt-ins' and 'opt-outs' – risks creating a 'mosaic' or 'patchwork' in the area of freedom, security and justice.

Consistent with the direction for policy development that had already been set, the Reform Treaty establishes a common European asylum system as a Treaty objective for the first time. Its Article 63 specifies the aim to move from 'minimum standards' – as exemplified by the implementation of the Amsterdam Treaty – to 'uniform standards' for the processing of asylum applications and the treatment of applicants. These standards should include common application procedures and reception conditions and shared information on countries of origin. Asylum policies should also be governed by the principles of solidarity and 'fair sharing' between EU member states.

The standard decision-making procedure in the area of freedom, security and justice will be the Commission exercising the right of initiative with the Council (deciding by QMV) and the EP as co-decision-makers. Use of co-decision and QMV will thus be extended to legal migration, visa policy and TCN integration policies. The output will be standard Community instruments (i.e., regulations, directives and decisions). These will strengthen the role of the EP through the creation of a single legislative procedure, while the role of national parliaments will be strengthened in the evaluation of measures in the area of freedom, security and justice through a new Title II of the Treaty, 'Provisions on Democratic Principles'. The role of the ECJ will also be enhanced, in that it will be given the general jurisdiction to interpret and review the validity of acts adopted in the area of freedom, security and justice.

Consistent with earlier developments – particularly Maastricht and Amsterdam – we see some variable geometry, as opt-outs remain for the UK, Ireland and Denmark. The difference, however, is that these states are unable to opt out of measures that derive from agreements that they have already entered into. So, for example, as the UK has opted into the EU asylum system as it has so far developed, it will either participate in the planned further development of this system or face being removed completely from this area of EU action.

The Reform Treaty marks another step towards common migration and asylum policies, one which bundles political authority in the EU, but it does so in a way consistent with key aspects of member state policies and in light of major changes, particularly the geo-political reconfiguration of Europe after the end of the Cold War and the rapid expansion in the number of member states. The Treaty could be seen as 'progress', in the sense that it deepens European integration in the areas of migration and asylum. An alternative reading of the term 'progress' would, however, also require that we look closely at the content of the measures agreed. It does seem fair to speculate that the current security impulse will remain a strong factor underlying policy development, with an associated focus on 'unwanted' forms of migration, such as asylum-seekers and irregular migrants. The next section moves on to consider alternative 'economic' framings of migration and the possibility of EU action on admissions policies.

New directions on labour migration?

Admission policies remain a matter for member states, although both the Amsterdam and Reform Treaties have created scope for common policies in this area. There do seem to be sound reasons why these would remain a national prerogative. Meyers (2002, 2004) argues that, as there is a large pool of potential workers prepared to migrate to Europe and as states, acting unilaterally, have been able to tap into this pool, then there is little incentive to develop a common approach. This is because European states have been able to recruit migrant workers as and when they need them and do retain the authority to curtail recruitment as and when economic conditions deteriorate (although not for family migrants, as we have seen). Why, then, would states agree to common policies on extra-EU labour migration if, firstly, they have been able to act unilaterally to attain their labour recruitment objectives and, secondly, the development of supranational measures may bind them to a common framework that could inhibit their capacity to reduce recruitment in times of economic downturn?

The analytical puzzle that presents itself is that there are now proposals on the table for EU action on admissions policy through the creation of what was labelled the EU 'blue card' – with obvious reference to the US 'green card'. A mechanistic neo-functional argument would not account for this development, as it would overstate Commission autonomy in this process and downplay the impact of member state migration policies in the formulation of an EU approach to an admissions policy that, in fact, fits neatly with selective national immigration policies favouring the highly skilled. Strict intergovernmentalism is, however, equally limited as an explanation, because if such measures on extra-EU migration were to be agreed and supranational legislation brought forward, then this would present a potential EU constraint on domestic admissions policies, with scope, too, for future unintended effects.

A more credible approach to this analytical puzzle, following Meyers (2002, 2004), would be to analyse the linkages between the type of admissions policy proposed by the Commission and other important aspects of European integration. Thus, it becomes possible to see how a selective approach to extra-EU labour migration connects with broader EU economic reform objectives, the quest for competitiveness, the impact of demographic change on labour markets, and the belief that greater mobility can facilitate economic reform. Making these kinds of connections and issue linkages has been the challenge for the European Commission as it has sought to create political space for EU-level measures in these areas (CEC, 2005c, 2005d). As was seen in the preceding section, it has thus far been easier at EU level to connect migration with an internal security frame, which has then driven responses to asylum and irregular migration.

Competence in this area was created by the Amsterdam Treaty and strengthened by the Reform Treaty. What were then needed were concrete proposals and political will. The first of these was accomplished in October 2007 when the Commission proposed a draft framework directive on the admission of highly qualified migrants to the EU (this would create the so-called EU blue card). This would apply only to workers with a signed work contract in the EU with remuneration at least three times that member state's minimum wage. This proposal is, therefore, focused on highly skilled workers and reinforces the point made above about the selectivity of EU action, consistent with national approaches to migration management. The 'blue card' would entitle workers to some socio-economic rights and favourable conditions for family reunification. The proposal would, however, limit residence to two years, although if workers can find employment with the same conditions they can then move to a second EU country and tot-up periods of residence in different member states to obtain long-term EU residence (after five years).

This draft directive also grants legally employed TCNs socio-economic rights similar to the rights of intra-EU migrants. This is set to include a 'one-stop shop', with a single application procedure, access to information on required documents, the obligation for member states to provide reasons for the rejection of an application, and a requirement that decisions be made within 90 days of the application.

The Commission has also announced its intention to bring forward in 2008 proposals on seasonal workers, remunerated trainees and intra-corporate transfers. Again, Commission proposals on admissions policies and labour migration have, thus, been consistent with the selective management of extra-EU migration, with a clear and strong preference for the highly skilled and linkage to EU economic reform and demographic change.

Conclusion

The developments identified in this chapter demonstrate that since the Amsterdam Treaty it has become meaningful to talk about a common European migration and asylum policy. Further, the Reform Treaty now expressly states the commitment to common policies on asylum, immigration and external borders, while also making this subject to standard institutional procedures. Amsterdam built on well established patterns of co-operation in an area within which interior ministry officials and security professionals had already been 'busy bees' since the 1970s. It is no great surprise to see, therefore, that EU action tended to reflect concern about 'unwanted' migration flows of asylum-seekers and irregular migrants, as EU action became a forum for the pursuit of domestic policy objectives by other means. Amsterdam contributed to 'boundary build-up' in the changed geo-political setting after the end of the Cold War and in light of deepening economic integration, EU enlargement and the terror attacks of the 2000s. Amsterdam also induced 'boundary shift', as the EU began to seek to spread its ideas about migration and asylum policy management to those states that wanted to join the EU, or those that would not join the EU but were migrant-sending or transit countries.

Through existing patterns of co-operation and their acceleration and formalisation after Amsterdam, we are also able to view elements of convergence around certain migration and asylum policies. Principles were established in the 1980s and 1990s regarding, for example, the basic framework of an EU asylum system. The Amsterdam Treaty took these further and established a framework within which these nascent forms of co-operation could become a more regular part of the EU legal framework, through the issuing of regulations and directives. The Reform Treaty now proposes to move from 'minimum' to 'uniform' standards. This is an important shift in how we think about European migration and asylum policy. In effect, the creation of law-making capacity at EU level in relation to certain aspects of migration and asylum demonstrates a shift into areas of high politics, but also that the 'venue shift' to EU level was closely tied to domestic policy objectives articulated through networks of transgovernmental co-operation. While there was some convergence, this was not imposed from above. Its origins are actually slightly more complex, because convergence did not come straightforwardly 'from below' either. Rather, there was an intensification of sectoral co-operation around internal security issues that both reflected and contributed to a changed meaning of security in Europe. As those who have adopted a more 'sociological' approach to these issues have shown, it began to make more sense to discuss a European 'field' in relation to migration and asylum, which could not be straightforwardly explained in terms of some intergovernmental versus supranational dichotomy (Favell, 1998).

Intensified EU action on migration and asylum relates directly to the core theme of this book. What impact did changed border relations within and between EU member states have on understandings of and responses to migration? The post-Cold War, post-single market and pre-enlargement context had an important effect on the Amsterdam negotiations. Border management was a key issue, but so, too, were debates associated with organisational borders of work and welfare, and conceptual borders of belonging, entitlement and identity. Migration became part of a broader discussion about the boundaries of Europe in a way that reflected not only on territory and its management, on population and its control, but also on issues related to the organisation and operation of labour markets and welfare states, and to basic understandings of entitlement, belonging and identity. It was not that migration somehow drove these concerns – it would be implausible to contend that it could – but that migration provides a lens through which we can view these changes. This is why the migration components of the Amsterdam Treaty were so important: because they give us cause to reflect on the EU's understanding of itself as a unique form of regional organisation.

Notes

1 The final report of the Kahn Commission is available as ECCCRX, *Final Report*, ref. 6906/1/95 Rev. 1, LIMITE, RAXEN. See also Council Regulation 1035/97, 2 June 1997, *Official Journal*, L151, 1997.

2 For the most recent iteration of the visa list, see Council Regulation (EC) No. 1932/2006, of 21 December 2006, amending Regulation (EC) No. 539/2001, listing the third countries whose nationals must be in possession of visas when crossing the external borders and those whose nationals are exempt from that requirement, *Official Journal*, L405/23, 30 December 2006.

3 Treaty of Amsterdam amending the Treaty on European Union, the Treaties establishing the European Communities and certain related acts – Consolidated version of the Treaty establishing the European Community, *Official Journal*, C340, 10 November 1997, P. 0173.

4 The co-decision procedure is fiendishly complicated, but the basic steps are as follows. (i) The Commission draws up a proposal for legislation. (ii) Opinions of the Economic and Social Committee and the Committee of the Regions are sought. (iii) The EP gives the proposal a first reading, with a rapporteur appointed to draft an opinion, which is debated in plenary session and can be adopted by simple majority. (iv) The Commission can amend the proposal to include EP suggestions that improve the legislation or increase the likelihood of eventual adoption. (v) A Council working group comprising member state representatives will have analysed the Commission proposal concurrent with EP activity. The Council can then: accept without alteration the Commission's proposal, which the EP has not amended, and the legislation can be adopted; accept all the EP's amendments which the Commission has incorporated into its amended proposal, and the legislation can be adopted; in all other cases, adopt a common position. (vi) If the Council adopts a common position, then this is forwarded to the EP, with the Commission also sending its views to the EP. The EP has three months to take action and can by absolute majority (367 votes) approve, reject or amend the common position. (vii) If the EP amends, then the Commission expresses its views to the Council, which can either approve them by QMV or unanimously if the Commission has delivered a negative opinion. (viii) If amendments are not accepted, then a conciliation committee is formed, with equal representation from the Council and EP. Each delegation to the conciliation committee must approve the joint text in accordance with its own rules: qualified majority for the Council's delegation (unanimity in cases where the Treaty specifies an exception to QMV) and simple majority for the EP's delegation. If the conciliation committee can approve a joint

text, then the legislation is adopted. This is a condensed overview; for a full description go to the Commission's web page on co-decision, http://ec.europa.eu/codecision/stepbystep/text/index_en.htm.

5 Council of the European Union, *Role and Future Activities of the Strategic Committee on Immigration, Frontiers and Asylum (SCIFA)*, 6370/00 LIMITE ASIM 6, 22 February 2000.

6 Council of the European Union, *SCIFA Mandate*, 7123/06 LIMITE ASIM 11, 8 March 2006.

7 Council decision providing for certain areas covered by Title IV of Part Three of the Treaty establishing the European Community to be governed by the procedure laid down in Article 251 of that Treaty, *Official Journal*, L396/45, 31 December 2004.

8 Council decision concerning the definition of the Schengen *acquis* for the purpose of determining, in conformity with the relevant provisions of the Treaty establishing the European Community and the Treaty on European Union, the legal basis for each of the provisions or decisions which constitute the *acquis*, 12 May 1999, 8054/99 LIMITE SCHENGEN 39.

9 Action Plan of the Council and the Commission on how best to implement the provisions of the Treaty of Amsterdam on an area of freedom, security and justice. Text adopted by the Justice and Home Affairs Council of 3 December 1998, *Official Journal*, C19/1, 23 January 1999.

10 Laeken European Council, *Presidency Conclusions*, 14–15 December 2001. Available online at www.consilium.europa.eu/ueDocs/cms_Data/docs/pressData/en/ec/68827.pdf.

11 Tampere European Council, *Presidency Conclusions*, 15–16 October 1999. Available online at www.consilium.europa.eu/ueDocs/cms_Data/docs/pressData/en/ec/00200-r1.en9.htm.

12 *Ibid.*

13 Council of the European Union, French Presidency, *Seminar on Illegal Immigration*, Paris, 20–21 July 2000, 12211/00 LIMITE JAI 109 ASIM 22.

14 The British paper can be accessed at www.ecre.org/eu_developments/debates/ukletter.pdf.

15 Council of the European Union, *The Hague Programme: Strengthening Freedom, Security and Justice in the European Union*, 16054/04 JAI 559, 13 December 2004.

7

Social and political spaces for migrants at EU level?

Introduction

This chapter shifts the focus from the management of territorial borders to the operation of organisational and conceptual borders of work, welfare, belonging and entitlement. These were brought more clearly into view not only by the Amsterdam Treaty but also by the much broader development of economic and political integration. Through them we see the shape, form and content of nascent EU debates about 'immigrant integration'. The chapter analyses the constitution of an EU policy field and the types of political opportunity for pro-migrant interests that have been created. It then asks how, why, when and with what effects EU legislation has developed in areas relating to residence and movement by TCNs and anti-discrimination. The empirical focus is on EU laws affecting residence and movement within the EU for legally resident TCNs, including entry to the labour market, social entitlements and family reunification, as well as on laws that counter discrimination on grounds including racial or ethnic origin. There is interest, too, in the underlying conceptualisation or 'framing' of integration as a concept, a process, a practice and a European issue.

The legal basis for measures relating to the status and conditions of TCNs was provided by Article 63(3,4) of the Amsterdam Treaty (signed in 1997) and by the subsequent Tampere agreement of October 1999 (see Chapter 6), which called for TCNs to be given uniform rights as near as possible to those enjoyed by EU citizens. On the basis of these Treaty provisions, a September 2003 directive on family reunion and a November 2003 directive on the rights of long-term residents are analysed.[1] The basis for action on anti-discrimination was provided by Amsterdam's Article 13, which enabled the Council, acting by unanimity, to take appropriate action to combat discrimination based on sex, racial or ethnic origin, religion or belief, disability, age or sexual orientation. Two directives – on race equality and equality in employment – were agreed by the member states in June and November 2000.[2]

The importance of these issues transcends the EU context, not only because they demonstrate some rather particular features of the EU as a political system, but also because they relate to a much broader debate about Europe's response to migration-related diversity. This response has been seen as representing a backlash against multiculturalism, even in the form of what has been called a 'repressive liberalism' evident in requirements such as that migrants satisfy 'integration' criteria (Joppke, 2007). The swirling cross-currents of debate across Europe about the integration of migrants provide not only a frame for EU discussion, but also for ideas that have been very influential in shaping EU debate (Groenendijk, 2004). The term 'integration' is used in this chapter because it is the point of reference for much national and EU policy debate, even though its meaning is unclear (integration into what, exactly?). The debate is also highly charged, because it provides a particularly intense focus for wider discussion of social integration, rights, belonging, entitlement and inclusion that affect all Europeans, as is seen when the issues are placed in the fuller context of debates about economic integration and European welfare states. We see a clear reflection of this debate in the insistence of some member states on 'integration' conditions being placed in the EU directives on long-term residence and family reunion.

The chapter begins by exploring the broader context of debates about migration, welfare, work, belonging and entitlement, by looking at the literature on European welfare states and at the EU's social dimension. It then relates these to the EU's institutional context, which, it is argued, channels debates about migrant integration in a particular way, one that is closely linked to sources of power at EU level, where there is a specific emphasis on the deployment of expert knowledge in policy development processes. The task then, obviously, is to specify what these sources of power are. This is the chapter's third element. Since 2000, there has been agreement on EU directives covering anti-discrimination, family reunion and the rights of long-term residents, in the context of what the European Commission now calls 'A Common Agenda for Integration' and a 2007–13 budget framework that allocates €825 million to an 'Integration Fund'. Moreover, there has been the introduction of what in EU parlance are known as 'new modes of governance', with an emphasis on lesson-learning and the sharing of best practice through, for example, the creation of 'national contact points' on integration, who meet regularly, and the publication of the *Handbook on Integration for Policy-Makers and Practitioners* by the Directorate-General for Freedom, Security and Justice in 2005. These developments shift debate towards implementation and the impact of the empowerment of EU institutions (the Commission, the ECJ and EP) on the shape and direction of policy. There is a certain technical nature to EU debate that facilitates the mobilisation of *expertise* (particularly legal expertise) as an integral element of the development of EU policy, in this case by those seeking to represent 'migrants' interests'.

Migration, welfare and labour markets

Organisational borders of work and welfare in EU member states are key arenas within which issues of inclusion and exclusion are mediated. They relate strongly to the organisation and operation of welfare states and labour markets. The relationship between states and markets themselves and the balance between them is a perennial issue in European politics and one that has acquired EU resonance too, because of single market integration and EMU. At national level, legal residence and contribution rather than nationality usually serve as qualifications for welfare entitlements for migrants (Guiraudon, 2000). The organisational and conceptual boundaries of welfare also equate to an underlying notion of entitlement and the definition of a 'community of legitimate receivers of welfare state benefits' (Bommes and Geddes, 2000: ch. 1).

Figure 7.1 shows support for equal social rights to be the view of the majority of respondents in all but five member states (Malta, Hungary, Belgium, Austria and Germany). Support was highest among newer member states (Romania, Estonia, Poland, Czech Republic, Slovenia and Slovakia).

It is important to note the use of the plural when referring to welfare states: there are many different types of welfare state organisation. Similarly, there are different types of labour market, although there is a general tendency for migrant workers to be evident in particular economic sectors, often at the highest and lowest end of the skills spectrum. Migrants, for example, are often intensely present in agriculture, food processing, information and communications technology, construction, health care and domestic employment. These sectors have different characteristics (such as

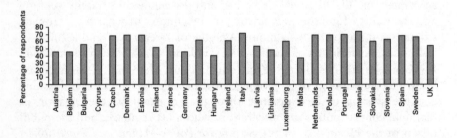

Figure 7.1 Support for equal social rights for migrants (2003). Percentage of respondents in the 25 member states of the EU and two candidate countries (Bulgaria and Romania) agreeing with the Eurobarometer survey statement 'Legally established immigrants [from outside the EU] should have the same rights as … citizens [nationality same as that of respondents]'. *Sources:* Calculated from *Eurobarometer Eurobarometer* 59.2, 2003, and *Eurobarometer* 2003.2, candidate countries survey.

tendencies to irregular employment in sectors such as food processing and construction) and gender distinctions (for example domestic employment has a predominance of female employees), and can see migrants in ancillary roles supporting other migrants (such as low-paid migrants who clean the offices of high-paid migrants). The point here is that labour migrants do not so much 'move into' countries as 'move into' particular areas of countries and particular types of economic activity. This can, of course, change the reference for debates about integration from 'the nation' to the more everyday workplace and neighbourhood. The discussion in this chapter focuses on the organisation of welfare states and the ideas that animate notions of belonging and entitlement, or, put another way, the relationship between migration and organisational and conceptual borders of work, welfare, entitlement and belonging.

Debates about welfare provision and the challenges faced by welfare states have long been salient political issues across Europe (Pierson, 1994). A European dimension has been added to these debates by the development of EU capacities in the 'social dimension'. Yet when compared with the 'avalanche' (Pierson, 1998: 777) of recent work on the welfare state, the questions raised by migration – by both free movement within the single market and extra-EU migration by TCNs – have been less frequently explored. There have been exceptions to this, such as the debate about 'posted workers' when EU provision for free movement by service providers enabled cheaper construction labour from countries such as the UK, Ireland and Portugal to be employed on German construction sites (Hunger, 2000). More recently, A8 accession led to restrictions being imposed on labour migration by all but three EU member states because of fears that cheaper migrant labour from new member states would undermine wages and working conditions (the initial exceptions were Ireland, Sweden and the UK).

The relationship between migration, work and welfare is central to analysis of migrant integration. In his analysis of labour migration to Germany, Martin (2002) argues that it has been easier to integrate migrants into the welfare state than into the labour market, because of labour market rigidities and inflexibilities. This has tended to lead to higher levels of unemployment for TCNs than for national citizens (British Council, 2004). Immigration could thus be construed as a challenge to the welfare state, because, as Kitschelt (1995: 270) asks, could 'the multiculturalization of still by and large homogenous or ethnically stable Western Europe ... lead to a decline of the welfare state?' Freeman (1986: 61) argued that immigration has been 'a disaster' in the sense that 'it has led to the Americanization of European welfare politics'. Or, in Martin's (2002: 2) terms, migration challenges a 'relatively structured and rigid labour market and economy'. There are others who challenge the extent of this erosion and contend that welfare states are a changed, but durable and valued, aspect of the European political scene, and serve as an important source of political legitimacy for national governments (Flora, 1986; Banting, 1995; Rhodes and van Apeldoorn, 1998).

More recently, the opening of the door to new labour migration from within and outside the EU has been linked to the perceived need for new workers to offset some aspects of demographic change and to close specific labour market gaps. Labour migration is unlikely to 'rescue' the welfare state and is equally unlikely to destroy it. Such arguments push debate in an apocalyptic direction, with the scale and effects of migration exaggerated (either positively or negatively). Larger-scale labour migration has been, is and will continue to be an important structural feature of European economies. It has generated, is generating and will continue to generate wealth, but has generated, is generating and will continue to generate use of welfare services. The effects of migration will often focus on certain types of economic activity and the effects of it will be unevenly distributed within member states. So, while there are likely to be overall benefits in terms of gross national product, there are likely to be some losers, such as lower-paid workers facing competition from migrant workers.

National welfare state systems are located in a wider EU context. Ferrera (2005: 2) sees European integration and other challenges, such as migration, as 'weakening and tearing apart those spatial demarcations and closure practices that nation states have built to protect themselves'. Ferrera then moves on to identify three elements of the relationship between national welfare states and European integration that are predicated on an understanding of social citizenship as a basis for the distinction between insiders and outsiders; this distinction is 'a crucial aspect of national sovereignty', albeit weakened because states have seen a diminution of their ability to 'lock in' actors and resources (Ferrera, 2005: 11–12). First, external closure can facilitate solidarity within boundaries, with the result that boundaries can promote social bonding; hence there can be a relationship between 'bounding' and 'bonding'. Second, welfare state boundaries have shifted in quite considerable ways and take highly diverse forms across the EU. Third, thinking about boundaries and borders pushes analysis in the direction of the concept of 'bounded space' as a geographical and membership area, which then raises the question of to what extent the EU can imitate 'bounding–bonding' processes previously integral to national welfare states. Social rights function as 'institutional stabilisers'. Concomitantly, phenomena, such as immigration, that are seen to challenge the provision of social rights could be destabilising, or at least be seen by some people as destabilising.

If the capacity of welfare state boundaries to 'cage' actors and resources has diminished, then issues such as European integration and immigration challenge the territorial basis upon which welfare states are organised, as well as the symbolic functions of group membership and welfare state identities, and, as a result, become a basis for political contention (Ferrera, 2005: 20). This contention centres on the management/protection of territory and the basis for codes of distinction, such as national citizenship. European integration and immigration encounter 'thick' national citizenship spaces, where practices and ideas of entitlement and belonging are relatively well established and where migration can generate complex and difficult politics. The EU offers only a thin alternative to this thick national material, such that European integration may represent not just a rebalancing of the relationship between politics and markets, but may actually be *'destructive* of deep seated social and political equilibriums' (Ferrera, 2005: 51, original emphasis). We can now look at actual EU social policy more closely.

The development of EU social policy

Social policy lagged behind economic integration and risked being dismissed 'as a pipe dream or as an afterthought to the EU's main project of economic integration' (Pierson and Liebfried, 1995: 4). EU social entitlements are linked to the functional right of free movement for workers. Market-making rather than market-correcting objectives drove the establishment of a supranational framework that sought to guarantee transferable social entitlements. The concern of policy has tended to be with protecting 'the civil right to enter into contracts and not with industrial and social rights relating to their outcome' (Streeck, 1996: 72). This emphasis on securing the conditions for factor and labour mobility within the single market has meant that EU policy has been largely concerned with 'technical matters' rather than with 'social conscience' (Lodge, 1989: 310). Streeck (1996: 64–5) notes a strongly normative aspect to work on EU social policy:

> given that the Community's 'really existing' social policy seemed so minimal in comparison to what it was supposed to become, it was discussed much more in terms of what it was not, or not yet, rather than what it was – which largely explains the analytical shallowness and the normative declaratory tone of most of the debate. Overcoming this requires that the basic institutional properties of the EU as we now know them be taken into account, which in turn implies breaking once and for all with the teleological federalism that has informed most of the past debate.

The EU's competencies developed in order to establish transferable social entitlements, in order to buttress free movement; and it did so in forms of 'encapsulated federalism' (Streeck, 1996: 76), where member states allowed supranational policy competence for areas such as gender equality, workplace consultation and working hours. There have often been strong arguments based on national interests for the extension of competence in these areas, derived from fear of so-called social dumping, where member states compete on the basis of lowering standards of social protection. In addition to this were some largely rhetorical commitments, such as the placing in the Treaty of Rome's preamble of the objective of securing 'economic and social progress of the member states' and 'the constant improvement of the living and working conditions of their peoples'. Article 2 contained a commitment to high employment standards and high levels of social protection. Articles 118–23 contained other social policy provisions, relating to, for instance, gender equality (Article 119) and the creation of a European social fund (Article 123). These complex and fragmented arrangements were replaced by a 2004 directive that created a single legal basis for EU citizens and their family members to move and reside freely within the EU by a new regulation amending Regulation 1612/68 and repealing nine other directives (see Chapter 3, note 8).

Article 51 of the Treaty of Rome made clear the connection between free movement and social entitlement. It gave the Council the power to adopt measures for social security provision for migrant workers who were nationals of an EC member state. Measures had to be agreed unanimously. The provision for unanimity was not altered by subsequent amendments of the Treaty. Article 51 applied to the aggregation and payment of benefits to nationals of one member state residing in another.

The Treaty of Rome did leave open the possibility that free movement rights could be extended to TCNs, but when the Treaty's provisions were given effect, free movement rights were restricted to workers who were nationals of a member state. The early rules covering transferable social entitlements were contained in Regulations 3/58 and 4/58 of 1958, which attempted to ensure co-ordination of entitlement for workers and self-employed people moving between member states. These regulations established the principles of equal treatment for all workers (holding the nationality of a member state) and the aggregation of benefits within the EEC and transferability of social benefits. These regulations also made it clear that the aim of EEC policy was *co-ordination*, not *harmonisation*.

In the aftermath of Regulation 1612/68, which provided for free movement for workers, Regulation 1408/71 updated provisions with respect to the application of social security schemes. Regulation 1408/71 sought the co-ordination of national social security legislation, with a view to guaranteeing to all workers holding the nationality of a member state and their dependants equality of treatment and entitlement to social security benefits, irrespective of their place of employment and residence. Regulation 1408/71 was the basis for the development of a complicated policy framework. Regulation 574/72 established detailed rules for the implementation of Regulation 1408/71.

There was some scope for inclusion of TCNs and their family members within these social entitlement provisions. In the case of *Dzodi* v. *Belgium*, the ECJ allowed for spouses: to move with the holder of the right; to remain permanently resident in the host state; to be admitted to that state's education system on the same conditions as the nationals of that member state; and to have the right to work and have access to social security benefits in the host state.[3] In the *Kziber* case, the social provisions of the Treaty were for the first time interpreted in such a way as to include a TCN as a result of an Association Agreement with a third country. The ECJ ruled that a Moroccan national covered by the Agreement between the EC and Morocco did have the right to special unemployment benefits for school leavers. Clause 41(1) of the EC–Morocco Association Agreement covering equal treatment in social security was ruled capable of creating direct effects.[4]

Although TCNs were to be excluded from the EC's SAP, arguments for their inclusion were made. The Commission's first SAP (in 1975) did initially include migrants who were not nationals of an EC member state and contained an extensive section covering problems encountered by TCNs in relation to living and working conditions, social security, vocational training, social services, housing, the education of children, health, and information and training. The Council did not share the Commission's expansive understanding of the term 'migrant' and focused instead on migrant workers holding the nationality of a member state. Member states argued that there was no Treaty basis for a more expansive interpretation of matters that would bring TCNs within the remit of the SAP. Council Resolution 311/76, which set up an action programme for migrant workers and their families, was less broad in its scope and spoke only of encouragement of equal treatment for TCNs, of consultation on immigration policies and co-operation on illegal immigration. Neither 'encouragement' nor 'co-operation' had legal effect. The resolution concentrated on measures designed to facilitate social policy necessary for the smoother operation of the common market, ensuring the necessary levels of social protection for EC workers moving between member states.

Other SAP measures had the potential to affect TCNs but, as it turned out, little real impact. In 1977, for instance, Council Directive EEC 486/77, on the education of the children of migrant workers, watered down a Commission proposal that had included *all* children (including those of TCNs) within its remit. Again, for the Council, the term 'migrant workers' applied to nationals of an EC member state moving within the EC, not TCNs. Article 2 of the directive required member states, in accordance with their national circumstances and legal systems, to ensure that the children of migrant workers who were EC nationals received free tuition to facilitate their initial reception. This included instruction in the language of the host country. Article 3 made provisions for teaching in the mother tongue, again in accordance with national circumstances and the legal system in member states. A non-binding declaration attached to the directive did express the political will of the member states to extend the measures to children who were TCNs, but this was merely a costless declaration. A 1984 Commission report criticised patchy implementation of the 1977 directive (CEC, 1984). Handoll (1995: 256) argued that this was hardly surprising, given the loose obligations contained in its Articles 2 and 4 and the Commission's preference, stated in a 1994 report on the education of migrants' children, for 'a gradual approach based on a mixture of persuasion, co-operation and pressure to ensure respect of Community law' (CEC, 1994b).

In 1986 the SEA gave fresh impetus to EU social policy, but without altering the basic fact that nationality of a member state was usually the key that opened the door to EU-level entitlements. The Council adopted the Community Fundamental Charter on the Basic Social Rights of Workers (better known as the Social Charter) on 30 October 1989. It 'acts as a gloss on the limited legal basis of social policy law' (Nielsen and Szyszcak, 1991: 26). The Charter (now superseded) was a non-binding statement of policy principles that outlined 12 fundamental social rights. It essentially reaffirmed the free movement rights of the Treaty of Rome, although its reference to 'workers of the EC' with respect to free movement and associated social entitlements did raise the question of whether TCNs were included (Handoll, 1995: 248). The British Conservative government refused to sign the Social Charter, which meant that it became an agreement between the other 11 member states. On the back of the Social Charter, the second SAP was launched in 1989. The thrust of previous policy was maintained and attention was directed towards the social rights and entitlements of nationals of member states (Streeck, 1995).

The Maastricht Treaty added the Social Chapter for the 11 participating member states – again, the British Conservative government refused to sign. It covered issues such as improved living and working conditions, proper social protection and the combating of exclusion, which affect all workers and – importantly – not only those who are nationals of a member state. The protocol allowed for QMV in four policy areas, although social security, social protection and conditions of employment for TCNs required unanimity.

Further consultation on the main objectives of social policy continued through the early 1990s. In 1994 a Commission White Paper attempted to plot a way forward for EU social policy (CEC, 1994c). It served as the basis for the third SAP, launched in 1995. Emphasis was placed on balancing fears about lack of European competitiveness in key economic sectors – as discussed in the Commission's 1993 White Paper *Growth, Competitiveness and Employment* – with maintenance of the 'European social model', which was viewed as providing a buttress for prosperity and stability. In a key section, the 1994 social policy White Paper addressed issues associated with the establishment of a European labour market. It recognised that legally resident TCNs 'suffered multiple disadvantages' because they were not covered by the same provisions as EU citizens. As a first step, the Commission stated that they should be entitled to necessary health care benefits (CEC, 1994c: 28). The White Paper also noted that: 'An internal market without frontiers in which the free movement of persons is ensured logically implies the free movement of all legally resident TCNs for the purpose of engaging in economic activity. This objective should be realised progressively' (CEC, 1994c: 29–30). This drive towards economic reform has formed the background for debates about the extension of rights to TCNs. The 'Lisbon process' of economic reform, launched in 2000, aims to make Europe the world's leading knowledge-based economy by 2010, but also sees labour migration and greater mobility within the EU as elements of this drive for greater competitiveness. This theme was taken forward in the Commission's *Policy Plan on Legal Migration* (CEC, 2005c).

The EU context has thus been 'thin' in the terms outlined by Ferrera, focused mainly on the portability of social entitlements, and largely excluding TCNs from its scope, because access to EU rights has tended to derive from holding the nationality of a member state. This basically sums up the position until the end of the 1990s. A lot has changed since then, with the effect that it has become more meaningful to discuss immigrant integration at EU level. Such analysis of immigrant integration will be both in the context of what Ferrera (2005) calls Europe's 'new spatial politics of social protection' and in the institutional context that 'channels' this debate.

Institutional channelling

The EU's institutional context structures debate about migrant integration and provides opportunities for and constraints upon groups seeking to represent migrants' interests in EU decision-making. This shapes an EU 'political opportunity structure' as a basis for mobilisation and for turning some issues of social inclusion and immigrant integration into 'problems of European integration'. It has been argued that the discussion of supranational rights for TCN migrants 'touch only the fringe, not the core of the European project' (Joppke, 1998: 30). Laws agreed since 2000 covering rights of residence, family reunion and anti-discrimination show that the debate has moved on and that the meaning and practice of 'integration' have acquired EU resonance.

In 2006, Eurobarometer surveys into public attitudes towards discrimination in the 25 member states of the EU plus the two candidate countries, Bulgaria and Romania, were conducted. Figure 7.2 shows that in Sweden, Poland, France, Latvia, Denmark, Hungary, Italy, Lithuania, Slovakia and the Czech Republic a majority of respondents thought that more needed to be done. Even in countries such as the UK and the Netherlands, with highly developed responses to anti-discrimination and that played a key role in shaping EU anti-discrimination legislation, there remains a substantial minority of respondents who see the need for more effort to be made to counter discrimination (45.5 per cent and 43.2 per cent, respectively).

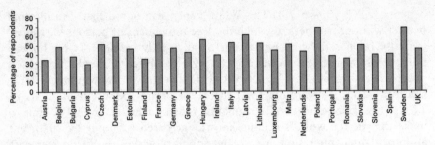

Figure 7.2 Percentage of respondents (2006) in the 25 member states of the EU plus the two 2007 accession countries responding 'No, not really' or 'No, definitely not' to the Eurobarometer survey statement 'In general, would you say that enough effort is made in ... [country same as that of respondent] to fight all forms of discrimination?' *Source:* Special *Eurobarometer*, Discrimination in the European Union, January 2007.

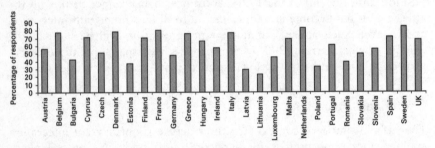

Figure 7.3 Percentage of respondents (2006) in the 25 member states of the EU plus the two 2007 accession countries indicating 'very widespread' or 'fairly widespread' in relation to 'Discrimination on the basis of ethnic origin' in the respondent's country. *Source:* Special *Eurobarometer*, Discrimination in the European Union, January 2007.

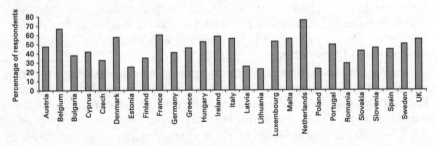

Figure 7.4 Percentage of respondents (2006) in the 25 member states of the EU plus the two 2007 accession countries indicating agreement with the Eurobarometer survey statement 'In general, would you say that ethnic discrimination has increased in ... [country same as that of respondent] in the last five years?' *Source:* Special *Eurobarometer*, Discrimination in the European Union, January 2007.

Figure 7.3 shows that there is a general perception that discrimination based on ethnicity is fairly widespread across the EU, with Swedes, Dutch, French and Belgians, in particular, thinking that there is fairly widespread discrimination in their countries. Figure 7.4 then shows perceptions of the growth or decline of ethnic discrimination over the previous five years. Interestingly, in 'older' countries of immigration, such as Belgium, France, the Netherlands and the UK, there was a sense among a majority of respondents that discrimination had become more widespread, as there was in newer immigration countries, such as Ireland and Italy.

These perceptions play into an EU-level debate about immigrant integration. Groenendijk (2004) has identified three underlying conceptualisations of foreigners/TCNs at work in EU debates about immigrant integration. Each conceptualisation identifies a particular element of this policy field that has played some role in shaping EU action. The first of these – equal treatment and non-discrimination – draws clearly from Treaty provisions that prohibited discrimination on grounds of nationality and gender and from the 1976 equal treatment directive. The second conceptualisation – citizenship and nationality – remains largely a matter for the member states. The third – integration conditions – would seem to connect with the second because it highlights the linkage now made in many member states between admissions policies and the perceived integration capacities of new migrants. This has been identified as an important recent element of national approaches in Austria, Germany and the Netherlands, and may form the basis of future developments with EU-wide implications. For example, the long-term residents directive (discussed below) extends free movement rights to TCNs, although with the proviso that member states can impose integration requirements on them, including the requirement to attend language training courses.

To understand how these conceptualisations entered the policy stream, became the subject of debate and proposals and then, at certain points in time, became a basis for legislative action requires close analysis of the understanding and articulation of policy problems, the ways in which solutions to these problems developed and the identity of participants in this policy process. It should not be assumed that problems and solutions followed neatly one from the other. Since the 1990s the EU-level 'problems stream' contained racism and xenophobia, EU citizenship, anti-fascism, anti-discrimination and equal treatment, the drive for closer economic integration, the democratic deficit, the promotion of human rights and, most recently, the integration of Europe's Muslim communities. We can then ask why particular sets of ideas were influential at EU level at certain points in time and which actors were involved as participants in this process of issue framing.

For much of the 1980s and 1990s, claims for inclusion on behalf of migrants could be batted back with the simple response 'Where's the legal basis?' This changed after the Amsterdam Treaty, when specific competencies for anti-discrimination and the rights of long-term residents were included. Just because they were included did not mean, however, that they would be turned into Community law. That is why it is necessary to explore the relationship between constitutionalisation – through inclusion in the Treaty framework – and institutionalisation – in terms of turning Treaty commitments into laws that bind the member states (Sandholtz and Stone Sweet, 1998). The close relation between the institutional context at EU level and the structure of political opportunity means that the focus is not on 'ethnic mobilisation' (Rex and Drury, 1994) but on the mobilisation of expertise (Radaelli, 1999). Mobilisation may possess an ethnic dimension, but is 'channelled' (Ireland, 1994) through an EU policy context where forms of interest group politics are well established and where a tone reminiscent of the heyday of corporatism informs the EU's desire to initiate dialogue with what are called the 'social partners', such as the Union of European Industrialists, the European Trades Unions Confederation and the Confederation of Agricultural Producers (Mazey and Richardson, 1993). Research has also focused on the scope for the 'Europeanisation of conflict' (Marks and McAdam, 1996; Tarrow, 1998). In this context, the mobilisation of migrant interests has been seen as offering only weak weapons for the weak, because of the often marginal social and political position of migrants and the difficulty in developing a 'migrant interests' agenda that exhibits coherence, given the sheer diversity of migrant and migrant-origin communities living in EU member states (Guiraudon, 2001).

Pro-migrant groups at EU level tend to act as umbrella groups for national organisations. The formulation of an EU-level migrants' interest agenda necessarily involves attempts to ensure that it is representative of the communities on whose behalf it purports to speak. Successful collective action has been connected with organisational capacity, group consciousness and levels of social control (McAdam, 1982). The diverse origins of migrant communities prompts relatively low levels of group consciousness and diverse sub-national, national and transnational settings for debate and action, while high levels of social control are exerted through restrictive immigration policies and internal securitisation. These factors connect with the coherence of the agenda, which, when combined with the representativeness and authoritativeness of those who seek to represent migrants' interests, will affect the success or failure of attempted political mobilisation by pro-migrant NGOs when seeking to operate at EU level (Favell and Geddes, 2000).

Migrant organisations based in member states with longer-established policy responses to migration have exerted most influence on the arguments put forward by these umbrella groups. British and Dutch understandings, for example, had particular influence on the EU anti-discrimination frame. A potential weakness with such groups acting at EU level is that they rely on horizontal co-ordination, which can be a 'weak substitute for consolidated formal organisation at national level' (Streeck, 1996: 85). However, EU institutions, particularly the Commission, sponsor and co-opt interest groups – including pro-migrant organisations – into consultation, development, evaluation and benchmarking processes, as a way of enhancing the legitimacy of both EU processes and the Commission's role as a policy actor.

EU-level umbrella groups could be seen as facilitators of transnational action that involves 'regular interactions across national boundaries when at least one actor is a non-state agent or does not operate on behalf of a national government or an intergovernmental organisation' (Risse-Kappen, 1995: 3). Transnational mobilisations also raise questions about the strategies, motivations and calculations of migrant organisations in these new EU spaces. For instance, is lobbying on behalf of migrants, with the use of independent resources, indicative of a struggle for inclusion based on 'strategies of resistance' or does it, when such lobbying draws on official resources, illustrate quiescence and a willingness to abide by the rules of the game? This is an important question because inclusion 'may be of more relevance to the stability of the system than to the interests of the included. But inclusion may also open the door to greater leverage in some circumstances' (Cerny, 1990: 39). Acts of recognition, participation and compliance contribute to the development of a new 'political field' in Europe, with its own forms of culture, capital and habitus, within which EU patterns of political activity develop (Favell, 1998; Favell and Geddes, 2000).

There are three potential – and overlapping – avenues for representation of migrants' interests: the mobilisation of expertise by lobby groups (particularly via the Commission); a 'democratic' route (via the EP); and judicial avenues (via the ECJ). Pro-migrant mobilisation based on expertise was focused on the Commission and EP but, since the introduction of anti-discrimination, long-term residence and family reunion laws, has shifted to a focus on implementation.

The mobilisation of expertise

The Commission has incorporated lobby groups into consultation processes. In part this stems from the Commission's small size (around 25,000 staff, of whom around half are administrators or translators), which means that it often relies on the kinds of expertise that lobby groups can bring to the policy process. Units within the Commission, such as the small anti-discrimination unit in the Directorate-General for Social Affairs, were allies of pro-migrant lobby groups but were hampered throughout the 1990s by the absence of a legal basis for EU action relating to TCNs. When the costs of Europeanised policy are concentrated and its benefits diffuse, incentives to organise are strong for the opponents of the policy, who bear the costs, and weak for those who actually benefit from it. In such circumstances, but only where the Treaty framework permits, the Commission can play an important role as the protector of diffuse and/or poorly organised interests (Majone, 1996). Where there is 'an important margin of autonomy and capacity to influence outcomes in the political process', the Commission can play an entrepreneurial role (Laffan, 1997: 423) and not only respond 'to opportunities for action' but also facilitate the emergence of these opportunities and thereby to become a 'purposeful opportunist' (Cram, 1994: 199). If such a role were to be played, then a clear legal basis for Commission action was necessary. Articles 13 and 63(3,4) of the Amsterdam Treaty provided just such a legal basis.

The European dimension introduces a new strategic element into the operation of migrant organisations, such as the opportunities provided by the designation of 1997 as the European Year Against Racism, which directed 4.7 million ecu towards projects in member states designed to raise awareness of racism and xenophobia, and of 2007 as the European Year of Equal Opportunities for All, with a budget allocation of €7.65 million. Commission funding has also been made available for other projects that seek the social integration of non-national immigrants in member states, to combat racism and xenophobia, and to assist refugees.

As EU migration policy responsibilities developed, so too did activity by groups seeking to represent the interests of migrants at EU level, such as Amnesty International, Caritas, the Starting Line Group (SLG), the Migration Policy Group (MPG) and the EU Migrants' Forum (EUMF). EU-level action focused on border controls and the restriction of migration, and this made it an uphill struggle to develop a pro-migrant agenda. Interestingly, though, while pro-migrant groups often advance a powerful critique of EU migration policy as currently constituted, the 'solutions' they propound tend to centre on *more* not *less* 'Europe', based on human rights principles and the attainment of economic and political integration. A quick comparative case analysis looks at alternative routes of 'ethnic co-option' by the Commission, through its creation of the EUMF and, in contrast, the mobilisation of expertise by the SLG.

Ethnic co-option as a strategy for Commission legitimisation

The EUMF was established as an umbrella group for migrant organisations in each member state, as well as for regional groups composed of migrants of similar ethnic or national origin (Danese, 1998: 719). It was originally intended as a broad inter-community forum, encompassing migrant and non-migrant groups, such as trade unions, which would include institutions and associations opposed to racism (EP, 1985). When it was finally established with Commission funding in 1991, the EUMF had a narrower remit than in the original proposal and was more concerned with providing a forum for the expression of migrants' opinions than with pursuing broader cross-community strategies against racism. EUMF funding from the

Commission accorded with a fairly standard model of interest co-option pursued by the Commission across a range of policy areas. The EUMF did, however, face difficulties. There was the basic definitional question of who was a 'migrant'. There are millions of people of migrant origin in EU member states who are wrongly thought to be migrants when in fact they are citizens of the member state in which they reside, and they can resent the imputation of temporariness. UK groups were more concerned to act against racism than to pursue a 'migrant' agenda.

There were also internal divisions within the EUMF. At its general assembly on 16–17 December 1993, the representatives of 14 Turkish associations walked out because they felt under-represented on the executive board. Turks constituted a third of 'migrants' (this depends on the definition employed) and a move to limit the voting weight of any ethnic group to a maximum of 10 per cent was seen as 'anti-Turkish' (*Migration Newssheet*, 133/94).

Following issues associated with financial mismanagement, the EUMF was wound down. The EUMF reflected the problems mentioned earlier about co-ordination of groups that operate in diverse national settings. There was also dissatisfaction from senior Commission officials with the fact that, while EU money was paying for it, the EUMF did not much engage with specific EU initiatives but tended to focus instead on national debates (EUMF, 1996).

Expertise as a base for pro-migrant mobilisation

The SLG is a good example of the mobilisation of expertise to make specific, often legally based claims for extended EU action against discrimination. The SLG was founded in 1992 by a group of independent experts from six member states, with the support of the Churches Commission for Migrants in Europe, the British Commission for Racial Equality and the Dutch National Office Against Racism. The original intention was to prepare a draft directive outlawing racial discrimination that would be modelled on the 1976 Equal Treatment Directive and use the wide-ranging Article 235 as its Treaty base for anti-discrimination legislation with direct effect. The SLG's proposal, known as the 'Starting Line' (SLG, 1998), was endorsed by national lobby groups and by the EP. The SLG was particularly effective at mobilising legal expertise to make specific proposals about the content of legislative measures and then initiating EU-level and national-level strategies to try to inform the thinking of key actors. The SLG also had close relations with the Commission and EP as supranational allies.

The 'democratic' route

There has been less scope for a democratic route to representation and influence, because the EU's only directly elected institution has been marginal to policy development. The Amsterdam Treaty gave the EP the right to be consulted on policy development, but this was a far cry from the powers of co-decision that it acquired in other policy areas. The EP has been a vigorous critic of intergovernmental immigration and asylum policy co-operation, and claims it reinforces 'lowest common denominator' policies of restriction and offers inadequate scope for scrutiny of decisions or for decision-makers to be called to account. The EP has long sought the supranationalisation of immigration and asylum policy, combined with a strengthened commitment to anti-discrimination and the combating of racism and xenophobia. The EP was a vigorous critic of the extreme right and an advocate of EU action against racism and xenophobia. In the aftermath of the extreme right's breakthrough at the 1984 European elections – when the Front National won 10 of the 80 seats available in France – the Committee of Inquiry into the Rise of Fascism and Racism was established. The resulting report (the Evrigenis report; EP, 1985) concluded that patchy national measures needed to be complemented by European-level initiatives. The first step, it was argued in the report, should be a joint declaration by the main EC institutions against racism and xenophobia. In June 1986 the Council, Commission and EP signed the Joint Declaration Against Racism and Xenophobia, which expressed bold sentiment when calling for the prevention of all 'acts or forms of discrimination'. The 1986 Joint Declaration was, however, 'a false dawn' (EP, 1998: 9). In 1989 the EP requested that the Commission bring forward proposals based on the 1986 Declaration, but the Commission responded that it was unable to do so, because there was no legal basis for such action in the Treaty of Rome. The Commission suggested a non-binding resolution that would urge member states without existing provisions to introduce anti-discrimination legislation. The final Council resolution was much watered down and signified disagreement among member states about the appropriateness of EC action against racism.

In 1990 the EP set up a second Committee of Inquiry into Racism and Xenophobia. Its report – the Ford report (EP, 1991) – made 77 recommendations for action. The report acknowledged the Commission's difficulties and recognised its intent to bring forward measures combating racism and xenophobia, but stated that 'initiatives are either subject to long delays in the Council of Ministers or they are watered down, if not completely abandoned, by the Commission on the grounds of political necessities, believing that unanimous approval will not be obtained' (EP, 1991: 99). The EP worked closely with the anti-racism lobby. In 1993 and 1994 resolutions were passed that called for the SLG's anti-discrimination proposals (SLG, 1998) to serve as the basis for Commission proposals for an amendment to the Maastricht Treaty that would extend anti-discrimination competencies. The EP's limited competence meant that action was more likely to emanate from other EU institutions, upon which the EP could seek to exert influence.

In the context of later discussion of the negotiation of the June and November 2000 anti-discrimination directives, the resonance of an anti-racism and anti-fascism frame can be added to the analysis. Concerns about racism and xenophobia prompted a shift in approach discernible at the Corfu summit held in December 1994. A Franco-German initiative led to the establishment of the Consultative Commission on Racism and Xenophobia. The Kahn Commission (named after its chair, Jean Kahn, President of the European Jewish Congress) called for binding legislation to combat racial discrimination. It argued that the EU had already displayed determination to combat discrimination based on gender: 'it is appropriate that it should be given a similar mandate, and that it should adopt similar measures, to combat discrimination on grounds of race, religion or ethnic or national origins' (European Council Consultative Commission on Racism and Xenophobia, 1995: 59). The EP endorsed the Kahn report and called for an amendment to the Maastricht Treaty to deal specifically with racial discrimination. The Commission's 1995 communication on racism, xenophobia and anti-Semitism reinforced this stance with its own call for the anti-discrimination provisions of the Treaty to be strengthened to cover racial discrimination (CEC, 1995b). The Commission's 1998 Action Plan Against Racism sought to 'mainstream' anti-racism by seeking integration across all sectors of EU activity, although this mainstreaming did not apply to immigration and asylum policy, which is a rather striking omission. The Commission has experienced other difficulties when trying to 'mainstream'. For instance, its proposals on parental leave and part-time work included specific non-discrimination sections that were then dropped from the final texts.

The judicial avenues

The disjunction between intra- and extra-EU migration policy hindered the ECJ's role until specific EU competencies related to anti-discrimination and the rights of long-term residents were introduced by the Amsterdam Treaty, in 1999. ECJ competence has also been restricted in Title IV areas, by the provision that involvement can occur only following reference from courts of final instance in member states (see Chapter 6). ECJ competencies suggest the potential for the opening of EU-level social and political spaces for migrants and their descendants. Moreover, the ways in which legal norms contained within international legal standards have contributed to forms of 'post-national membership' have also been stressed by those who emphasise new patterns of claims-making (Soysal, 1994; Jacobsen, 1996). The development of new powers around anti-discrimination and rights of residence has led to a greater role for the ECJ. It also demonstrates how the spatial shift to the EU level, designed as a 'venue shift' to escape domestic constraints, might encounter new forms of constraint at EU level, through ECJ jurisprudence, that are indicative of a temporal shift as EU competencies bed down. Social and political spaces for migrants that opened at national level may then open at EU level, too.

Council measures on anti-discrimination, long-term residence and family reunion

The anti-discrimination directives

In June and November 2000 the EU introduced two anti-discrimination directives. The racial equality directive of June 2000:

- implements the principle of equal treatment of all people, irrespective of racial or ethnic origin;
- provides for protection against direct and indirect discrimination in employment and training, education, social protection (including social security and health care), social advantages, membership and involvement in organisations of workers and employers, and access to goods and services, including housing.

With regard to enforcement, once a complainant has established facts that suggest discrimination, then the respondent has to prove that there has been no breach of the equal treatment principle. The racial equality directive was to be transposed into national law by 19 July 2003.

The employment equality directive is based on the same principles of direct and indirect discrimination that inform the racial equality directive and implements the principle of equal treatment in employment and training irrespective of religion or belief, disability, age or sexual orientation. The employment equality directive was to be transposed into national law by 2 December 2003.

Both directives allow scope for positive action. They are ambitious in a number of ways, not least because they go well beyond the traditional area of employment and into fields such as social advantage, health care, education and access to goods and services.

These directives are important developments, as EU institutions acquire powers through them to act and intervene in areas related to immigrant integration that have been closely linked to national sovereignty and seen as quite deeply embedded in particular and distinct processes in national polities. The two directives also demonstrate how particular sets of ideas were mobilised at EU level during the 1990s by umbrella groups such as SLG and how these influenced thinking within the Commission. The SLG was particularly effective at bringing legal expertise to bear on the issue of the EU's under-developed capacity to deal with discrimination. The arguments that were elaborated made more general claims about human rights, but also drew from very specific ideas about operative principles in EC law of equal treatment and action against gender-based discrimination.

Concern about racism and xenophobia informed the desire during the negotiation of the Amsterdam Treaty to move beyond declarations of opposition to racism and to put in place more concrete measures. The difficulty was then to decide on the shape and form of such measures. The insertion of Article 13 into the Amsterdam Treaty was a significant step towards creating a more substantial capacity in this area but, to be given effect, measures introduced under it required agreement from all member states. Given that member states had diverse approaches to immigrant integration issues, then agreement on anti-discrimination measures may well have been unlikely or, if it were reached, might be a 'lowest common denominator' response. The fact that the racial equality and employment equality directives were agreed and actually represented a significant levelling up of the response merits close attention.

Ideas about the scope for strengthened EU action against discrimination had been in circulation for much of the 1990s, with the SLG playing a key role. As discussed above, the SLG was able to bring to the European debate national legal responses and took 'ethnic minorities' as the policy reference. We are still left with the puzzle of why other member states would agree to this. Why, for example, would France, with its starkly contrasting 'Republican' policy response, agree to measures that appeared to mimic the UK 'race relations' and 'ethnic minorities' policy response? To answer this question requires that we delve a little deeper into the negotiation over the June 2000 racial equality directive. Negotiations began on the basis of a Commission proposal presented in December 1999. The fact that agreement was reached little more than six months later has been described as a 'world record' for a directive that involved breaking new ground for the EU (Tyson, 2001). In an analysis of those negotiations, it was found that the key factor explaining the rapid pace of the translation of proposals into a final legal form was the entry into the Austrian coalition government in February 2000 of Jörg Haider's extreme right-wing Freedom Party (Geddes and Guiraudon, 2004). This energised action against racism and xenophobia. The French government, in particular, was keen to assert its opposition to the neo-fascists in the Austrian government. For example, the French social affairs minister Martine Aubry refused to have her photograph taken with the Austrian government representatives in the usual post-meeting group photo opportunity. It was then difficult for the French at the Council negotiating table to block anti-discrimination legislation. France, with Denmark, Austria and Italy, underlined the problem of counting numbers of 'racial' or 'ethnic' groups and rejected statistical elements of the UK definition of indirect discrimination.[5] The two directives created scope for supranational action and provided resources that could feed into national debates.

'Talk' and 'decision' are one thing; 'action' is another (Brunsson, 1993, 2002). Some member states failed to implement the racial equality directive in time: they were required to notify the Commission of implementation by 19 July 2005, but by December 2005 Austria, Poland, the UK, France, Germany, Lithuania and Portugal had failed to do so. Infringement proceedings were initiated by the Commission against Luxembourg, Finland, Germany and Austria.[6] The Commission also noted issues for central and east European countries, because of the difference between 'ethnic' and 'national' minorities. There were also calls for more information about the new legislation to be disseminated (CEC, 2006b).

It is still early to judge the effects of this legislation but, in the context of many influential accounts of European immigration politics, it is worth noting that there are now European laws that are justiciable by the ECJ, represent a significant levelling-up rather than lowest common denominator response and do create scope for outcomes that may well not have been intended by member states at the time they entered into these agreements. The issue is now whether EU 'talk' and 'decision' translate into 'action' in terms of implementation. Also, it is important to see how the anti-discrimination directives relate to those on long-term residence and family reunion, within which there has been a strong emphasis on integration by migrant newcomers. We now move on to analyse those two directives more closely, beginning with that covering the rights and status of legally resident TCNs.

Rights of residence

As already mentioned, specific provisions of the Amsterdam Treaty empowered the Council to act on the basis of a proposal from the Commission to bring forward measures relating to the residence of TCNs. Denmark, Ireland and the UK had opt-outs from such measures. Before the Amsterdam Treaty had been ratified, the Commission proposed (in July 1997) a Convention on the Rules for the Admission of TCNs to the Member States of the EU (CEC, 1997d). The Convention was introduced using Maastricht's third pillar provisions and stood no chance of adoption as proposed, but the Commission announced its intention to resubmit a proposal for a directive following ratification of the Amsterdam Treaty. The draft Convention marked an attempt by the Commission to stake a claim for a leading role in shaping post-Amsterdam arrangements for free movement, immigration and asylum policy, as a way of attempting to ensure future communitarisation of these policy areas. The proposed Convention chimed with many issues raised by NGOs regarding the rights of TCNs, in that it would break the connection between nationality and free movement and the transferability of social entitlements within the EU. If such a development were to occur, then the deterritorialisation of social entitlement would fit more easily with a model of membership and entitlement that transcended the national, albeit with the qualification that entitlements would arise from membership of national welfare states, in which the criteria governing entitlement would still be largely determined by the criteria of national welfare states.

The British-based Immigration Law Practitioners' Association (1997: 1) called the Commission's proposed Convention 'revolutionary stuff indeed'. This was certainly the case when compared with the previous perception of Commission inactivity in these areas. The Convention proposed enforceable rules on employment, self-employment, study and training. It also proposed the creation of a right to enjoy family life. This right would not be extended to the same degree as for EU citizens, however, and member states would still retain an element of discretion over treatment of TCNs that had long since been ceded to the EU for intra-EU migration. Member states would, though, be obliged to justify any use of national discretion on the admission of family members of TCNs. The draft Convention also contained free movement provisions that created a right for long-term resident TCNs to move to any member state to take up employment. It also listed a series of basic rights that they would take with them. These included equal treatment with EU citizens as regards employment, self-employment, training, trade union rights, the right of association, access to housing, whether in the private or public sector, and schooling.

The SLG also proposed, in a draft directive, strengthened social rights for TCNs by way of access to rights of free movement and social entitlements. The SLG's proposal stipulated that, after three years' legal employment (compared with the Commission's proposal of five years) in one member state, a TCN would enjoy free access to paid employment or self-employment in any member state. The proposed directive then went on to outline provisions for employment and free movement, the right of establishment, the provision of services and family reunion. The directive mirrored the free movement provisions of Regulation 1612/68, by allowing those TCNs who qualified and who were exercising the right of free movement to be issued with a residence permit for five years, with the possibility of automatic renewal. It was also seen as essential that TCNs exercising the right of free movement be granted equal social treatment to other EU citizens. Provisions were, therefore, made for access to employment and self-employment, vocational guidance and training, trade union rights, the right of association, access to public and private sector housing, social welfare, education, health care, and the provision of goods, facilities and services. These provisions would guarantee equal treatment for TCNs.

The original Commission proposal did include refugees and people benefiting from subsidiary forms of protection, but this provision was deleted, with the intention that it be covered in later legislation. According to the directive, the status of 'long-term resident' would be obtained after legal and continuous residence of five years. This status allows TCNs to move, under certain conditions, from one member state to another while maintaining the rights and benefits acquired in the first member state. The status of long-term resident is permanent because the person is entitled to a permit valid for at least five years and which is automatically renewable. Long-term residents are allowed equal treatment with nationals as regards:

- access to employment and self-employed activity;
- education and vocational training, including study grants, in accordance with national law;
- recognition of professional diplomas, certificates and other qualifications;
- social security, social assistance and social protection, as defined by national law;
- tax benefits;
- access to goods and services, including housing;
- freedom of association, affiliation and membership, including trade union membership.

A key issue in the negotiation of the directive on the rights of long-term residents was the requirement for certain integration conditions in member states to be met by TCNs exercising rights under this directive. This is a reflection of the point made by Groenendijk (2004) about the emphasis on perceived 'integration capacity' in the conceptualisation of 'the foreigner' in Community law. A paper to the Council's Strategic Committee considering the directive, from the Austrian, Dutch and German delegations, emphasised the importance from their point of view of integration conditions: 'full participation of TCNs can be encouraged by the implementation of integration policies'.[7] Articles 5(2) and 15(3) of the directive allow member states to require that TCNs satisfy integration conditions in accordance with national law. Article 15(3) provides that TCNs moving to a second member state may be required to attend language courses or to comply with other integration measures. Such integration requirements could be seen as a restriction on free movement, as there is no such condition for EU citizens moving from one member state to another, and the directive creates lower minimum standards at the EU level than already exist in some member states for those TCNs already resident. It has been argued that these provisions could amount to 'five paces forwards and three back' and also be an 'Achilles' heel' of the directive, because they could be used as 'a vehicle to erode the basic rationale of the directive: to promote the integration of third-country nationals who have been long-term residents in EU Member States' (Boelaert, 2005: 1011). What it also shows is that an increased onus on adaptation by migrant newcomers has entered the EU framework as a reflection of strands of debate in prominent member states.

Family reunion
Family migration is an essential part of contemporary European migration history because it was supported by national and international laws protecting the right to family life; it was also an important part of the transition

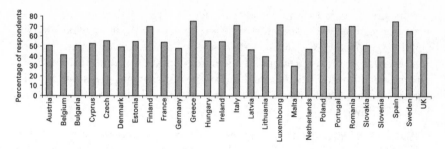

Figure 7.5 Percentage of respondents (2003) in the 25 member states of the EU plus the two 2007 accession countries indicating agreement with the Eurobarometer survey statement 'Legally established immigrants [from outside the EU] should have the right to bring members of their immediate family into ... [country same as that of respondent]'. *Sources:* Calculated from *Eurobarometer* 59.2, 2003, and *Eurobarometer* 2003.2, candidate countries survey.

to settled migrant and ethnic minority communities in 'older' European immigration countries. In addition, court decisions on family migration helped open 'social and political spaces' for migrants and their families (Hollifield, 1992). Figure 7.5 shows that a majority in most EU member states supports family reunion, but in Malta, Lithuania, Slovenia, Belgium, the UK, Latvia, the Netherlands, Germany and Denmark a minority supported the right to family reunion. The results in Belgium, the UK, the Netherlands, Germany and Denmark seem particularly significant, as they are 'older' countries of immigration, for which the 'family route' has been a key source for immigration.

The directive on the right to family reunification was agreed after a negotiating period of three years and after three different Commission proposals. During the negotiation process there was a movement away from the Commission's more liberal initial proposals to a stronger emphasis on integration by migrants and their families. Initially, the Commission had conceptualised 'integration' in relation to the promotion of social stability, through, for example, access to training and education for family members. Throughout the negotiation process Austria and Germany were particularly insistent on the inclusion of integration provisions, in accordance with national laws, for those availing themselves of rights created by the directive.

The directive determines the right to family reunification of TCNs who reside lawfully in the territory of an EU member state and the conditions under which family members can enter into and reside in a member state. It also determines the rights of the family members, once the application for family reunification has been accepted, regarding, for example, education and training. The EP sought annulment of the directive, based on the powers given to it by the Treaty of Nice. It argued that certain articles were not in line with fundamental rights, such as those specified by the ECHR (specifically Article 8 on the right to family life and Article 14 on non-discrimination on grounds of age) and a number of other international agreements, although the Council did point out that the EU is not actually a party to these agreements. According to the EP, the specific problems were as follows:

- Article 4 (1) specifies that member states are to authorise entry and residence for dependent, unmarried children below the age of majority in the member state they move to. There is a derogation that allows member states to require that children aged over 12 who arrive independently of the rest of their family may be required to satisfy the integration conditions set down in national law in the country they move to.
- Article 4(6) specifies a derogation that member states may require that applications for family reunification for minor children be submitted before the age of 15.
- Article 8 states that member states may require the sponsor to have been legally resident for two years prior to family members joining him or her. There is then a derogation that allows a member state to take into account its 'reception capacity' and to extend the waiting period to three years.

The ECJ rejected the EP's action for annulment on the grounds that, while member states must have regard to a child's interests, the framework of fundamental rights does not create an individual right for family members to enter the territory of a member state. Member states are thus entitled to a 'certain margin of appreciation' when examining applications for family reunification. Similarly, the ECJ held that member states would still be obliged to examine requests made by children of more than 15 years old in light of the interests of the child and with a view to promoting family life. The requirement for 'integration' conditions was viewed as a legitimate factor to be taken into account, but not as the basis for a quota system or a three-year waiting period imposed without regard to the particular circumstances of specific cases.[8]

Overview
There is a 'glass half-full or half-empty' issue here, in that all the measures that have been examined on anti-discrimination, long-term residence and family reunion mark a significant advance on what was previously evident at EU level. For analysts of European immigration politics they represent highly significant developments in areas of high politics that touch on the core of the European project. When the focus shifts to the content of these measures, then there may be more grounds to be equivocal. The anti-discrimination directives did represent a significant levelling up in

terms of provision, which may be why some member states had difficulty adjusting to what were, in the context of some national legal frameworks, ground-breaking new principles. The long-term residence directive is highly significant not only because of the deterritorialisation for which it provides, but also because of the emphasis within it on perceived integration capacity. New modes of migration governance have provided a great opportunity for some national officials to learn about policy orientations in other member states where 'integration challenges' have been salient political concerns, such as the Netherlands. The family reunion directive encroaches squarely upon the right to family life, which was central to secondary migration flows. The EU framework was watered down during negotiations, to amount to little more than a restatement of national frameworks. In a sense, the situation is now perfect for EU-level NGOs and think-tanks and their supranational allies in the Commission and EP: much has been done, but from their point of view, there is still much to do.

Conclusion

This chapter has focused on organisational borders of work, welfare, belonging and entitlement as a way of viewing the emerging EU debate about 'immigrant integration'. This is an area of EU action where, similar to the regulation of international migration, there has been an explosion of activity since the end of the 1990s. There has been a profusion of 'softer' initiatives, designed to promote sharing of ideas and best practices concerning integration.[9] There have also been 'harder' legal measures, dealing with anti-discrimination, equal treatment, rights of residence and family reunion.

To what extent can these developments be said to have created social and political spaces for migrants at EU level? To address this question, the chapter considered three issues. First, it analysed the relationship between migration, work and welfare in the context of European integration. This was done in order to demonstrate the centrality to debates about immigrant integration in the EU of the reconfiguration of organisational and conceptual borders of work, welfare, belonging and entitlement. The EU offers only a thin alternative to processes of welfare state bonding, which have primarily been located within nation states. The EU has also tended to derive its rationale for social policy action from market-making rather than market-correcting objectives. This helped create a particular setting for EU action, which was directly related to the second set of issues explored in this chapter. These related to the constitution of an EU policy field in the area of migrant integration and the types of political opportunity that have been created for pro-migrant interests. It was shown that the mobilisation of expertise has been a particularly salient aspect of pro-migrant action at EU level and that this has tended to facilitate close relations between pro-migrant groups and EU institutions, such as the Commission and EP. This, in turn, has helped create pro-European integration alliances, with a strong emphasis on the need for new EU-level measures and more power to EU institutions to address various 'problems of European integration', such as racism and xenophobia, the democratic deficit, inadequate rights frameworks and disappointing levels of socio-economic integration. Indeed, as has been pointed out in this chapter and others, participants in a well populated 'solutions stream' have been looking for problems to which they could attach their own particular ideas. It is this link between solutions and problems that was central to the exploration of the specific EU legislation on anti-discrimination, long-term residence and family reunion. Here, too, we see the power of ideas and, in particular, framings of integration that place more emphasis on adaptation by migrant newcomers to *national*, not EU, contexts. These ideas did not come from EU actors, but from the member states. Germany, Austria and the Netherlands took the lead, but others were sympathetic to their arguments. In the broader context of the analysis of EU action that has been developed in this book, it is also clear that the borders and boundaries of the EU political system and the sources of social and political action enabled by it and within it now play a much more important role than ever before in the politics of migrant integration, but this is a very particular, elite-level, EU-focused debate, detached to quite an extent from 'everyday' concerns, where national citizenship appears to remain the key concern (Koopmans et al., 2005). The 'national' has, however, played a key role in defining the 'European'.

Notes

1   Council Directive 2003/86/EC, of 22 September 2003, on the right to family reunification, *Official Journal*, L251/12, 3 October 2003; Council Directive 2003/109 EC, of 23 November 2003, covering the status of TCNs who are long-term residents, *Official Journal*, L16/44, 23 January 2004.

2   Council Directive 2000/43/EC, of 29 June 2000, implementing the principle of equal treatment between persons irrespective of racial or ethnic origin, *Official Journal*, L180/22, 19 July 2000; and Council Directive 2000/78/EC, of 27 November 2000, establishing a general framework for equal treatment in employment and occupation, *Official Journal*, L303/16, 2 December 2000.

3   Joined cases C-297/88 and C-197/89 [1990] ECR 3783.

4   Case C-18/90 [1991] ECR I-199.

5   Council of the EU, Social Questions Working Party, Proposal for a Council Directive implementing the principle of equal treatment between persons irrespective of racial or ethnic origin, 19 May 2000, 8675/00 LIMITE SOC 192, JAI 54.

6   Judgement against Luxembourg in case C-320/04 and Finland in case C-327/04, 22 February 2005, against Germany in case C-329/04, on 28 April 2005, and against Austria in case C-335/04, on 4 May 2005.

7   Council of the EU, Note from the German, Dutch and Austrian delegations to the Strategic Committee on Immigration, Frontiers and Asylum, 23 September 2002, 12217/02, LIMITE, MIGR82, p. 1.
8   Case C-540/03, 27 June 2006.
9   On integration, see www.integrationindex.eu.

8

Exporting EU migration and asylum policy

Introduction

This chapter analyses one of the most important recent developments in EU migration and asylum policy – its external dimension. This means attempts by the EU and its member states to influence migration from, and the migration policies of, non-EU states. This external dimension of migration policy is not in itself new. Attempts to influence the composition of flows were, for example, a prominent feature of US immigration policy as far back as the eighteenth century and are probably as old as migration policies themselves (Zolberg, 2006). What is new in the European context is the attempt to relate and co-ordinate action at EU level and – in certain policy areas – formulate common policies. Europe organised *as a region* with a geo-political form and important material and symbolic aspects is seeking to exert influence on neighbouring states and regions (Lavenex, 2001, 2006; Lavenex and Uçarer, 2002, 2004; Boswell, 2003; Geddes, 2006). By doing so, the EU is acting as an international organisation as it deals with one of the most difficult ethical and practical dilemmas in contemporary international politics: international population flows and their consequences. By exploring these issues we also explore the EU's international identity and its capacity to shape what is seen as 'normal' in international politics (Manners, 2000). We also see the 'domestic' origins of external action because, as Heisler (1992) suggests, these are simultaneously societal and international issues and must be analysed over both these levels. External action can be seen as an attempt to maintain organisational and conceptual borders of welfare, work, belonging, entitlement and identity (Geddes, 2005a).

The chapter begins by exploring the initial phase in the external dimension of EU migration and asylum policy, when, following the end of the Cold War, there were systematic attempts to export migration and asylum policies and practices to accession states in central, eastern and southern Europe. This was a response to the geo-political widening of migration, as it began to affect new immigration countries in southern and eastern

Europe. There were fears that the end of the Cold War would lead to large, uncontrolled migration. The ability of a prospective member state to demonstrate that it was in control of its borders and could allay such fears was an important part of the accession process that culminated in membership for the Czech Republic, Estonia, Hungary, Latvia, Lithuania, Poland, Slovakia, Slovenia (collectively known as the A8), plus Cyprus and Malta, on 1 May 2004. Romania and Bulgaria took membership to 27 when they joined on 1 January 2007. This marks a significant shift in EU borders, and there are still other countries in south-east Europe in the queue for membership, including Turkey (Kirisci, 2002).

The chapter then explores a second phase in the development of the external dimension of EU migration and asylum policy, which is the elaboration of a concept of a European 'neighbourhood' and, through this, the management of migration relations with migrant-sending countries in, for example, sub-Saharan Africa. A common factor uniting the EU's neighbours relations is the development of new forms of 'international migration relations', with a key role played by the EU as a regional bloc (Geddes, 2006).

The empirical focus of the chapter is thus on what are called *phase 1* developments, before the May 2004 'big bang' accession, and *phase 2* developments, centred on the operationalisation of the 'neighbourhood' concept. The implications of developments during these two phases are particularly significant for the 'challenges' posed by asylum-seeking and illegal/irregular migration flows.

The chapter shows how the EU has moved beyond 'fortress Europe' to notions of managed migration and some openness to labour migration (particularly by the highly skilled). The opening of 'small doors' to certain types of labour migration has, however, been accompanied by ever-increasing vigour in the EU's self-described 'fight against illegal immigration'. One important aspect of this fight is against trafficking and smuggling and the modern-day forms of slavery associated with it. There may well be other consequences of the focus on reinforcing territorial borders, as efforts to tighten external frontier controls (managed by a new European border control agency, FRONTEX, based in Warsaw[1]) may make it increasingly difficult for asylum-seekers to enter the territory of EU member states. This in turn risks creating the previously unknown category of the 'illegal asylum-seeker', because the only routes of entry will be those rendered 'illegal' by member state policies (Morrison and Crosland, 2000).

Migration and asylum in a wider Europe

The concept of boundary build-up was introduced in Chapter 2 to explain the ways in which market liberalisation can be accompanied by a toughening of both practices and discourses associated with Europe's borders (Nevins, 2002). A distinction was then made between territorial, organisational and conceptual borders, to highlight the ways in which 'sense-making' processes (Weick, 1995) within organisations – processes here concerning ostensibly new migration 'challenges' and associated processes of categorisation into different migration types – develop and change over time. The 'European project' is also a 'sense-making' exercise, in that it contains unfinished elements – that will likely remain unfinished in the EU's compound or partial polity – and has been engaged in an almost continual process of boundary shift and redefinition since its formation, with enlargements in 1973, 1981, 1986, 1995, 2004, 2007 and with more to come. The 2004, 2007 and likely subsequent enlargements raised and will continue to raise particular concerns about migration, asylum and border control on the part of existing member states.

The EU's attempts to manage territorial borders and regulate migration have been to the fore in discussions of EU enlargement. Zielonka (2001: 508) argued that 'The very notion of a hard, external border as envisaged by the single market project and the regime of Schengen is basically flawed and unlikely to survive ... enlargement'. This is because, he argues, the EU is less of a 'post-Westphalian state' – with hard and fixed external borders, socio-economic homogeneity, a European cultural identity, one type of citizenship and 'absolute sovereignty' – than it is a 'neo-medieval empire', with overlapping authorities, divided sovereignty, varied institutional arrangements, multiple identities and diversified types of citizenship, with different sets of rights and duties. Zielonka argues that enlargement will accelerate trends towards diversity, multiplicity and differentiation, which means that the EU will also require overlapping authority, multiple cultural identities and flexible institutional arrangements to promote free movement within and across its borders.

EU member states have sought, through their migration and asylum policies, to maintain what Scharpf (1996: 22) calls 'the precarious balance' between closed states and open economies as capitalist systems develop in ways that 'transform the given boundaries of any political system'. In the practical arrangements put in place to deal with enlargement and 'neighbourhood' relations, the EU has been concerned to ensure the development of capacity to regulate external migration. There have also been fears about the potential for large migration flows from accession states. The general concern appears to have been with, to borrow Zolberg's (1989) metaphor, building walls high enough to keep out the 'unwanted' migrants but leaving 'small doors' through which certain types of migrant can pass. One result has been an increased focus on highly skilled migrants (operationalised thus far in national, *not* EU policies), but the other side of the coin has been increased irregular or illegal immigration. There is a strong relationship between so-called legal and illegal migration flows, because 'illegals' often do the lower-skilled, lower-paid, lower-status jobs that sustain higher-skilled migrants and support the EU's bold aspirations to create 'the world's leading knowledge-based economy', as EU leaders declared when launching the 'Lisbon process'. In such terms, regular and irregular migration flows are not simply the European manifestation of some external push factor that impels migrants to seek opportunities in EU member states.

Phase 1: migration and EU enlargement

Adaptation by potential member states in central and eastern Europe to the migration and asylum framework in the 1990s and 2000s was almost entirely a consequence of the requirements of EU accession. The main emphasis was on developing the capacity to deal with various types of migration flow. This capacity was then linked to accession to the Schengen system. Prior to the 2004 enlargement, there were also concerns about migration from central and eastern European countries. These concerns led to the imposition of transitional arrangements (for up to seven years) on the A8 after 2004 and on Bulgaria and Romania when they joined in 2007.

Lavenex (2001, 2006) argues that adaptation for the A8 was shaped by two competing paradigms, or 'frames'. On the one hand, there were security concerns on the part of the existing 15 member states about borders and the scope for uncontrolled migration; on the other, there were more liberal concerns, often mobilised by NGOs, that derived their force and purchase from human rights standards embedded in national and international law. To this could be added an economic frame, linking migration from central and eastern Europe to changes in both labour markets and welfare states. There are major differences in the shape and form of organisational borders across the member states of the EU. Indeed, much discussion of migration from the A8 states has focused on its economic effects on the organisation of work and welfare. The UK government allowed free access for A8 nationals to its labour market, but with some welfare state restrictions. In the context of the more structured German welfare state, concerns were expressed about the potential for the undercutting of the domestic workforce and the lowering of social standards. The 'Polish plumber' became a particularly powerful metaphor for the impact of A8 migration on the diverse and complex organisational borders of work and welfare, where, as Ferrera (2005) has shown, core issues of 'bonding' and 'bounding' arise that shape social citizenship (see Chapter 7).

The sub-text for these developments was the potential for large-scale east–west migration. Between 1989 and 2001, migrants from central and eastern European countries were estimated to comprise around 15 per cent of EU total immigration, with 2.5 million people moving, although precise numbers were hard to specify (Organisation for Economic Co-operation and Development, 2001). Post-Cold War alarmist stories about 'floods' and 'invasions' fuelled a security-oriented perception of eastern enlargement. Such predictions even made their way into some academic analyses, with Turnbull and Sandholtz (2001) contending that the end of the Cold War 'unleashed a flood of immigrants from the east and seemed to open the way to criminal organizations from the east to move to the EU'. Predictions of large-scale migration – or of 'floods', to put it emotively – informed debate about migration and contributed to migration's 'securitisation' (Wæver et al., 1993; Bigo, 2001; Huysmans, 2006). Such debates do little, however, to illuminate the complexity of migration flows. It makes little sense to use the single term 'immigration' to cover all forms of migration and mobility from and across central and eastern Europe, which will include intra-regional flows of workers, movement by workers from developing countries, migration by workers from western Europe, return migration, ethnic migration, asylum-seeking, or migration defined as illegal by state policies. This picture, as Iglicka (2001: 8) puts it, is then superimposed on a 'complex mosaic of relatively short-term movement based on "labour tourism" and petty trading and comprising a highly intensive shuttling back and forth across international borders to make a living'. As the Organisation for Economic Co-operation and Development (2001: 68) tellingly observed, central and eastern Europe is 'a theatre of much more complex movements' than just a straightforward move to the west.

Four key factors were at play when the requirements for accession by the A8 were specified during the 1990s (Geddes, 2003: 176–7). First, unpredictable migration pressures could lead to perceptions of loss of control. Second, the scale and extent of borders raised 'control' issues. Poland's 'green' (i.e. relatively unpopulated) borders run for 407 km with Belarus and for 526 km with the Ukraine. It was also likely that the costs of control would need to be shared, because new member states were unwilling (and likely unable) to absorb all these costs themselves. Third, the development of new border controls could hit potentially desirable activities, such as cross-border trade. Fourth, there were considerable complications caused by the presence of national minorities, such as the three million Magyars who do not live in Hungary but in neighbouring states and the substantial numbers of Russians living in the Baltic states.

While the general management of enlargement was dealt with at a senior political level, that is, by foreign ministers and their officials, it spilt over into a range of policy sectors. The Copenhagen summit meeting of EU heads of government in 1993 linked the accession of central and eastern European countries to 'political conditionality'. This meant 'membership requires that the candidate country has achieved stability of institutions guaranteeing democracy, the rule of law, human rights and the respect of and protection of minorities'.[2] Migration and asylum were late onto the agenda because there was some member state resistance to Commission influence in these areas, which became more formally established only post-Amsterdam. The detail of migration and asylum policy was dealt with by interior ministries and their officials, and gave rise to an extension of networks of intensive transgovernmental action beyond existing member states to include potential member states and key international organisations, such as the International Organization for Migration and the UNHCR. Applicant states were obliged to adopt the formal conventions and instruments, informal and non-binding measures, and the agreed elements of draft instruments that were in negotiation.

Before 2001 the main focus was on transposition into national law of the relevant measures. Formal transfer need not mean that a particular state possesses either the authority or the capacity to implement such measures. After 2001 the focus shifted to their implementation, which meant support for the development of administrative and judicial capacity in accession states. It was also agreed that accession to Schengen would occur in a two-step process. Step 1 would involve the development of border controls, and step 2 the imposition of transitional arrangements on the A8 states.

Step 1 comprised four main elements (Geddes, 2003: 182–4). First, a series of unilateral and bilateral processes were initiated that linked the EU with accession states. The 'Budapest process', for example, focused on co-operation on border guards, combating trafficking in human beings, and building capacity. Second, a range of measures were put in place to enforce the principles of the Dublin Convention on asylum applications (see Chapter 4). These were important developments, because the Dublin system, with its 'one-stop shop' system, was an integral element of the EU migration and asylum framework. The EU defined the applicant states as 'safe' and implemented 'safe third country' and other rules, plus readmission agreements that provided for the return of asylum applicants to safe countries. A complex web of readmission agreements was to develop, beginning with one between the Schengen states and Poland in 1991. The key issue with such readmission agreements was the incentive that could be offered for a sending or transit country to enter into one with the EU. In the case of Poland, EU member states were able to offer the incentive of relaxations on short-term visas for Poles and the provision of financial assistance for the development of border control and surveillance technologies. The EU has pushed for readmission agreements as a standard element of the 'external' dimension of migration policy. The reasons for doing so are clear if we take the case of the agreement between Germany and Romania. In 1992 there were 100,000 asylum-seekers from Romania in Germany. A readmission agreement was signed in 1994. Between 1993 and 1995, Germany paid DM120 million to Romania for resettlement costs (Munz and Ulrich, 1998). In 1995 there were 3,500 Romanian asylum-seekers in Germany. Between 1993 and 1995 around 85,000 people were returned to Romania. The readmission agreements also had a knock-on effect, as applicant states were encouraged to reach their own readmission agreements with neighbouring states and to extend the 'safe country' principle, even if there were some doubts about exactly how safe they were or how well equipped they were to deal with asylum-seekers and refugees (Abell, 1999). The third element was the export of the EU visa policy, with adaptation to the common visa format agreed by a Council regulation in 1995 and the attempt to develop 'white' and 'black' lists of countries as a base for the issuance of visas (see Chapter 5). Finally, efforts were made to develop asylum systems in central and eastern European countries, although Lavenex (1999) argued that this put the cart before the horse, because the definition of countries as 'safe' preceded the development of asylum systems.

Following the development of border controls, step 2 of accession to Schengen would be the lifting of internal border controls with existing member states (Adinolfi, 2005; Carrera, 2005). In the interim, there has been what has been described as 'a "re-nationalisation" of free movement against the premises of equality inherent in the [EU] citizenship concept' (Reich, 2005: 675). The German government led calls for a seven-year transition period before introduction of full rights to free movement for the purposes of work (leaving open freedom of establishment and of service provision), during which full free movement rights would not be granted to nationals of the A8 states. The final agreement was for a 2 + 3 + 2 formula from 2004 until 2011, whereby full rights would be granted at the end of seven years, or possibly earlier after the situation had been reviewed at two years and then again after a further three. Sweden, Ireland and the UK allowed free movement from the date of accession. The Commission reported positive labour market effects of that migration after A8 accession and urged the remaining 12 member states to lift their restrictions. Finland, Greece, Italy, Spain and Portugal lifted the transitional arrangements on 1 May 2006. Belgium, Denmark, France, Luxembourg and the Netherlands announced their intention to relax restrictions before 2009. Austria and Germany seemed likely to maintain restrictions until 2011. When Bulgaria and Romania joined in 2007, they were also subject to the 2+3+2 formula, with only Sweden and Finland of the 15 older member states opening their labour markets with immediate effect. Of the 2004 accession states, only Malta and Hungary imposed restrictions.

Phase 2: migration in Europe's 'neighbourhood'

Alongside the accession of the A8 in May 2004 there was also the operationalisation of the concept of Europe's 'neighbourhood', comprising 16 states, from Belarus in the north-east to Morocco in the south-west (CEC, 2003e, 2004). In relation to migration, asylum, visas and border security, the 'neighbourhood' represents an attempt to put in place migration 'partnerships' and bilateral and multilateral forums, in an attempt to influence migration flows via various forms of dialogue and co-operation. This attempt to build partnerships is evident in various other areas, including political dialogue with African, Caribbean and Pacific states, political dialogue with Mediterranean partners (Bicchi, 2007), dialogue with and between regional and sub-regional organisations, including the Economic Community of West African States and the African Union, and specific regional initiatives, such as the EU–Africa ministerial conference of 58 European and African states at Rabat in July 2006. The European Neighbourhood Partnership applies to countries that share EU land and sea borders and then looks for analogous organisations in other parts of the world that can be credible interlocutors, such as the African Union. Together, these various partnership initiatives are part of an attempt to form a coherent EU approach to migration management that is strongly focused on border management and measures to deter flows of irregular migrants and asylum-seekers, and that seeks to export EU action to neighbouring transit countries and countries of origin.

The Tampere summit of EU heads of government in October 1999 identified four key elements of a common EU approach to migration and asylum, one of which was partnership with countries of origin (the others were a common asylum system, fair treatment of TCNs and management of migration flows – see p. 129). These objectives were renewed and updated by the Hague Programme to carry through EU action until 2010 (see Chapter 6). The Hague Programme included partnership with third countries to improve their asylum systems, to tackle illegal immigration and to implement resettlement programmes, as well as a policy to expel and return illegal immigrants to their countries of origin and the creation of a fund for the management of external borders operated by FRONTEX.

New integration 'laboratories', such as the Prüm Convention, have also developed, to pursue in smaller, more select groupings the security implications of a deeper and wider EU.

In 2005, the member states issued a strategy for the external dimension of justice and police co-operation in the context of terror attacks, organised crime and global migration flows (the issue 'frame' for migration is not too difficult to detect).[3] Such attacks and threats provide institutional opportunities and impel co-operation and integration, but 'security policy is never *compelled* by external events' (Walker, 2004: 11, original emphasis). A security 'frame' is well established at EU level and was a key driver of co-operation long before the terror attacks of the 2000s. The EU strategy uses enlargement to align various linked policy objectives.

As far back as 1994, the Commission's communication on immigration had registered the need for co-operation with non-EU states and hence recognised the growing 'foreign policy' dimension (CEC, 1994a). This external dimension raised what are known in EU jargon as cross-pillar issues, as they bridge 'external' and 'internal' security and render visible both the domestic and the international politics of migration (as well as the links between them) (Geddes, 2006). Cross-pillar dimensions were also evident in the work of the High Level Working Group on Asylum and Migration, which was a Dutch government initiative established in December 1998 to provide action plans for countries of origin and transit of migrants and asylum-seekers. That Working Group brings together officials from interior, foreign and development ministries. It has issued reports on Afghanistan and the neighbouring region, Morocco, Somalia, Sri Lanka, Iraq and Albania and the neighbouring region. The reports on Afghanistan, Morocco, Somalia, Sri Lanka and Iraq were submitted to the October 1999 Tampere European Council. The report on Albania was approved in June 2000.[4] The reports all called for a 'common approach' that was comprehensive, long term and responsive to changes in the situation. Implementation was seen to require that the Council, the Commission and member states work closely together, that there be agreement on financial and human resources, that there be close consultation with relevant international organisations, and that the plans be based on 'genuine partnership', with the definition of 'reciprocal undertakings'.[5] Each report covered foreign policy, development and economic assistance, migration and asylum. It was agreed that:

> Important components of the approach are protection of human rights, support for democratisation and rule of law, social and economic development, alleviation of poverty, support for conflict prevention and reconciliation, co-operation with UNHCR and human rights organisations, observance of refugees' and asylum-seekers' rights to protection, integration of migrants and the fight against illegal immigration *inter alia* (through Community readmission agreements).[6]

Strong criticisms were directed at the report that indicate problems with EU attempts to build 'migration partnerships' and, by doing so, impart an EU dimension to what is seen as 'normal' in international politics (Manners, 2000; Boswell, 2003). First, the countries about which the reports were written did not always feel like real partners. When visiting Morocco in October 2000, the EU delegation was told that the action plan lacked balance, particularly in its emphasis on the 'security dimension'. Morocco called for more emphasis on the socio-economic dimension (CEC, 2003f). The work of the High Level Working Group was also hampered by difficulties co-ordinating national administrations, the absence of a budget line to support implementation, the need to link more clearly to the development agenda, and the need, as the EU Council put it, to 'dissipate those mis-understandings regarding an apparent imbalance' in favour of security.[7]

If the concern is that the external dimension is a vehicle for the EU to impose its migration and asylum priorities on non-member states, then what value would such agreements possess? Also, in practical terms, what incentive is there for non-member states to agree to participate in such processes if the onus is on them to adapt to EU requirements? In this context, it is useful to consider the meaning of 'partnership'. The most developed state-ment of the principles underlying migration partnership can be found in the Cotonou Agreement between 77 African, Caribbean and Pacific states and the EU, of June 2000. Article 13 specifies that migration partnership involves in-depth dialogue consonant with commitments in international law to respect human rights and eliminate all forms of discrimination based particularly on origin, sex, race, language and religion. Three broad areas for dialogue can be identified:

- The first relates to residence and employment, including fair treatment of TCNs, integration policy that grants rights and obligations comparable to those of citizens, enhancement of non-discrimination in economic, social and cultural life and the development of measures against racism and xenophobia. In employment, the treatment by each member state of legally employed workers shall be free from discrimination based on nationality as regards working conditions, remuneration and dismissal, relative to its own nationals. The June and November 2000 directives on anti-discrimination and the November 2003 directive on the rights of long-term residents covered most of these areas, but labour migration rules remain a national competence and EU action to shape migration opportunities for nationals of non-member states remains very limited.
- The second area relates to addressing 'root causes', which includes efforts to 'normalise' migration flows, through poverty reduction, improving living and working conditions and creating employment. Partnership should also include provision for training and education, such as schemes to facilitate access to higher education (the links between migration and economic development are considered below).
- The third area is a particular concern of EU states and relates to their 'fight against illegal immigration' through return and readmission policies, with bilateral agreements governing specific obligations for readmission and return (CEC, 2006a). At time of writing, the EU has re-admission agreements with Hong Kong, Sri Lanka, Macao and Albania, and is negotiating with Morocco, Russia, Pakistan, the Ukraine and Algeria (Abell, 1999; Schieffer, 2003).

If partnership is to work in the interests of both parties, then it should be based on shared interests. The EU may be able to exercise leverage in order to provide incentives to co-operation. For those non-EU states with the prospect of eventual accession, such as those in the western Balkans, then incentives are linked to membership. For states that do not have the prospect of membership, other incentives are necessary. In its 2002 com-munication on migration and development, the Commission discussed incentives for co-operation (CEC, 2002). Links between migration and development are famously 'unsettled' (Papademetriou and Martin, 1991). Evidence does, however, suggest that successful poverty-reduction strategies can lead to increased migration, by boosting both the motives and the resources necessary for movement and creating a 'migration hump' (Heisler, 1992). Or, put another way, 'poverty reduction is not in itself a migration-reducing strategy' (Nyberg-Sorensen et al., 2002: 5). While emigration from sending states can relieve labour market and political pressures, provide education and training, generate remittances, and lead to eventual return by successful migrants, there can also be more negative effects, including loss of skills ('brain drain') and under-deployment of skills ('brain waste'). Also, it can be difficult to put in place principles of 'circulation'; the circulation of migrant workers, that is, back to the country of origin without precluding a later move back to an EU member state, can be beneficial, but runs counter to the current restrictionist direction of EU migration policies.

In its 2002 communication on migration and development, the Commission sought to integrate migration issues into relations with non-EU states based on four key principles (CEC, 2002: 4–5):

- maintaining the coherence of external policies and actions through a comprehensive approach, of which a part is migration and which is differentiated by country;
- addressing root causes;
- including migration within regional and country strategy papers;
- extending additional funding through the EU budget.

The Council then called for action in five areas:[8]

1 *Facilitating 'brain circulation' (extending free movement) and encouraging return.* Here the basic problem is that migrants are likely to be concerned that if they leave the EU they will not be able to re-enter. In its 2007 communication on 'circular migration and mobility partnerships' the Commission raised the possibility of creating routes for migrants to enter, leave and re-enter and linking this to tougher border controls in sending states (CEC, 2007).

2 *More efficient use of remittances, with cheaper and more reliable transmission and efforts to channel their use towards productive investment.* Remittances from migrants, which often flow to kith and kin in countries of origin, far exceed development aid as a source of funding for developing countries (World Bank, 2005, 2007). Although these are private flows and their uses cannot easily be controlled or necessarily channelled towards productive investment, remittances have tended to have a positive impact on development. Governments, international organisations and NGOs can encourage remitting behaviour through incentive schemes and improved financial infrastructures. They can also seek to channel remittances towards productive investment.

3 *Better integration of legally resident TCNs living in EU member states, with rights and obligations comparable to those of other EU residents*

and opportunities to participate in education and vocational training
(see Chapter 7 on the 2003 directive on the status of long-term resident
TCNs).

4 *Possible tensions between high-skilled recruitment and development.* If
   EU member states cherry-pick skilled migrants, then an EU approach to
   labour migration may not be in the interests of developing countries, as
   they may lose their brightest and best, but it has been argued that wider
   channels for migrants who work in lower-skilled occupations could
   choke off some of the demand for irregular migration.

5 *Readmission agreements.* The Council called on the Commission to step
   up negotiation of readmission agreements and to consider ways in which
   financial and technical assistance could be used to develop reception
   capacity and 'durable solutions' to asylum in developing countries. This
   issue of readmission is right at the top of the EU agenda.

At the core of the debate about partnership is the tension between
the EU's 'fight against illegal immigration' and all the attendant concerns
about border security and the attempt to integrate migration issues within
a development agenda. A Commission communication on policy priorities
in the fight against illegal immigration specified partnership with third
countries as an essential element in the EU's southern and eastern neigh-
bourhoods, with intensified engagement in the Balkans (CEC, 2006a).
The Commission also produced annual reports on the development of
a common policy on illegal immigration, smuggling and trafficking of
human beings, external border controls and the return of illegal residents.
The 2006 report analysed relations with third countries and identified
European Neighbourhood Partnership action plans with 10 countries,
with a commitment on both sides to co-operate on migration, as well
as a technical dialogue with Libya on illegal immigration. Monitoring
mechanisms have been established to evaluate levels of co-operation from
Albania, China, Libya, Morocco, Russia, Serbia and Montenegro, Tunisia
and the Ukraine. The EU's 'leverage' clearly differs quite markedly among
this array of states (CEC, 2006b).

There is also the question of money. If the EU is to attain its objectives,
then it has to back up its commitments with some financial resources.
These resources have expanded considerably since 2000, especially for
border management in third countries. The EU has worked through various
regional programmes, such as MEDA for Mediterranean states, CARDS
and SAP for the western Balkans and TACIS for eastern Europe and central
Asia. Within the budget, so-called 'Title B5-8 appropriations', devoted to
the creation of the EU as an area of freedom, security and justice, rose
from €29.5 million in 1998 to €56 million in 2003, with the European
Refugee Fund scooping up half, mainly to facilitate the return of failed
asylum-seekers (CEC, 2003e). In 2003, spending on asylum, immigration

and the management of external frontiers amounted to just under 1 per cent of spending on EU internally directed policies (CEC, 2003b). Between 2001 and 2004 a specific €42.5 million budget line (called B7-667) funded projects relating to co-operation with non-EU states. Between 2002 and 2004, Morocco got around €50 million to assist with border control.

In March 2004 the AENEAS programme was established to provide financial and technical assistance to non-EU states in the areas of migration and asylum.[9] Between 1 January 2004 and 31 December 2008, €250 million was allocated to promote more efficient management of migration flows, in co-operation with third countries engaged in preparing or implementing a readmission agreement. This linkage is central to the external dimension of EU migration and asylum policy. In all its agreements with non-member states, the EU seeks a standard readmission clause. To further these objectives, a variety of programmes could be supported by EU cash, including: information campaigns and advice; maintaining links between emigrants and their countries of origin; information from non-EU states about migration potential; support for institutional and legislative capacity; support for the development of border controls; the development of regional and sub-regional dialogue; and support for the building of reception centres for asylum-seekers. The 2007–13 budget settlement allocated a grand total of €4,020 million to 'Solidarity and Management of Migration Flows'. This includes €1820 million to external borders, €676 to a return fund, €699 to the European Refugee Fund and €825 to the Integration Fund.

The ambitions of EU member states in these areas remain bold. The Brussels European Council in December 2006 called for a strengthening and deepening of co-operation and dialogue with third countries of origin and transit, through specific EU delegations to African countries in 2007, closer integration of migration and development policies, coherent EU follow-up to the United Nations High Level Dialogue on Migration and Development, measures on return and readmission, measures against smuggling and trafficking, and new thinking on legal migration, while emphasising that these remain areas of member state competence.

Understanding migration and asylum in Europe's neighbourhood

The external dimension of migration and asylum needs to be considered in the context of the 'internal governance' patterns discussed in this book's other chapters and the ways in which Europe's borders have now moved (Guild, 2001). The internal governance of migration is centred on the relationship between the management of territory, the maintenance of organisational borders of work and welfare, and the definition of conceptual borders of belonging and entitlement. The burgeoning external dimension needs to be seen in this context, because the foreign or external dimension has strong domestic or internal motives. It also suggests a key issue for the EU as boundary build-up is accompanied by boundary shift. More than this, boundary shift occurs in the context of the EU expanding its membership to include countries that are closer to major migrant-sending regions or are seen to have significant 'sending potential', such as Turkey. While this external dimension is not new – states have long sought to influence migration flows – what is novel is the focus on the EU as a specific form of regional governance with developing migration and asylum powers. Moreover, migration and asylum have now become component elements of the EU's foreign policy agenda and thus relate quite closely to the identity of the EU as an actor in international politics.

Thus far, the external dimension of EU action has been largely concerned with exporting the pre-occupations of member states with immigration controls. It has been difficult to integrate development concerns into this agenda, because that would involve thinking about routes for legal entry into EU member states, which until now have remained the jealous pre-serve of the member states. EU action in this area has also replicated the patterns we saw in earlier chapters, in the sense that it has been dominated by the executive and strongly focused on the resolution of domestic policy priorities, namely to curb asylum-seeking and irregular flows. In terms used earlier, this external dimension and the specific content of external action represent a 'transgovernmental' extension of EU action, which cannot be understood in simple intergovernmental versus supranational terms. There is now a greater intensity and denser structuring of EU action, plus an unwillingness to embrace the supranational method, which would be difficult anyway when dealing with non-EU states not bound by the EU legal framework (Wallace et al., 2005).

There are analogies between the kinds of action being pursued by EU states and those strategies of similar non-European states; this suggests that boundary build-up and boundary shift are more general components of responses by liberal states to migration pressures. To make this analogy clearer requires that a distinction is made between the kinds of processes through which the EU acts (and which, it must be said, have been to the fore in this and other chapters) and the types of policy action that result from these processes. So, while the EU is clearly a unique form of supra-national governance (there is no other international organisation like it), there are some parallels between the kinds of things the EU does and the kinds of things that states experiencing similar migration dilemmas have pursued (Geddes, 2007). For example, Australia has sought to externalise its response to asylum through the so-called 'Pacific solution' (Maley, 2003; Rajaram, 2003). There was much interest – stimulated by the UK – in Australian-style extra-territorial processing of asylum claims. There are also important parallels between boundary build-up and the EU's 'fight against illegal immigration' and similar processes evident at the US–Mexico border, not the least of which is the shocking loss of life at both of these international borders of inequality (Cornelius, 2001; Nevins, 2002).

Boundary build-up and boundary shift are thus not unique to Europe. They represent new phases in the pursuit of territorially focused strategies to achieve security, based, of course, on a particular understanding of the relationship between migration and security. As external strategies, they are closely linked to organisational and conceptual borders of work, welfare, belonging and entitlement, which play a key role in defining the relationship between Europe and international migration as Europe makes sense of itself and seeks to make sense of complex international migration flows.

Conclusion

This chapter has completed the analysis of EU migration and asylum policy by exploring the growing importance of an external dimension that seeks to export key elements of EU migration and asylum priorities to new and non-EU member states. A variety of processes and mechanisms have been identified that show how this has occurred and the kinds of measures that have been transferred, as well as some of the difficulties that the EU has experienced. The chapter has also explored the underlying framing of the issues to pinpoint an EU pre-occupation with border controls and action against unwanted forms of migration. This pre-occupation has made it more difficult to attain the EU's objective of integrating migration issues within relations with non-EU states. The chapter made a broad distinction between phase 1 development, which was linked to enlargement and where EU leverage has been most evident, because of the carrot of membership, and phase 2 development, linked to the elaboration of a concept of 'neighbourhood' (and through that to transit and sending countries), where action has been more problematic, because of both the content of policy (the security focus) and the leverage problems. Phase 1 has seen intra-EU migration become a major policy concern, with the supposed virtues of intra-EU migration encountering a hostility linked to perceptions of adverse welfare state and labour market effects. A particularly significant issue in phase 2 has been the absence of EU competencies for legal migration channels, which are integral to the relationship between migration and development.

The conceptualisation, location and operation of borders have been central to this book's analysis. Similarly, the moving of Europe's borders is central to this chapter's focus on the external dimension of EU action. Through this intensification of external action, we also see how the EU is developing forms of international migration relations that are complex because of the range of issues and countries involved, but that highlight the interplay between the internal and external governance of migration and the capacity of the EU as a powerful regional presence to shape perceptions of what is 'normal' in the international politics of migration. This extends the moral and practical resonance of the discussion of migration far beyond the domestic political realm and locates it squarely in debate about global justice and the international or global governance of migration.

Notes

1 Council Regulation (EC) No. 2007/2004, of 26 October 2004, establishing a European Agency for the Management of Operational Cooperation at the External Borders of the Member States of the European Union, *Official Journal*, L349, 25 November 2004, pp. 1–11.
2 European Council, Copenhagen, Conclusions of the Presidency, 21–22 June 1993.
3 Council of the EU, *A Strategy for the External Dimension of JHA: Global Freedom, Security and Justice*, 14366/3/05, REV 3 LIMITE JAI 417, RELEX 628, 30 November 2005.
4 Council of the EU, High Level Working Group on Migration and Asylum: Draft Action Plan for Albania and the Neighbouring Region, 7886/1/00, REV 1, LIMITE JAI 40 AG 41, 6 June 2000.
5 Council of the EU, *High Level Working Group on Migration and Asylum: Adoption of the Report to the European Council in Nice*, 13993/00 LIMITE JAI 152, AG 76.
6 *Ibid.*: 5.
7 *Ibid.*: 4.
8 Council of the EU, Communication from the Commission to the Council and the EP: Integrating migration issues in the European Union's relations with third countries, Draft Council conclusions on migration and development, 8927/03 LIMITE, DEVGEN 59, RELEX 160, JAI 123, ASIM 25, 5 May 2003.
9 Council of the EU, Regulation (EC) No. 491/2004 of the EP and of the Council, of 10 March 2004, establishing a programme for financial and technical assistance to third countries in the areas of migration and asylum (AENEAS), *Official Journal*, L080, 18 March 2004, pp. 1–5.

9

Conclusion

Migration in context

This book has placed the development of EU migration and asylum policy and politics in the context of broader patterns of European integration dating back more than 50 years. It has shown that it does now make sense to analyse a common EU migration and asylum policy, albeit with a partial policy framework (one covering some but not all aspects of policy). This has occurred in a wider Europe that now comprises 27 countries, with a total population of more than 500 million. The implications of these developments are wide-reaching and of great significance to our understanding both of responses to international migration and of the EU as a regional organisation with important effects on the politics both of its member states and of neighbouring states. The developments are complex, not least because they tend to be couched in the rather particular language that the EU has evolved to describe itself. Indeed, it can be difficult to disentangle the mass of activity from the broader setting within which these developments have occurred. The task of this concluding chapter is to attempt to locate the development of EU migration and asylum policy in its broader setting. To do this, this conclusion will focus on the constitutive elements of the European governance of migration, on the remaking of European migration politics and policy, on the motives for and form taken by EU policy (the why and how), and on the making and remaking of Europe's borders.

The European governance of migration

While international migration may typically be processed as a domestic concern, this book has demonstrated that the societal and international issues that simultaneously underpin it have generated significant interdependencies within the EU. These interdependencies have been intensified by the links between migration and asylum and other elements of the European project, particularly economic integration and the development of an internal security field. The result has been the emergence of a complex, multi-level field of social and political action around migration and asylum. This action cannot be understood in terms of some supranational versus intergovernmental dichotomy, as though it can be reduced to a discussion of whether the member states or supranational institutions are in charge. While it is accurate to note that member states have been to the fore in co-operation and integration thus far, they have developed new ways of working together for more than 30 years on internal security and, during the last 10 years or so, have begun to legislate at EU level on migration and asylum issues. This book has argued (*pace* Wallace, 2005) that this amounts to the consolidation of networks of transgovernmental action on migration and asylum. More particularly, it has shown that these networks serve to link more informal sources of social and political action to more formally constituted and institutionalised forms of action on migration and asylum, within what has been characterised as the Brussels 'field'. This has been particularly significant in the development of migration and asylum policy because of the co-operation that occurred *around* rather than *within* formal Treaty structures. Variously referred to as a 'wining and dining culture' or as 'laboratories' for the development of later EU action, the growth, development and consolidation of these networks are an integral component of the story that has been told in this book. More particularly, the European governance of migration has been particularly focused on the binding of freedom and security as the EU sought to realise free movement objectives in a frontier-free and wider Europe. Security agencies – and the kinds of expertise they were able to mobilise – were the dominant players in the development of the EU policy field, although other actors, such as pro-migrant NGOs, have sought to make their voices – or their expertise – heard too. Indeed, it was shown that the mobilisation of expertise has been a key constitutive element of the migration and asylum policy field at EU level.

The growth and consolidation of networks of action and the mobilisation of expertise have contributed to a European governance of migration, but there are two senses of this term, both of which can help us think about the *Europeanness* of this EU action. The first is the way in which action has been focused on particular types of EU process and output. Here there can be little doubt that there is a unique form of supranational regional integration occurring, with major implications for migration and asylum, that is without parallel anywhere else in the world (there is no other international organisation like the EU). The second is the way in which EU action differs from that seen in other parts of the world. Here the argument of the book was that there are actually interesting parallels between what has been happening in Europe and what has been happening in similar states elsewhere. If the USA has been involved in its own 'fight' against illegal immigration that mimics in some senses that seen in the EU, or if Australia has been seeking to externalise its response to asylum, then to what extent is the EU's action distinctly *European*? The argument was that the EU has engaged in forms of boundary build-up that are similar to those seen in comparable states in other parts of the world, in seeking to manage the tensions between increased openness to flows of goods, services and capital, but relative closure to the movement of people (Nevins, 2002). A key difference in Europe, however, is that boundary build-up has been accompanied by major boundary shifts as the EU widened to include 12 new member states and more than 130 million people between 1995 and 2007. Moreover, enlargement moved the EU closer to major migrant-sending countries and regions, and meant that Europe's borders became more pronounced international borders of inequality, which reveal the ethical and practical dilemmas at the heart of 'managed migration'.

The remaking of European migration politics and policy

The implications of a wider Europe have been integral to this book. While too much can be made of newness and novelty – at the expense of broader contextual factors – it is the case that much has changed in European migration politics and that these changes have played a major part in the development of EU action. It is now the case that all 27 EU member states are sending, receiving and/or transit countries (usually a combination of all three). This geo-political widening of migration means that analyses of European migration politics cannot focus on a small group of 'older' immigration countries in north-west Europe. The core dilemmas of EU migration and asylum policy are often to be found on the EU's eastern and southern borders. In addition to this, there has been a conceptual widening of migration politics and policy in response to ostensibly new migration flows that challenge systems for the control and regulation of migration. The word 'ostensibly' was used because this book has shown how processes of categorisation are central elements of state responses to migration. The closing of the door to lower-skilled migration may well have induced an increase in irregular/illegal flows. It may, then, be the labels and categories that have changed, rather than the motives for migration. These 'widenings' have been accompanied by the relocation of some elements of the policy response to EU level, in the form of the European governance of migration assessed just above. There has also been a renewed openness to labour migration, made evident by the recruitment of foreign workers across the EU in the face of demographic and labour market changes. This has been far from uncontroversial and has contributed to the increased political salience of migration (from both within and outside the EU). Again, while ostensibly new, the core challenge remains a perennial element of migration policy: how to strike a balance between openness and closure or, as Zolberg (1989) put it, to construct walls while leaving small doors open in these walls. This dilemma is not new; what is new is the context within which EU member states address it.

Why and how

Thus far in this concluding chapter, a great deal of emphasis has been laid on the distinct features of the EU as a unique form of regional governance with supranational elements that distinguish it from any other international organisation. This underpins some elements of novelty in the form taken by the European governance and politics of migration. This book has also tried to develop a better understanding of why and how EU member states have sought co-operation and integration in the areas of migration and asylum policy.

In terms of 'why', the answer given was that EU member states have been keen to use the EU as an alternative arena in which to resolve troubling or difficult domestic issues, while also potentially increasing their capacity to deal with these issues by working together rather than alone. In this sense, EU action on migration and asylum does not mark the end of state sovereignty in Europe or signify that EU states have 'lost control'. Rather, it can be seen as part of a more general orientation of European integration towards the sustenance of core state functions, in this instance to regulate access to territory through the development of EU co-operation and integration. National sovereignty has not ended, but it has changed. It was also seen that the executive-dominated form of EU action on migration and asylum minimises the scope for involvement by judicial and legislative authority at both national and EU level. The result could be seen as an 'escape to Europe', whereby national actors see Europe as an arena that allows national executives a freer reign over migration and asylum. This book has argued that while this view offers a powerful interpretation of events, it tends to give a rather partial account of European integration. Or, put another way, it offers an explanation for the spatial relocation of decision-making to EU level, but has less to say about the subsequent potential for temporal shift as EU competencies accrue over time and the scope increases for EU-level legal and political action to affect domestic political systems. This points to the relevance of the Europeanisation of migration and asylum, which is not a theme that has been to the fore in this book. That said, the significant developments of the last 10 years or so do create real scope for EU migration and asylum policy to penetrate domestic systems, with effects on both the regulation of migration and the integration of migrants.

This leads us to the 'how' question, which points us in the direction of exploring the types of measures that the EU has adopted. First of all, it is important to note the rapid pace of EU development. In less than 10 years there has been a mass of legal outputs, which, taken together, can be seen as constituting a common EU migration and asylum policy. When we explore these measures in more detail, two points become particularly apparent. First, EU action has been strongly focused on co-operation and integration to reduce or minimise the scope for those forms of migration defined as unwanted by state and EU policies, particularly asylum-seeking migration and irregular/illegal immigration. The EU has thus far been unable to develop a common approach to admissions policy, although that does not mean that it will not be able to do so. Second, there is a growing concern within EU policy to elaborate a common approach to the integration of migrants, one that makes some reference to the perceived capacity of migrants to integrate. This was evident in the directives on the rights of long-term residents and family reunion. Thought about another way, the fact that we now discuss the content of EU measures relating to such core issues as the rights and status of TCNs is a measure of how far EU migration and asylum policy has come.

The making and remaking of Europe's borders

The consideration of why and how EU member states have co-operated and, in some areas, integrated leads to the final issue addressed by this book, namely the effects of this action. At this point we can return to the core question posed in this book's introduction: how have changed border relationships within and between EU member states shaped understandings of and responses to international migration? Territorial, organisational and conceptual borders were identified as those sites at which the relationship between European societies and migrant newcomers is mediated. This allowed free movement, extra-EU migration and asylum policy to be linked to strategies of territorial management and population control, as well as broader changes in labour markets and welfare states across the EU and notions of entitlement, identity and belonging. It also allowed domestic change to be linked to regional integration and to the broader patterns of complex international interdependency within which the EU and its member states are embedded. The core argument here is that the 'internal' and 'external' governance of migration are closely connected. If we are to understand the current trends towards 'externalisation' of migration and asylum, then it is also necessary to understand the relation of external governance to free movement within the common market, to the creation of the single market, to the elaboration of a common approach to migration and asylum after the Maastricht Treaty and to the development of common policies after the Amsterdam Treaty. Internal and external governance are linked because the export of EU measures on migration and asylum has been predicated on the maintenance of Europe's organisational and conceptual borders in all their diversity. This can help explain the action that has occurred as well as its limits, and can also help to locate it within the much bigger picture of economic and political integration more generally. This reaffirms a point made throughout this book, that we should not see international migration in all its diversity as some kind of external challenge to the EU, but as integrally connected to the European state system, to the EU as a manifestation of both the transformation and the continuing power of that state system, and thus to fundamental questions about the EU's identity as a regional organisation. The contemporary European challenge is for the EU to make sense of itself; in doing so, it may make sense of migration and this, in turn, may help it to define its relations with the rest of the world.

Bibliography

Abell, N. A. (1999) 'The compatibility of readmission agreements with the 1951 refugee convention relating to the status of refugees', *International Journal of Refugee Law*, 11(1): 60–83.

Adinolfi, A. (2005) 'Free movement and access to work of citizens of the new member states: the transitional measures', *Common Market Law Review*, 42(2): 469–98.

Alexander, W. (1992) 'Free movement of non-EC nationals: a review of the case law of the Court of Justice', *European Journal of International Law*, 3(1): 53–64.

Anderson, B. (2000) *Doing the Dirty Work: The Global Politics of Domestic Labour*, London: Zed Books.

Anderson, M. (2004) *Frontiers: Territory and State Formation in the Modern World*, Cambridge: Polity.

Anderson, M. and E. Bort (2001) *The Frontiers of Europe*, Basingstoke: Palgrave Macmillan.

Bade, K. (2003) *Migration in European History*, Oxford: Blackwell.

Badie, B. (1995) *La Fin des Territoires: Essai sur le Désordre International et sur le Utilité Social de Respect*, Paris: Fayard.

Baganha, M. (ed.) (1997) *Immigration in Southern Europe*, Oeiras: Celta Editora.

Baldwin-Edwards, M. (1991) 'The socio-political rights of migrants in the European Community', in G. Room (ed.), *Towards a European Welfare State?*, Bristol: School for Advanced Urban Studies, pp. 189–234.

Baldwin-Edwards, M. (1997) 'The emerging European immigration regime: some reflections on implications for southern Europe', *Journal of Common Market Studies*, 35(4): 497–520.

Baldwin-Edwards, M. and J. Arango (1999) *Immigrants and the Informal Economy in Southern Europe*, London: Frank Cass.

Baldwin-Edwards, M. and M. Schain (eds) (1994) *The Politics of Immigration in Western Europe*, London: Frank Cass.

Bank, R. (1998) 'The emergent EU policy on asylum and refugees', paper presented to the European Forum on International Migrations, European University Institute, Florence, 22 January.

Banting, K. (1995) 'The welfare state as statecraft: territorial politics and social policy', in S. Liebfried and P. Pierson (eds), *European Social Policy: Between Integration and Fragmentation*, Washington, DC: Brookings Institution, pp. 269–300.

Beyers, J. (2005) 'Multiple embeddedness and socialization in Europe', *International Organization*, 59 (fall): 899–936.

Bicchi, F. (2007) *European Foreign Policy-Making Towards the Mediterranean*, New York: Palgrave.

Bieber, R. (1994) 'Links between the third pillar (Title VI) and the European Community (Title II) of the Treaty on European Union', in J. Monar and R. Morgan (eds), *The Third Pillar of the European Union*, Brussels: European Interuniversity Press, pp. 37–47.

Bigo, D. (1996) *Polices en réseaux, l'expérience Européene*, Paris: Presses de la Fondation Nationales des Sciences Politiques.

Bigo, D. (2001) 'Migration and security', in C. Joppke and V. Guiraudon (eds), *Controlling a New Migration World*, London: Routledge.

Bigo, D. and R. Leveau (1992) *L'Europe de la sécurité intérieure*, Paris: Institut des Hautes Etudes de Sécurité Intérieure.

Boelaert, S. (2005) 'Non-EU nationals and Council Directive 2003/109/EC on the status of TCNs who are long-term residents: five paces forward and possibly three paces back', *Common Market Law Review*, 42(4): 1011–52.

Bogusz, B., R. Cholewinski, A. Cygan and E. Szyszczak (eds) (2004) *Irregular Migration and Human Rights: Theoretical, European and International Perspectives*, Leiden: Martinus Nijhoff.

Bommes, M. and A. Geddes (eds) (2000) *Welfare and Immigration: Challenging the Borders of the Welfare State*, London: Routledge.

Boswell, C. (2003) 'The external dimension of EU immigration and asylum policy', *International Affairs*, 79(3): 619–38.

Bourdieu, P. (1993) 'Esprits d'états', *Actes de la Recherche en Sciences Sociales*, 96–97 (March): 49–62.

British Council (2004) *European Civic Citizenship and Inclusion Index*, Brussels: British Council.

Brubaker, R. (1992) *Citizenship and Nationhood in France and Germany*, Cambridge, MA: Harvard University Press.

Brunsson, N. (1993) 'Ideas and actions: justification and hypocrisy as alternatives to control', *Accounting, Organizations and Society*, 18(6): 489–506.

Brunsson, N. (2002) *The Organization of Hypocrisy: Talk, Decisions and Actions in Organizations* (2nd edition), Chichester: Wiley.

Brym, R. (1991) 'The emigration potential of Russia and Lithuania: recent survey results', *Innovation*, 3(4): 29–32.

Buller, J. and A. Gamble (2002) 'Conceptualising Europeanisation', *Public Policy and Administration*, 17(2): 4–24.

Bunyan, T. (1991) 'Towards an authoritarian European state', *Race and Class*, 32(3): 19–27.

Byrne, R. (2003) 'Harmonisation and burden redistribution in the two Europes', *Journal of Refugee Studies*, 16(3): 336–59.

Byrne, R., G. Noll and J. Vedsted-Hansen (2003) *New Asylum Countries? Migration Control and Refugee Protection in an Enlarged European Union*, Leiden: Brill.

Calavita, K. (1994) 'Italy and the new immigration', in W. Cornelius, P. Martin and J. Hollifield (eds), *Controlling Immigration: A Global Perspective*, Stanford, CA: Stanford University Press, pp. 303–26.

Callovi, G. (1992) 'Regulation of immigration in 1993: pieces of the European Community jig-saw puzzle', *International Migration Review*, 26(2): 353–72.

Canovan, M. (1999) 'Populism and the two faces of democracy', *Political Studies*, 47(1): 2–16.

Caporaso, J. (1996) 'The European Union and forms of state: Westphalian, regulatory or post-modern?', *Journal of Common Market Studies*, 34(1): 29–52.

Carrera, S. (2005) 'What does free movement mean in theory and practice in an enlarged EU?', *European Law Journal*, 11(6): 699–721.

Carrera, S. and F. Geyer (2007) *The Reform Treaty and Justice and Home Affairs: Implications for the Common Area of Freeedom, Security and Justice*, Brussels: Centre for European Policy Studies.

Castles, S. and G. Kosack (1973) *Immigrant Workers and Class Structure in Western Europe*, Oxford: Oxford University Press.

Castles, S. and M. Miller (2003) *The Age of Migration* (3rd edition), London: Macmillan.

Castles, S., H. Booth and T. Wallace (1984) *Here for Good: Western Europe's New Ethnic Minorities*, London: Pluto Press.

CEC (Commission of the European Communities) (1977) *Freedom of Movement for Workers Within the Community*, Brussels: Office for the Official Publications of the European Community (OOPEC).

CEC (1984) *Commission Report on the Implementation of Directive 77/486*, COM (84) 54 final, Brussels: CEC.

CEC (1985a) *White Paper on the Completion of the Internal Market*, COM (85) 310 final, Brussels: CEC.

CEC (1985b) *Guidelines for a Community Policy on Migration*, COM (85) 48 final, Brussels: CEC.

CEC (1988a) *Communication on a People's Europe*, COM (88) 331 final, Brussels: CEC.

CEC (1988b) *Communication on the Abolition of Controls of Persons at Intra-Community Borders*, COM (88) 310 final, Brussels: CEC.

CEC (1990) *Policies on Immigration and the Social Integration of Migrants in the EC, Expert's Report Drawn Up on Behalf of the Commission of the European Communities*, SEC (90) 1813, Brussels: CEC.

CEC (1991) *Communication on Immigration*, COM (94) 596 final, Brussels: CEC.

CEC (1993) *Proposal for a Decision Based on Article K3 of the Treaty on European Union Establishing a Convention on the Crossing of the External Frontiers of the Member States*, COM (3) 684 final, Brussels: CEC.

CEC (1994a) *Communication on Immigration and Asylum Policies*, COM (94) 23 final, Brussels: CEC.

CEC (1994b) *Report on the Education of Migrant Workers' Children in the European Union*, COM (94) 80 final, Brussels: CEC.

CEC (1994c) *European Social Policy: A Way Forward for the Union*, COM (94) 333 final, Brussels: CEC.

CEC (1995a) *Commission Report for the Reflection Group*, Luxembourg: OOPEC.

CEC (1995b) *Communication from the Commission on Racism, Xenophobia and Anti-Semitism and Proposal for a Council Decision Designating 1997 as European Year Against Racism*, COM (95) 653 final, Brussels: CEC.

CEC (1996) *Commission Opinion: Reinforcing Political Union and Preparing for Enlargement*, COM (96) 90 final, Brussels: CEC.

CEC (1997a) *An Action Plan for Free Movement of Workers. Communication from the Commission*, COM (97) 586 final, Brussels: CEC.

CEC (1997b) *Proposal for a Joint Decision on a Joint Action Adopted by the Council Introducing a Programme of Training, Exchanges and Co-operation in the Field of Asylum, Immigration and Crossing of External Borders*, COM (97) 364 final, Brussels: CEC.

CEC (1997c) *Proposal to the Council for a Joint Action Based on Article K.3(2)(b) of the Treaty on European Union Concerning Temporary Protection for Displaced Persons*, COM (97) 93 final, Brussels: CEC.

CEC (1997d) *Proposal for a Decision on Establishing a Convention on Rules for the Admission of TCNs to the Member States of the European Union*, COM (97) 387 final, Brussels: CEC.

CEC (2002) *Communication: Integrating Migration Issues in the European Union's Relations with Third Countries COM(2002) 703 final*, Brussels: CEC.

CEC (2003a) *Communication: The Implementation of Directive 96/71/EC in the Member States*, COM(2003) 458 final, Brussels: CEC.

CEC (2003b) *Reference Document for Financial and Technical Assistance to Third Countries in the Area of Migration and Asylum AENEAS Programme 2004–2006*, http://ec.europa.eu/europeaid/projects/eidhr/pdf/themes-migration-annexe2_en.pdf, accessed 24 March 2007.

CEC (2003c) *Communication. A More Efficient Common European Asylum System: The Single Procedure as the Next Step*, COM(2004) 503 final, Brussels: CEC.

CEC (2003d) *Communciation: On Regional Protection Programmes*, COM(2005) 388 final, Brussels: CEC.

CEC (2003e) *Communication: Wider Europe – Neighbourhood: A New Framework for Relations with Our Eastern and Southern Neighbours*, COM(2003) 104 final, Brussels: CEC.

CEC (2003f) *Staff Working Paper: Intensified Co-operation on the Management of Migration Flows with Third Countries. Report by the Commission's Services on the Implementation of the Council Conclusions on Intensified Co-operation on the Management of Migration Flows with Third Countries of 18 November 2002*, SEC (2003) 815, Brussels: CEC.

CEC (2004) *European Neighbourhood Policy: Strategy Paper*, COM(2004) 373 final, Brussels: CEC.

CEC (2005a) *Proposal for a Regulation of the EP and of the Council on Community Statistics on Migration and International Protection*, COM(2005) 375 final, Brussels: CEC.

CEC (2005b) *Communication: A Common Agenda for Integration*, COM (2005) 389 final, Brussels: CEC.

CEC (2005c) *Policy Plan on Legal Migration*, 21 December, Brussels: CEC.

CEC (2005d) *Green Paper on an EU Approach to Managing Economic Migration*, COM(2005) 0811 final.

CEC (2006a) *Communication. On Strengthened Practical Co-operation, New Structures, New Approaches: Improving the Quality of Decision-Making in the Common European Asylum System*, COM(2006) 67 final, Brussels: CEC.

CEC (2006b) *Communication. Policy Priorities in the Fight Against Illegal Immigration*, COM(2006) 402 final, Brussels: CEC.

CEC (2006c) *Communication. The Application of Directive 2000/43/EC of 29 June 2000 Implementing the Principle of Equal Treatment Between Persons Irrespective of Racial or Ethnic Origin*, COM(2006) 643 final, Brussels: CEC.

CEC (2006d) *Communication. Strengthened Practical Co-operation. New Structures New Approaches: Improving the Quality of Decision-Making in the European Asylum System*, SEC (2006) 67 final, Brussels: CEC.

CEC (2007) *Communication. On Circular Migration and Mobility Partnerships Between the European Union and Third Countries*, COM(2007) 248 final, Brussels: CEC.

Cecchini, P. (1988) *The European Challenge 1992: The Benefits of a Single Market*, Aldershot: Wildwood House.

Cerny, P. (1990) *The Changing Architecture of Politics: Structure, Agency and the Future of the State*, London: Sage.

Checkel, J. (2005) 'International institutions and socialization in Europe: introduction and framework', *International Organization*, 59 (fall): 801–26.

Closa, C. (1995) 'Citizenship of the Union and nationality of the member states', *Common Market Law Review*, 32(2): 487–518.

Codagnone, C. (1999) 'The new migration in Russia in the 1990s', in K. Koser and H. Lutz (eds), *The New Migration in Europe: Social Constructions and Social Realities*, London: Macmillan, pp. 38–59.

Cohen, M., J. March and J. Olsen (1972) 'A garbage can model of organisational choice', *Administrative Science Quarterly*, 17(1): 1–25.

Cornelius, W. (1994) 'Spain: the uneasy transition from labor exporter to labor importer', in W. Cornelius, P. Martin and J. Hollifield (eds), *Controlling Immigration: A Global Perspective*, Stanford, CA: Stanford University Press, pp. 331–69.

Cornelius, W. (2001) 'Death at the border: efficacy and unintended consequences of US immigration control policy', *Population and Development Review*, 27(4): 661–85.

Cornelius, W., P. Martin and J. Hollifield (1994) 'Introduction: the ambivalent quest for immigration control', in W. Cornelius, P. Martin and J. Hollifield (eds), *Controlling Immigration: A Global Perspective*, Stanford, CA: Stanford University Press, pp. 3–41.

Cram, L. (1994) 'The European Commission as a multi-organization: social policy and IT policy in the EU', *Journal of European Public Policy*, 1(2): 195–217.

Crossick, S., M. Kohnstamm and J. Pinder (1997) 'The Treaty of Amsterdam', in *Challenge Europe: Making Sense of the Amsterdam Treaty*, Brussels: European Policy Centre, pp. 1–4.

Danese, G. (1998) 'Transnational collective action in Europe: the case of migrants in Italy and Spain', *Journal of Ethnic and Migration Studies*, 24(4): 715–34.

Dawson, R. and K. Prewitt (1969) *Political Socialization*, Boston, MA: Little Brown.

Delors, J., et al. (Committee for the Study of Economic and Monetary Union) (1989) *Report on Economic and Monetary Union in the EC*, Luxembourg: OOPEC.

den Boer, M. (1996) 'Justice and home affairs: co-operation without integration', in H. Wallace and W. Wallace (eds), *Policy-Making in the European Union*, Oxford: Oxford University Press, pp. 389–409.

den Boer, M. (1998) *Taming the Third Pillar. Improving the Management of Justice and Home Affairs Co-operation in the EU*, Maastricht: European Institute for Public Administration.

Donnan, H. and T. Wilson (1999) *Borders: Frontiers of Identity, Nation and State*, Oxford: Berg.

Duff, A. (1994) 'The main reforms', in A. Duff, J. Pinder and R. Pryce (eds), *Maastricht and Beyond: Building the European Union*, London: Routledge, pp. 19–35.

Dunsire, A. (1978) *Implementation in a Bureaucracy*, Oxford: Martin Robertson.

ECRE (European Council on Refugees and Exiles) (1997a) *Comments from ECRE on the Proposal of the European Commission Concerning Temporary Protection of Displaced Persons*, Brussels: ECRE.

ECRE (1997b) *Position of ECRE on Temporary Protection in the Context of the Need for a Supplementary Refugee Definition*, Brussels: ECRE.

ECRE (1997c) *Position on the Functioning of the Treaty on European Union in Relation to Asylum Policy*, Brussels: ECRE.

ECRE (1997d) *Analysis of the Treaty of Amsterdam in so far as it Relates to Asylum Policy*, Brussels: ECRE.

Ehlermann, H-D. (1998) *Differentiation, Flexibility, Closer Co-operation: The New Provisions of the Amsterdam Treaty*, Working Papers of the Robert Schuman Centre, Florence: European University Institute.

Eichenhofer, E. (ed.) (1997) *Social Security of Migrants in the European Union of Tomorrow*, Osnabrück: Universitätsverslag.

Entzinger, H. (1985) 'The Netherlands', in T. Hammar (ed.), *European Immigration Policy: A Comparative Study*, Cambridge: Cambridge University Press.

EP (European Parliament) (1985) *Report of the Committee of Inquiry into the Rise of Fascism and Racism in Europe*, Brussels: OOPEC.

EP (1991) *Report of the Committee of Inquiry on Racism and Xenophobia*, Brussels: OOPEC.

EP (1998) *EU Anti-Discrimination Policy: From Equal Opportunities Between Men and Women to Combating Racism*, Research Working Document, Public Liberties Series LIBE 102, Brussels: EP Directorate General.

EUMF (European Union Migrants' Forum) (1996) *Proposals for the Revision of the Treaty on European Union at the Intergovernmental Conference 1996*, Brussels: EUMF.

European Council Consultative Commission on Racism and Xenophobia (1995) *Final Report*, ref. 6906/1/95, Rev 1 Limite Raxen, Brussels: General Secretariat of the European Council.

Faist, T. (2000) *The Volume and Dynamics of International Migration and Transnational Social Spaces*, Oxford: Oxford University Press.

Faist, T. and A. Ette (eds) (2007) *The Europeanization of National Policies and Politics of Immigration: Between Autononmy and the European Union*, Basingstoke: Palgrave Macmillan.

Favell, A. (1998) 'The Europeanisation of immigration politics', *European Integration On-Line Papers*, 2(10), http://eiop.or.at/eiop/texte/1998-010a.htm.

Favell, A. and A. Geddes (2000) 'Immigration and European integration: new opportunities for transnational mobilisation', in P. Statham and R. Koopmans (eds), *Challenging and Defending the Fortress: Political Mobilisation over Ethnic Difference in Comparative and Transnational Perspective*, Oxford: Oxford University Press.

Ferrera, M. (2005) *The Boundaries of Welfare: European Integration and the New Spatial Politics of Social Protection*, Oxford: Oxford University Press.

Fligstein, N. and I. Mara-Drita (1996) 'How to make a market: reflections on the European Union's single market programme', *American Journal of Sociology*, 102(1): 1–33.

Flora, P. (1986) 'Introduction', in P. Flora (ed.), *Growth to Limits: The Western European Welfare States Since World War Two. Volume I: Sweden, Norway, Finland and Denmark*, Berlin: De Gruyter, pp. vii–xxxvi.

Foreign and Commonwealth Office (1996) *A Partnership Among Nations*, London: FCO.

Fortescue, A. (1995) 'Opening statement', in S. Perrakis (ed.), *Immigration and European Union: Building on a Comprehensive Approach*, Athens: Sakkoulas, pp. 7–39.

Foucault, M. (1979) *Discipline and Punish: The Birth of the Prison*, New York: Vintage Books.

Foucault, M. (1991) 'Governmentality', in G. Burchell, C. Gordon and P. Miller (eds), *The Foucault Effect*, Hemel Hempstead: Harvester Wheatsheaf, pp. 87–104.

Franklin, N., M. Marsh and L. McLaren (1994) 'Uncorking the bottle: popular opposition to European unification in the wake of Maastricht', *Journal of Common Market Studies*, 18(3): 101–17.

Freeman, G. (1986) 'Migration and the political economy of the welfare state', *Annals of the American Academy of Social and Political Sciences*, 485(1): 51–63.

Freeman, G. (1995) 'Modes of immigration politics in liberal democratic states', *International Migration Review*, 29(4): 881–902.

Freeman, G. (1998) 'The decline of sovereignty: politics and immigration restriction in liberal states', in C. Joppke (eds), *Challenge to the Nation State: Immigration in Western Europe and the United States*, Oxford: Oxford University Press.

Geddes, A. (1995) 'Immigrant and ethnic minorities and the EU's "democratic deficit"', *Journal of Common Market Studies*, 33(2): 197–217.

Geddes, A. (2003) *The Politics of Migration and Immigration in Europe*, London: Sage.

Geddes, A. (2005a) 'Europe's border relationships and international migration relations', *Journal of Common Market Studies*, 43(4): 787–806.

Geddes, A. (2005b) 'Getting the best of both worlds: Britain, the EU and migration policy', *International Affairs*, 81(4): 723–40.

Geddes, A. (2006) 'The politics of domestic order', in K.-E. Jorgensen, M. Pollack and B. Rosamond (eds), *The Handbook of European Union Politics*, London: Sage.

Geddes, A. (2007) 'The Europeanisation of what? Migration and the politics of European integration', in T. Faist and A. Ette (eds), *The Europeanization of National Policies and Politics of Immigration: Between Autonomy and the European Union*, London: Palgrave, pp. 49–70.

Geddes, A. (2008) '*Il rombo dei cannoni?* Immigration and the centre-right in Italy', *Journal of European Public Policy*, 15(3): 349–66.

Geddes, A. and A. Favell (eds) (2004) *The Politics of Belonging: Migrants and Minorities in Contemporary Europe*, Aldershot: Ashgate.

Geddes, A. and V. Guiraudon (2004) 'Britain and France and EU anti-discrimination policy: the emergence of an EU policy paradigm', *West European Politics*, 27(2): 334–53.

Gilpin, R. (1987) *The Political Economy of International Relations*, Princeton, NJ: Princeton University Press.

Glassner, M. (1993) *Political Geography*, London: Wiley.

Goodwin-Gill, G. (1996) *The Refugee in International Law* (2nd edition), Oxford: Oxford University Press.

Green, S. (2004) *The Politics of Exclusion: Institutions and Immigration Policy in Contemporary Germany*, Manchester: Manchester University Press.

Groenendijk, K. (2004) 'Legal concepts of integration in EU migration law', *European Journal of Migration and Law*, 6(2): 111–26.

Guild, E. (1992) *Protecting Migrants' Rights: Application of EC Agreements with Third Countries*, Briefing Paper No. 10, Brussels: Churches Commission for Migrants in Europe.

Guild, E. (1998) 'Competence, discretion and TCNs: the European Union's legal struggle with migration', *Journal of Ethnic and Migration Studies*, 24(4): 613–26.

Guild, E. (2001) *Moving the Borders of Europe*, inaugural lecture, May 2001, Nijmegen: Catholic University of Nijmegen.

Guild, E. and J. Niessen (1996) *The Developing Immigration and Asylum Policies of the European Union: Adopted Conventions, Resolutions, Recommendations and Conclusions*, Den Haag: Kluwer Law International.

Guiraudon, V. (1997) *Policy Change Behind Gilded Doors: Explaining the Evolution of Aliens' Rights in France, Germany and the Netherlands, 1974–94*, PhD thesis, Harvard University.

Guiraudon, V. (1998) *International Human Rights Norms and Their Incorporation: The Protection of Aliens in Europe*, Working Paper No. 98/4, Florence: European University Institute.

Guiraudon, V. (2000) 'The Marshallian triptych reordered: the role of courts and bureaucracies in furthering migrant social rights', in M. Bommes and A. Geddes (eds), *Welfare and Migration: Challenging the Borders of the Welfare State*, London: Routledge, pp. 72–89.

Guiraudon, V. (2001) 'European integration and migration policy: vertical policy-making as venue shopping', *Journal of Common Market Studies*, 27(2): 334–53.

Guiraudon, V. (2003) 'The constitution of a European immigration policy domain: a political sociology approach', *Journal of European Public Policy*, 10(2): 263–82.

Guiraudon, V. and G. Lahav (2000) 'A reappraisal of the state sovereignty debate: the case of migration control', *Comparative Political Studies*, 33(2): 163–95.

Hailbronner, K. (2004) 'Asylum law in the context of a European migration policy', in N. Walker (ed.), *Europe's Area of Freedom, Security and Justice*, Oxford: Oxford University Press, pp. 41–88.

Hammar, T. (ed.) (1985) *European Immigration Policy: A Comparative Study*, Cambridge: Cambridge University Press.

Hammar, T., G. Brochmann, K. Tamas and T. Faist (1997) *International Migration, Immobility and Development: Multidisciplinary Perspectives*, Oxford: Berg.

Handoll, A. (1995) *Free Movement of Persons in the EU*, Chichester: Wiley.

Hansen, R. (2000) *Citizenship and Immigration in Britain*, Oxford: Oxford University Press.

Hansen, R. (2002) 'Globalization, embedded realism, and path dependence: the other immigrants to Europe', *Comparative Political Studies*, 35(3): 259–83.

Hantrais, L. (1995) *Social Policy in the European Union*, Basingstoke: Macmillan.

Hargreaves, A. (1995) *Immigration, 'Race' and Ethnicity in Contemporary France*, London: Routledge.

Hartley, T. (1978) 'The internal scope of the EEC immigration provisions', *European Law Review*, 3(2): 191–207.

Heisler, M. (1992) 'Migration, international relations and the New Europe: theoretical perspectives from institutional political sociology', *International Migration Review*, 26(2): 596–622.

Heitman, S. (1991) 'Soviet emigration in 1990: a new fourth wave?', *Innovation*, 3(4): 1–15.

Hix, S. and J. Niessen (1996) *Reconsidering European Migration Policies: The 1996 Intergovernmental Conference and the Reform of the Maastricht Treaty*, Brussels: Churches Committee for Migrants in Europe.

Hoffmann, S. (1966) 'Obstinate or obsolete? The fate of the nation state and the case of Western Europe', *Daedalus*, 95: 892–908.

Hoffmann-Nowotny, H-J. (1985) 'Switzerland', in T. Hammar (ed.), *European Immigration Policy: A Comparative Study*, Cambridge: Cambridge University Press.

Hollifield, J. (1992) *Immigrants, Markets and States: The Political Economy of Post-War Europe*, Cambridge, MA: Cambridge University Press.

Hollifield, J. (2004) 'The emerging migration state', *International Migration Review*, 38(3), 885–912.

Hooghe, L. (2005) 'Several roads lead to international norms, but few via international socialization: a case study of the European Commission', *International Organization*, 59 (fall): 861–998.

House of Lords European Union Committee (2007) *Schengen Information System II*, London: HMSO.

Hune, S. (1994) 'The UN Convention on the Protection of Migrant Workers and Their Families', in J. Cator and J. Niessen (eds), *The Use of International Conventions to Protect the Rights of Migrants and Ethnic Minorities*, Strasbourg: Churches Commission for Migrants in Europe/Commission of the European Communities.

Hunger, U. (2000) 'Temporary transnational labour migration in an integrating Europe: the challenge to the German welfare state', in M. Bommes and A. Geddes (eds), *Welfare and Migration: Challenging the Borders of the Welfare State*, London: Routledge, pp. 189–208.

Huysmans, J. (1995) 'Migrants as a security problem: dangers of "securitizing" social issues', in R. Miles and D. Thränhardt (eds), *Migration and European Integration: The Dynamics of Inclusion and Exclusion*, London: Pinter, pp. 53–72.

Huysmans, J. (2006) *The Politics of Insecurity: Fear, Migration and Asylum in the EU*, London: Routledge.

Iglicka, K. (2001) *Poland's Post-war Dynamic of Migration*, Aldershot: Ashgate.

Immigration Law Practitioners' Association (1997) *European Update*, London: ILPA.

Ireland, P. (1994) *The Policy Challenge of Ethnic Diversity: Immigrant Politics in France and Switzerland*, Cambridge, MA: Harvard University Press.

Ireland, P. (1995) 'Migration, free movement and immigrant integration in the EU: a bifurcated policy response', in S. Liebfried and P. Pierson (eds), *European Social Policy: Between Integration and Fragmentation*, Washington, DC: Brookings Institution, pp. 231–66.

Jacobsen, D. (1996) *Rights Across Borders: Immigration and the Decline of Citizenship*, Baltimore, MA: Johns Hopkins University Press.

Johansson, K.-M. (1999) 'Tracing the employment title in the Amsterdam Treaty: uncovering transnational coalitions', *Journal of European Public Policy*, 6(1): 85–101.

Joppke, C. (1996) 'Multiculturalism and immigration: a comparison of the United States, Germany and Great Britain', *Theory and Society*, 25(4): 449–500.

Joppke, C. (1997) 'Asylum and state sovereignty: a comparison of the United States, Germany and Britain', *Comparative Political Studies*, 30(3): 259–98.

Joppke, C. (ed.) (1998) *Challenge to the Nation State: Immigration in Western Europe and the United States*, Oxford: Oxford University Press.

Joppke, C. (2007) 'Beyond national models: civic integration policies for immigrants in western Europe', *West European Politics*, 30(1): 1–22.

Joppke, C. and E. Morawska (2003) *Toward Assimilation and Citizenship: Immigrants in Liberal Nation-States*, Basingstoke: Palgrave Macmillan.

Katznelson, I. (1973) *Black Men, White Cities: Race Relations and Migration in the United States 1900–1930 and Britain 1948–1968*, London: Oxford University Press for the Institute of Race Relations.

Kelemen, R. D. (2002) 'The politics of "Eurocratic" structure and the new European agencies', *West European Politics*, 25(4): 93–118.

Kelly, L. (2005) '"You can find anything you want": a critical reflection on research on trafficking in persons within and into Europe', in I. O. F. Migration (eds), *Data and Research on Human Trafficking: A Global Survey*, Geneva: IOM.

Keohane, R. (1989) 'International institutions: two approaches', in R. Keohane (ed.), *International Institutions and State Power: Essays in International Relations Theory*, Boulder, CO: Westview, pp. 158–79.

Kindleberger, C. (1967) *Europe's Post-war Growth: The Role of Labour Supply*, Cambridge, MA: Harvard University Press.

King, R. (1993) 'Why do people migrate?', in R. King (ed.), *The New Geography of European Migrations*, London: Belhaven Press, pp. 17–46.

Kingdon, J. (1984) *Agendas, Alternatives and Public Policies*, Boston, MA: Little, Brown.

Kirisci, K. (2002) 'Immigration and asylum issues in EU–Turkish relations: assessing the EU's impact on Turkish policy and practice', in S. Lavenex and E. Ucarer (eds), *Migration and the Externalities of European Integration*, Lanham, MD: Lexington Books, pp. 125–42.

Kitschelt, H. (1995) *The Radical Right in Western Europe: A Comparative Analysis*, Ann Arbor, MI: University of Michigan Press.

Knill, C. (2005) 'Introduction: cross-national policy convergence: concepts, approaches and explanatory factors', *Journal of European Public Policy*, 12(5): 764–74.

Koopmans, R. and P. Statham (2000) *Challenging and Defending the Fortress: Political Mobilisation Over Ethnic Difference in Comparative and Transnational Perspective*, Oxford: Oxford University Press.

Koopmans, R., P. Statham, M. Giugni and F. Passy (2005) *Contested Citizenship: Immigration and Cultural Diversity in Europe*, London: University of Minnesota Press.

Kostakopoulou, T. (1997) 'Why a "community of Europeans" could be a community of exclusion', *Journal of Common Market Studies*, 35(2): 301–8.

Kostakopoulou, T. (1998) 'European Union citizenship as a model of citizenship beyond the nation state: limits and possibilities', in A. Weale and M. Nentwich (eds), *Political Theory and the European Union: Legitimacy, Constitutional Choice and Citizenship*, London: Routledge, pp. 158–71.

Kuijper, P. J. (2000) 'Some legal problems associated with the communitarization of policy on visas, asylum and immigration under the Amsterdam Treaty and incorporation of the Schengen acquis', *Common Market Law Review*, 37: 345–66.

Laffan, B. (1997) 'From policy entrepreneur to policy manager: the challenge facing the European Commission', *Journal of European Public Policy*, 4(3): 422–38.

Lahav, G. (1998) 'Immigration and the state: the devolution and privatisation of immigration control in the EU', *Journal of Ethnic and Migration Studies*, 24(4): 675–94.

Lavenex, S. (1998a) 'Ironic integration: the Europeanization of asylum policies in France and Germany', paper presented to the European Forum on International Migrations, European University Institute, Florence, Italy, paper MIG/9.

Lavenex, S. (1998b) 'Transgressing borders: the emergent European refugee regime and "safe third countries"', in A. Cafruny and P. Peters (eds), *The Union and the World*, Den Haag: Kluwer, pp. 113–32.

Lavenex, S. (1999) *Safe Third Countries: Extending EU Asylum and Migration Policies to Central and Eastern Europe*, Budapest: Central European University Press.

Lavenex, S. (2001) 'Migration and the EU's new eastern border: between realism and liberalism', *Journal of European Public Policy*, 8(1): 24–42.

Lavenex, S. (2006) 'Shifting up and out: the foreign policy of European immigration control', in V. Guiraudon and G. Lahav (eds), *Immigration Policy in Europe: The Politics of Control*, London: Routledge.

Lavenex, S. and E. Uçarer (eds) (2002) *Migration and the Externalities of European Integration*, Lanham, MD: Lexington Books.

Lavenex, S. and E. Uçarer (2004) 'The external dimension of Europeanisation: the case of immigration policies', *Co-operation and Conflict*, 39(4): 417–43.

Layton-Henry, Z. (ed.) (1990) *The Political Rights of Migrant Workers in Western Europe*, London: Sage.

Lewis, J. (2005) 'The Janus face of Brussels: socialization and everyday decision-making in the European Union', *International Organization*, 59 (fall): 937–71.

Livi-Bacci, M. (1993) 'South–north migration: a comparative approach to North American and European experiences', in *The Changing Course of International Migration*, Paris: OECD, pp. 37–46.

Lodge, J. (1989) 'Social Europe: fostering a people's Europe?', in J. Lodge (ed.), *The European Community and the Challenge of the Future*, London: Pinter, pp. 303–18.

Loescher, G. and J. Milner (2003) 'The missing link: the need for comprehensive engagement in regions of refugee origin', *International Affairs*, 79(3): 595–617.

Lowi, T. (1972) 'Four systems of politics, policy and choice', *Public Administration Review*, 32(4): 298–310.

Maas, W. (2005) 'The genesis of European rights', *Journal of Common Market Studies*, 43(5): 1009–25.

McAdam, D. (1982) *The Political Process and the Development of Black Insurgency*, Chicago, IL: University of Chicago Press.

Majone, G. (1996) *Regulating Europe*, London: Routledge.

Maley, W. (2003) 'Asylum-seekers in Australia's international relations', *Australian Journal of International Affairs*, 57(1): 187–202.

Manners, I. (2000) 'Normative power Europe: a contradiction in terms?', *Journal of Common Market Studies*, 40(2): 235–58.

March, J. and J. Olsen (1989) *Rediscovering Institutions: The Organizational Basis of Politics*, New York: Free Press.

March, J. and J. Olsen (1998) 'The institutional dynamics of international political orders', *International Organization*, 52(4): 937–71.

Marks, G. and D. McAdam (1996) 'Social movements and the changing structure of political opportunity in the European Union', in G. Marks, F. Scharpf, P. Schmitter and W. Streeck (eds), *Governance in the European Union*, London: Sage, pp. 95–120.

Marshall, T. H. (1964) 'Citizenship and social class', in *Class, Citizenship and Social Development: Essays by T. H. Marshall*, New York: Anchor Books.

Martin, D. and E. Guild (1996) *Free Movement of Persons in the EU*, London: Butterworth.

Martin, P. (1993) 'The migration issue', in R. King (ed.), *The New Geography of European Migrations*, London: Belhaven Press, pp. 1–16.

Martin, P. (2002) *Germany: Managing Migration in the Twenty First Century*, Working Paper CIIP-1 2002, Institute of European Studies, University of California Berkeley.

Martiniello, M. (1994) 'Citizenship of the European Union: a critical view', in R. Baübock (ed.), *From Aliens to Citizens: Redefining the Status of Immigrants in Europe*, Vienna/Aldershot: European Centre/Avebury, pp. 29–47.

Mazey, S. and J. Richardson (eds) (1993) *Lobbying in the European Community*, Oxford: Oxford University Press.

Meehan, E. (1993) *Citizenship and the European Community*, London: Sage.

Meloni, A. (2005) 'The development of a common visa policy under the Treaty of Amsterdam', *Common Market Law Review*, 42(5): 1357–81.

Meny, Y. and Y. Surel (2002) *Democracies and the Populist Challenge*, London: Palgrave.

Messina, A. (1992) 'The two tiers of ethnic conflict in Western Europe', *Fletcher Forum of World Affairs*, 16(2): 51–64.

Messina, A. (2007) *The Logics and Politics of Post WWII Migration to Western Europe*, Cambridge: Cambridge University Press.

Meyers, E. (2002) *Multilateral Cooperation in International Labor Migration*, Working Paper No. 61, San Diego, CA: Center for Comparative Immigration Studies, University of California San Diego.

Meyers, E. (2004) *International Immigration Policy: A Theoretical and Comparative Analysis*, London: Palgrave Macmillan.

Milward, A. (1992) *The European Rescue of the Nation State*, London: Routledge.

Monar, J. (1994) 'The evolving role of the Union institutions in the framework of the third pillar', in J. Monar and R. Morgan (eds), *The Third Pillar of the European Union*, Brussels: European Interuniversity Press, pp. 69–83.

Monar, J. (1998) 'Justice and home affairs', *Journal of Common Market Studies*, 36 (annual review): 131–42.

Monar, J. (2001) 'The dynamics of Justice and Home Affairs: laboratories, driving factors and costs', *Journal of Common Market Studies*, 39(4): 747–64.

Monar, J. and R. Morgan (eds) (1994) *The Third Pillar of the European Union*, Brussels: European Interuniversity Press.

Moravcsik, A. and K. Nicolaïdis (1998) 'Federal ideals and constitutional realities in the Treaty of Amsterdam', *Journal of Common Market Studies*, 36 (annual review): 13–38.

Morrison, J. and B. Crosland (2000) *The Trafficking and Smuggling of Refugees: The End Game in European Asylum Policy?*, Geneva: UNHCR.

Müller-Graff, P-C. (1994) 'The legal basis of the third pillar and its position in the framework of the Union Treaty', in J. Monar and R. Morgan (eds), *The Third Pillar of the European Union*, Brussels: European Interuniversity Press, pp. 21–36.

Munz, R. and R. Ulrich (1998) 'Germany and its immigrants: socio-demographic analysis', *Journal of Ethnic and Migration Studies*, 24(1): 26–56.

Nevins, J. (2002) *Operation Gatekeeper: The Rise of the 'Illegal Alien' and the Making of the US–Mexico Boundary*, New York: Routledge.

Nielsen, R. and E. Szyszczak (1991) *The Social Dimension of the European Community*, Copenhagen: Handelshøjskolens Forlag.

Niessen, J. (1994) 'The role of non-governmental organisations in standard setting and promoting ratification', in J. Cator and J. Niessen (eds), *The Use of International Conventions to Protect the Rights of Migrants and Ethnic Minorities*, Brussels: Churches Commission for Migrants in Europe.

Noiriel, G. (1988) *Le creuset Français: Histoire de l'immigration XIXe–XXe siècles*, Paris: Seuil.

Noll, G. (2000) *Negotiating Asylum: The EU Acquis, Extra-territorial Protection and the Common Market of Deflection*, Leiden: Martinus Nijhoff.

Noll, G. (2003) 'Visions of the exceptional: legal and theoretical issues raised by transit processing centres and protection zones', *European Journal of Migration and Law*, 5(3): 303–41.

North, D. (1990) *Institutions, Institutional Change and Economic Performance*, Cambridge: Cambridge University Press.

Nyberg-Sorensen, N., N. Van Hear and P. Engberg-Pedessen (2002) 'The migration–development nexus: evidence and policy options. State-of-the-art overview', *International Migration*, 40(5): 3–47.

O'Keeffe, D. (1992) 'The free movement of persons and the single market', *European Law Review*, 17(1): 3–19.

O'Keeffe, D. (1994) 'Citizenship of the Union', in D. O'Keeffe and P. Twomey (eds), *Legal Issues of the Maastricht Treaty*, Chichester: Wiley, pp. 87–107.

O'Leary, S. (1996) *The Evolving Concept of Community Citizenship: From the Free Movement of Persons to Union Citizenship*, Den Haag: Kluwer.

Olsen, J. (2002) 'The many faces of Europeanisation', *Journal of Common Market Studies*, 40(5): 921–52.

Organisation for Economic Co-operation and Development (2001) *SOPEMI Report Trends in International Migration 2002*, Paris: OECD.

Papademetriou, D. (1996) *Coming Together or Pulling Apart? The European Union's Struggle with Immigration and Asylum*, Washington, DC: Carnegie Endowment for International Peace.

Papademetriou, D. and P. Martin (eds) (1991) *The Unsettled Relationship*, Westport, CT: Greenwood Press.

Peers, S. (1996) 'Towards equality: actual and potential rights of TCNs in the European Union', *Common Market Law Review*, 33(1): 7–50.

Peers, S. (2004) *Statewatch Briefing: Vetoes, Opt-Outs and EU Immigration and Asylum Law*, London: Statewatch, www.statewatch.org/news/2004/dec/eu-immig-opt-outs3.pdf, accessed 5 March 2007.

Peterson, J. (1995) 'Decision-making in the European Union: towards a framework for analysis', *Journal of European Public Policy*, 2(1): 69–93.

Pierson, C. (1998) 'Contemporary challenges to welfare state development', *Political Studies*, 46(4): 777–94.

Pierson, P. (1994) *Dismantling the Welfare State. Reagan, Thatcher and the Politics of Retrenchment*, Cambridge: Cambridge University Press.

Pierson, P. (1996) 'The path to European integration: an historical institutionalist approach', *Comparative Political Studies*, 29(2): 123–63.

Pierson, P. and S. Liebfried (1995) 'Multitiered institutions and the making of social policy', in S. Liebfried and P. Pierson (eds), *European Social Policy: Between Integration and Fragmentation*, Washington, DC: Brookings Institution, pp. 1–40.

Pinder, J. (1968) 'Positive and negative integration: some problems of economic union in the EEC', *World Today*, 24(3): 88–110.

Plender, J. (1988) *International Migration Law* (2nd edition), Dordrecht: Martinus Nijhoff.

Portes, A. and J. Borocz (1989) 'Contemporary immigration: theoretical perspectives on its determinants and modes of incorporation', *International Migration Review*, 23(3): 606–30.

Purcell, M. and Nevins, J. (2005) 'Pushing the boundary: state restructuring, state theory, and the case of US–Mexico border enforcement in the 1990s', *Political Geography*, 24(2): 211–35.

Putnam, R. (1988) 'Diplomacy and domestic politics', *International Organization*, 42(3): 427–61.

Radaelli, C. (1999) *Technocracy in the European Union*, London: Longman.

Radaelli, C. (2004) 'Europeanisation: solution or problem?', *European Integration On-Line Papers*, 8(16), http://eiop.or.at/eiop/pdf/2004-016.pdf.

Rajaram, P. K. (2003) '"Making place": the "Pacific solution" and Australian

Emplacement in the Pacific and on refugee bodies', *Singapore Journal of Tropical Geography*, 24(3): 290–306.

Ravenstein, W. (1889) 'The laws of migration', *Journal of the Royal Statistical Society*, 52(2): 241–305.

Reflection Group (1995) *Report of the Reflection Group*, Brussels: Secretariat General of the Council.

Reich, N. (2005) 'The constitutional relevance of citizenship and free movement in an enlarged European Union', *European Law Journal*, 11(6): 675–98.

Rex, J. and B. Drury (eds) (1994) *Ethnic Mobilisation in a Multi-cultural Europe*, Aldershot: Avebury.

Rhodes, M. and B. van Apeldoorn (1998) 'Does migration from less developed countries erode the welfare state?', paper presented to the conference Migration and the Welfare State in Contemporary Europe, European University Institute, Florence, 21–23 May.

Risse-Kappen, T. (ed.) (1995) *Bringing Transnational Relations Back In: Non-State Actors, Domestic Structures and International Institutions*, Cambridge: Cambridge University Press.

Rogers, R. (ed.) (1985) *Guests Come to Stay: The Effects of European Labor Migration on Sending and Receiving Countries*, Boulder, CO: Westview.

Rosamond, B. (2000) *Theories of European Integration*, Basingstoke: Macmillan.

Rosenau, J. (1997) *Along the Domestic–Foreign Frontier: Exploring Governance in a Turbulent World*, Cambridge: Cambridge University Press.

Ruggie, J. (1982) 'International regimes, transactions and change: embedded liberalism in the post-war economic order', *International Organization*, 36(2): 379–415.

Ruhs, M. and Chang, H-J. (2004) 'The ethics of labour immigration policy', *International Organization*, 58(1): 69–102.

Samers, M. (2004) 'An emerging geo-politics of illegal immigration in the European Union', *European Journal of Migration and Law*, 6(1): 23–41.

Sandholtz, W. and A. Stone Sweet (eds) (1998) *European Integration and Supranational Governance*, Oxford: Oxford University Press.

Sandholtz, W. and J. Zysman (1989) '1992: recasting the European bargain', *World Politics*, 27(4): 496–520.

Sartori, G. (1970) 'Concept misinformation in comparative politics', *American Political Science Review*, 64(4): 1033–53.

Sassen, S. (1996) *Losing Control*, New York: Columbia University Press.

Sayad, A. (2004) *The Suffering of the Immigrant*, Cambridge: Polity.

Scharpf, F. (1996) 'Negative and positive integration in the political economy of European welfare states', in G. Marks, F. Scharpf, P. Schmitter and W. Streeck (eds), *Governance in the European Union*, London: Sage, pp. 15–39.

Schieffer, M. (2003) 'Community readmission agreements with third countries – objectives, substance and current state of negotiations', *European Journal of Migration and Law*, 3(3): 343–57.

Schmidt, V. (2006) *Democracy in Europe: The EU and National Polities*, Oxford: Oxford University Press.

Schmitter, P. (1996a) 'Examining the present Euro-polity with the help of past theories', in G. Marks, F. Scharpf, P. Schmitter and W. Streeck (eds), *Governance in the European Union*, London: Sage, pp. 1–14.

Schmitter, P. (1996b) 'Imagining the future of the Euro-polity', in G. Marks, F. Scharpf, P. Schmitter and W. Streeck (eds), *Governance in the European Union*, London: Sage, pp. 121–50.

SLG (Starting Line Group) (1998) *Proposals for Legislative Measures to Combat Racism and the Promotion of Equal Rights*, Brussels: SLG.

Snyder, F. (1994) 'Institutional development in the European Union: some implications of the third pillar', in J. Monar and R. Morgan (eds), *The Third Pillar of the European Union*, Brussels: Interuniversity Press, pp. 85–95.

Soysal, Y. N. (1994) *Limits of Citizenship: Migrants and Postnational Membership in Europe*, Chicago, IL: Chicago University Press.

Soysal, Y. N. (1998) 'Towards a post-national model of membership', in G. Shafir (ed.), *The Citizenship Debates: A Reader*, Minneapolis, MN: University of Minnesota Press, pp. 189–220.

Spencer, M. (1990) *1992 and All That: Civil Liberties in the Balance*, London: Civil Liberties Trust.

Spencer, M. (1995) *States of Injustice*, London: Pluto Press.

Statewatch (1997) *Key Texts on Justice and Home Affairs in the European Union Volume I (1976–1993): From Trevi to Maastricht*, London: Statewatch.

Streeck, W. (1995) 'From market-making to state-building? Reflections on the political economy of European social policy', in S. Liebfried and P. Pierson (eds), *European Social Policy: Between Fragmentation and Integration*, Washington, DC: Brookings Institution, pp. 389–431.

Streeck, W. (1996) 'Neo-voluntarism: a new European social policy regime?', in G. Marks, F. Scharpf, P. Schmitter and W. Streeck (eds), *Governance in the European Union*, London: Sage, pp. 64–94.

Stubb, A. (1996) 'A categorization of differentiated integration', *Journal of Common Market Studies*, 34(2): 283–95.

Szczerbiak, A. and P. Taggart (2000) *Theorising Party-Based Euroscepticism: Problems of Definition, Measurement and Causality*, Sussex European Institute Working Paper 69, Brighton: University of Sussex.

Taggart, P. (1998) 'A touchstone of dissent: Euroscepticism in contemporary western European party systems', *European Journal of Political Research*, 33(2): 363–88.

Tarrow, S. (1998) 'The Europeanization of conflict: reflections from a social movements perspective', *West European Politics*, 18(2): 223–51.

Thym, D. (2002) 'The Schengen law: a challenge for legal accountability in the European Union', *European Law Journal*, 8(2): 218–45.

Travis, A. (1998) 'Fortress Europe's four circles of purgatory', *Guardian*, 20 October, p. 19.

Turnbull, P. and W. Sandholtz (2001) 'Policing and immigration: the creation of new policy spaces', in A. Stone-Sweet, W. Sandholtz and N. Fligstein (eds), *The Institutionalization of Europe*, Oxford: Oxford University Press, pp. 194–220.

Twomey, P. (1994) 'Title VI of the Union treaty: "matters of common interest" as a question of human rights', in J. Monar and R. Morgan (eds), *The Third Pillar of the European Union*, Brussels: European Interuniversity Press, pp. 49–66.

Tyson, A. (2001) 'The negotiation of the European Community directive on anti-discrimination', *European Journal of Migration and Law*, 3(2): 199–229.

UNHCR (United Nations High Commissioner for Refugees) (2006) *State of World's Refugees*, Geneva: UNHCR.

United Nations Population Fund (2006) *State of World Population 2006: A Passage to Hope: Women and International Migration*, New York: UNPFA.

Wacquant, L. (2005) *Pierre Bourdieu and Democratic Politics: The Mystery of Ministry*, Cambridge: Polity.

Wæver, O. (1996) 'European security identities', *Journal of Common Market Studies*, 34(1): 103–32.

Wæver, O., B. Buzan, M. Kelstrup and P. Lemaitre (eds) (1993) *Identity, Migration and the New Security Agenda in Europe*, New York: St Martin's Press.

Walker, N. (2004) *Europe's Area of Freedom, Security and Justice*, Oxford: Oxford University Press.

Walker, R. B. J (1998) 'Review: the elusive study of global change', *Mershon International Studies Review*, 42(2): 325–9.

Wallace, H. (1996) 'Politics and policy in the EU: the challenge of governance', in H. Wallace and W. Wallace (eds), *Policy-Making in the European Union*, Oxford: Oxford University Press, pp. 3–36.

Wallace, H. (2005) 'An institutional anatomy and five policy models', in H. Wallace, W. Wallace and M. Pollack (eds), *Policy-Making in the European Union* (5th edition), Oxford: Oxford University Press, pp. 49–89.

Wallace, H., W. Wallace and M. Pollack (eds) (2005) *Policy-Making in the European Union* (5th edition), Oxford: Oxford University Press.

Weick, K. (1995) *Sense-Making in Organizations*, London: Sage.

Weil, P. (1991) *La France et ses étrangers: l'aventure d'une politique de l'immigration*, Paris: Calmann-Lévy.

Weil, P. (1996) 'Nationalities and citizenships: the lessons of the French experience for Germany and Europe', in D. Cesarani and M. Fulbrook (eds), *Citizenship, Nationality and Migration in Europe*, London: Routledge, pp. 74–87.

Wiener, A. (1997) *European Citizenship Practice: Building Institutions of a Non-state*, Boulder, CO: Westview.

Wiener, A. and V. Della Sala (1997) 'Constitution making and citizenship practice – bridging the democracy gap in the EU', *Journal of Common Market Studies*, 35(4): 595–614.

Williams, A., R. King and T. Warnes (1997) 'A place in the sun: international retirement migration from northern to southern Europe', *European Urban and Regional Studies*, 4(2): 115–34.

Wimmer, A. and N. Glick Schiller (2002) 'Methodological nationalism and beyond: nation-state building, migration and the social sciences', *Global Networks*, 2(4): 301–34.

World Bank (2005) *Global Economic Prospects. The Economic Implications of Remittances and Migration*, Washington, DC: World Bank, www.worldbank. org/prospects/gep2006.

World Bank (2007) *Close to Home: The Development Impact of Remittances in Latin America*, Washington, DC: World Bank.

Zielonka, J. (2001) 'How new enlarged borders will reshape the EU', *Journal of Common Market Studies*, 39(3): 507–36.

Zolberg, A. (1989) 'The next waves: migration theory for a changing world', *International Migration Review*, 23(3): 403–30.

Zolberg, A. (2006) *A Nation by Design: Immigration Policy in the Fashioning of America*, Cambridge, MA: Russell Sage Foundation/Harvard University Press.

Zürn, M. and J. Checkel (2005) 'Getting socialized to build bridges: constructivism and rationalism, Europe and the nation state', *International Organization*, 59 (fall): 1045–79.

Index